PICTORIAL HISTORY OF

TANKS
OF THE
WORLD
1915~45

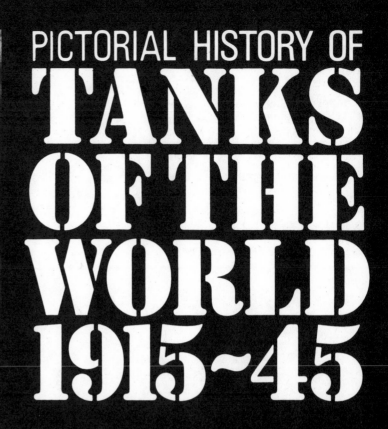

PICTORIAL HISTORY OF
TANKS OF THE WORLD 1915~45

Peter Chamberlain & Chris Ellis

GALAHAD BOOKS

Published by arrangement with
Stackpole Books,
Cameron and Kelker Streets,
Harrisburg,
Pa. 17105.

Library of Congress Catalog Card No. 73-92013

ISBN 0-88365-183-1

Printed in the United States of America

CONTENTS

PREFACE

The Pictorial History of Tanks of the World, 1915–1945 is intended to present the armoured vehicle enthusiast with a comprehensive coverage, in a single handy volume, of all fighting tanks, including those with special devices produced for the different armies of the world during the first forty years of tank development.

These were the great years of evolution for the armoured fighting vehicle — years of immense technological progress under the impetus of two world wars. As a result, in only about eight of the years covered in this book (ie: the combined period of the two world wars) tank design progressed in a couple of bounds from crude, slow, tractor-like contraptions to become the most complex and destructive of battlefield weapons. The small 'popguns' of 1915 had, by 1945, led to fully-stabilised, high-velocity weapons, sometimes with infra-red sights; hand operated 'crash' gear changing had been succeeded by a variety of sophisticated transmissions, sometimes automatic in action; brittle riveted armour plate (or even boiler plate) had given way to superbly machined armour often inches thick and fully welded. Tank production itself had progressed from what amounted to hand-building in small lots to the full mass-production flow-line techniques derived from (and in some cases supervised by) the automotive industry. The interwar period saw designs being slowly evolved, and new ideas tried, specially in the tactical field, while the technological progress generally in this period made possible the vast amount of AFV development carried out during World War II, mainly to meet ever changing operational requirements. (It is interesting to note in passing that in over a quarter-century since the end of World War II, AFV development has again slowed up and the tanks of today are, in most cases, little more than one step away from the best designs that had appeared in 1945.) Study of this book will give an instant visual idea of just what progress was made from the first design illustrated, 'Little Willie', up to the 1945 models shown in each reference section. Each reference section in this volume is devoted to a single country, and there is an introductory text to each, providing a brief outline of the development, production and employment of the tanks produced or used. In the illustrated reference sections we have adopted the procedure of showing each vehicle in turn, in a chronological order (although here it must be noted that much development work on projects ran concurrently with other models, so that some designs appeared within days of each other, some were shelved or delayed, thus disturbing the order of acceptance dates). Below the illustration of each vehicle is a concise development history, together with a note of basic characteristics, dimensions and data (including weight, crew, armament, armour, engine details, horsepower, speed and dimensions of length, width and height). In most cases the figures quoted denote the limits of the vehicle's capacity: for example, speeds given are road speed maxima (unless otherwise stated) which would have been considerably faster in most cases than cross-country speeds.

In certain cases the units of mensuration have been quoted in their original form, rather than conversions to avoirdupois. To assist the reader in these comparative aspects, conversion tables are provided at the end of the book.

Where there are many variants (as in the case of the Sherman tank) these are shown after the main entry with any major changes noted in the captions or appended notes. In some cases the development histories were so complex that the reference notes need to be longer than others: in such instances we have not attempted to go into similar complex details in the introductory text since this would simply repeat lengthy notes which are best given with the pictures of the vehicles concerned. Many tanks were used by more than one country: this was brought about either by one country supplying allies (e.g. Anglo-American Lend-Lease, 1942–5); by purchase by some countries from foreign arms suppliers (eg: Vickers in Britain, Skoda in Czechoslovakia, or Marmon-Herrington in USA); or by the use of captured vehicles (eg: by Germany in World War II). In general we have given the main details of such vehicles under the heading of the country of origin rather than the user country. There is then a cross-reference under the user country, in many instances showing a typical vehicle being used by its purchasers.

In the case of lesser nations, who almost always relied on purchase from the major producers, we have grouped such countries together, showing examples of the tanks they purchased and used. In these instances the reader should refer back to the indicated country of origin to read more details about the equipment concerned.

It should be noted that this book shows only the fighting tanks and combat tanks with special devices. It will be readily appreciated that there were also many special-purpose variants built on the basic tank chassis. Space considerations preclude the inclusion of these but in all major cases there is a reference to main variants in the text. In addition some fighting tank variants are mentioned in the text only, and not illustrated, since they are externally similar to adjacent illustrated models.

The preparation and research involved in this work took considerable time, in tracking down both pictures and information. The main authors have been considerably aided by the following who contributed sections for inclusion:

Raymond Surlémont: France, much of Japan, Sweden, some of Poland.

Charles Kliment: Czechoslovakia.

In addition John Milsom cross-checked parts of some sections. For additional assistance in the supply of photographs the authors are indebted to Col. R. J. Icks, USAR (Retd), R. Hunnicutt, Major J. W. Loop, US Army, and the staff of the photographic library, Imperial War Museum, London (especially D. Mayne, G. Pavey and E. C. Hine). To all other individuals who helped, the authors acknowledge their gratitude.

AUSTRALIA

Tractor Tank, 1933: A copy of the American Disston tank on a commercial agricultural tractor chassis. Trials only, not adopted.

3. Cruiser Tank Sentinel AC III: This was a close-support version of the AC I mounting a 25pdr howitzer in place of the 2pdr. This necessitated a larger turret ring and turret. The hull MG was eliminated and the triple engines were given a common crankcase. Prototype was tested in early 1943, but there was no production of this design.

I. VICKERS MEDIUM Mk IIA (Special Pattern)
Four Medium Mk IIA tanks were purchased in 1928, these differed from the English version by having the coaxial Vickers machine-gun on the left of the 3pdr gun, and a ball-mounted Vickers machine-gun on the right.

4. Cruiser Tank Sentinel AC IV: This was a further development of the AC III fitted with a 17pdr gun. Pending the availability of the 17pdr gun, twin 25pdr were fitted in order to simulate the high recoil of the 17pdr for test purposes. One test vehicle in the AC series was later fitted with torsion bar suspension for tests. The AC IV did not proceed beyond prototype stage. Details of the AC III and AC IV were generally similar to the AC I.

5. Test vehicles equipped with twin 25pdr guns.

2. CRUISER TANK, SENTINEL AC I
This was a design started late in 1940 for a tank intended for Australian production utilising only readily available materials and sources. Commercial truck engines were to be used, together with an adapted version of the American M3 Medium Tank final drive and transmission. Cast hull and turret with 2pdr gun were features of the finalised design. Work on the AC I was held in abeyance for a time while an alternative design (AC II) was studied. The latter proved too complicated, however, and AC I design was completed in September 1941 and the prototype was finished in January 1942. Production started in August 1942 and 66 vehicles were built. These were used only for training as there were by this time sufficient American medium tanks available to equip Australian units in the field. The design was very sound with good armour. 62,720lb; crew 5; 1 2pdr, 2 Vickers MG; armour 25–65mm; engine 3 Cadillac V8 117hp each; 20mph; 20ft 9in x 8ft 5in x 9ft 1in.

6. Test vehicle with torsion bar suspension.

Vickers Light Tank, Mk V: Ten vehicles were purchased from Britain in 1936.

7. Vickers Light Tank, Mk VI, VIA, VIB (above, VIA): A number of these vehicles were obtained from Britain in 1939, they were used for training. Australian units also took over some British tanks of this type (and some Light Mk IIs) in the Western Desert in 1940.

8. Infantry Tank, Mk II Matilda: Various marks of this vehicle were delivered from the British Army, 1942, armed with the 2pdr gun or with 3in howitzer. Some of these vehicles were modified by having an armoured shield welded to the hull top to protect the turret ring and anti-magnetic screens over the rear engine louvres.

Infantry Tank, Mk III Valentine: Small number supplied to Australians from 1943 onwards.

Light Tank, M3 Series: Various models in this series supplied to Australians by United States under Lend-Lease arrangements.

Medium Tank, M3 Grant: Many of the Grants superseded by Shermans in the 8th Army in late 1942–early 1943 were supplied to the Australians in the Pacific theatre.

9. MATILDA FROG, Mk I
Developed for operations against Japanese bunkers and pillboxes this tank-mounted flamethrower was initiated late in 1942. Based on the Matilda IV and V versions, the flamethrowing unit was carried inside the turret, the flame projector replacing the normal 2pdr gun. The majority of the flame fuel was stowed internally, the total capacity being 260 gallons. The main fuel tank was in the turret (80 gallons), four smaller tanks (combined capacity 32 gallons) were situated in the ammunition lockers adjacent to the turret, and there were two chain locker tanks (of 15 gallons). A 100 gallon jettisonable tank was carried outside at the rear of the vehicle. Twenty-five vehicles were converted by late 1945.

Matilda Murray FT: This was a modified version of the Frog Mk I, produced in 1945 with cordite operated flame-equipment instead of gas-pressure, this allowed the removal of batteries, motor and pumps, with an increase in storage capacity within the turret of 50 gallons of flame fuel.

Matilda Hedgehog: Seven spigot mortars were taken from a Naval Hedgehog projector and mounted in line, within an armoured box, at the rear of a Matilda tank. The spigot mortars that could be fired singly or as a salvo were elevated by hydraulic rams on each side of the vehicle.

Servicing Ram tanks in England.

Canadian Shermans advance in Normandy.

The Fifth Canadian Armoured Division in review order, 23 May 1945.

CANADA

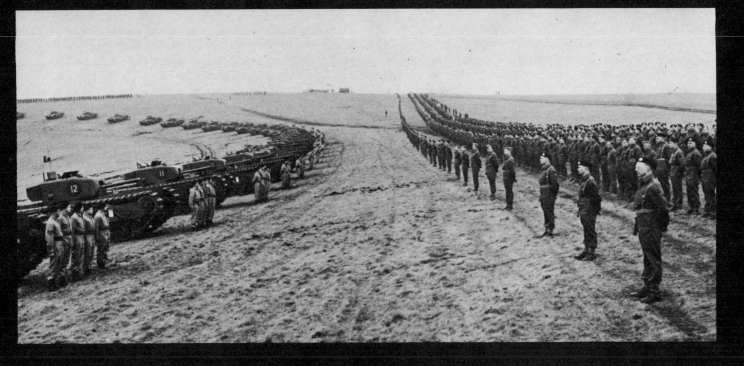

INTRODUCTION

The first Canadian Tank Corps had been formed early in 1918 and had been equipped with British Mk V heavy and French Renault light tanks, but with the armistice this corps had been disbanded.

During 1930 a batch of Carden-Loyd Mk VIb machine-gun carriers were purchased from England to equip the machine-gun platoons of the few Canadian regular infantry battalions, these being the first tracked fighting vehicles to go into military service since 1918.

In 1936, due to the international situation the Canadian Defence Department decided to form an armoured element, initially in cadre strength to train men in tank warfare in the event of war. A Tank Training School was set up at London, Ontario, with the Carden-Loyd Mk VIb carriers provided as training vehicles; these were supplemented by two Vickers Mk VI light tanks purchased from Britain. In the summer of 1939 a further 14 of the Light Tanks Mk VI series were ordered from Britain.

No attempt had previously been made to acquire tanks in quantity for Canada, partly on the grounds of expense, but mainly because it was considered that any tank requirement would be met by Britain in the event of a Canadian Expeditionary Force being sent once more to Europe. However, German military success in the invasion of Poland and subsequently France and Flanders showed that British tank production would have to be greatly expanded. In the spring of 1940 therefore, a British order for Valentine tanks was placed with the Canadian Pacific Railway Co of Montreal and in light of this a Canadian order was immediately placed with the same contractor to equip a Canadian Tank Brigade.

The fall of France, and the bombing offensive against Britain, led to a further decision that Canada be established as a source of light armoured vehicles and tanks. The authorization of two Canadian Armoured Divisions in the summer of 1940 necessitated a requirement for over 1,000 cruiser type tanks, this was in addition to the demands already raised for Valentine tanks. As it was obvious that these could not be supplied through United Kingdom production and that tank production in the United States was limited to British and American orders it was decided to construct a Tank Arsenal in Canada under the administration of Montreal Locomotive Works with the assistance of its parent organisation, American Locomotive. It was further decided that the Canadian built cruiser tank design would be based on that of the US M3 medium tank, then in its pilot stages, both to save time and to utilise mechanical and chassis components already in production for the M3. By the autumn of 1940, it became clear that many of the design features of the M3 would be far from satisfactory for the British and Canadian users, in particular the high silhouette, sponson-mounted main armament, inadequate armour protection and lack of radio in the turret. After lengthy consideration a decision was made in January 1941, to develop and produce in Canada a tank utilizing the mechanical components of the M3, but including turret, hull and armament features of Canadian design, together with a standard British main armament; this vehicle was to be known as the Ram tank.

A running prototype was completed in June 1941 and design and stowage details were worked out during the course of the year. It had been anticipated that production drawings of the 6pdr gun mount would be provided from the United Kingdom but as these did not materialise in time the mantlet, cradle and elevating gear were designed in Canada. Pending the final development and production of the 6pdr mounting, the first fifty vehicles were fitted with the 2pdr gun and designated Ram Mk I, production vehicles mounting the 6pdr gun then became the Ram Mk II. Rams were not used in action as gun tanks, most being used for training in Canada or Britain; many of them were subsequently converted for special purposes, notably as Kangaroo armoured personnel carriers.

In 1942, the United States brought into production the M4 (Sherman) tank to supersede the M3. This vehicle incorporated all the features of the Ram and met British requirements. Consideration was given to manufacturing it in Canada (concurrently with United States production) but this plan was discarded due to increased orders for the Valentine tanks and the expanded arsenal facilities in the United States. It was agreed, however, that at the earliest practical date, the Ram tank at the Montreal Locomotive Works would be superseded by the M4A1 Sherman. The specifications were laid down in September 1942 for Canadian produced M4A1's, to be known as 'Grizzlies', but it was not until August 1943 that the changeover in production was made; this was after 1944. 1941 Ram tanks had been built. While it had been planned to build large quantities of the Grizzly tanks in Canada, orders were cut back when it was realised that the production of Sherman tanks from the USA would be more than sufficient for the Allied requirements. Of the 188 Grizzly tanks built, some were allocated to British Forces but the bulk of them were retained for training.

I. Light Tank Mk VI, VIA, VIB: Small numbers of these Vickers light tanks were obtained from Britain for training purposes in 1939.

Tank Mk VIII: About 90 of these 1919 vintage vehicles were taken from store in 1940 and supplied by the USA for training purposes (see American section for further details).

2. Six Ton Tank (M1917): About 140 M1917 light tanks were supplied by the USA in 1940 for training purposes (See American section).

Valentine VI: Externally similar to the British Valentine IV, but with GMC diesel engine, cast noseplate instead of bolted as on the British vehicle; Besa machine-gun replaced by Browning .30 after sixteenth vehicle.

Valentine VI, VII, VIIA: The basic pattern was provided by the UK but considerable development work was necessary in Canada due to the unavailability of British components and the necessity to utilize Canadian production procedures and materials. In this connection it was necessary to redraw all British drawings and develop Canadian parts that were not available. The North

American engine and gearbox was fitted in lieu of the powerplant specified by the British, this involved the redesign of mountings, propeller shafts, accessories, controls etc. A one-piece cast turret and a cast hull nose were developed and put into production to replace the difficult fabricated UK design. A change was made from Besa to a Browning machine-gun in the coaxial mount and in addition it was necessary to re-design a multitude of detail parts. Orders were placed in early 1940, and production commenced in 1941 at the Angus Shops of the Canadian Pacific Railway. A total of 1420 vehicles were produced before production ceased in 1943, the great bulk of this production (1930) being shipped to Russia as Lease-Lend equipment; these were used in combat by the Red Army. Three Marks of the Valentine Tank were built in Canada.

Valentine VII: Improved Mk VI built in Canada, No. 19 Wireless set replacing No 11 and remote control grip and firing gear attachment added to Browning machine-gun.

Valentine VIIA: Improved Mk VII with jettisonable fuel tanks, studded tracks, protective cages over headlamps, and turret protection angles.

3. CRUISER TANK RAM MK I
The overall design was developed in Canada to incorporate the best United States, British and Canadian ideas of that time, that is to say the US engine and power train (as used in the M3) new cast upper hull and 360° cast turret mounting main armament and W/T set. The vehicle was in production at the Montreal Locomotive Works Tank Arsenal from the fall of 1941 until the summer of 1943. A limited number of these vehicles were equipped with a shoulder-controlled 2pdr gun, using a mount adapted from the Valentine tank. This was an expedient adopted so that vehicles could be produced in advance of the availability of the 6pdr gun mount and elevating gear. This version was known as the Ram I; fifty of these tanks were built most of which were shipped to England. 64,000lbs; crew 5; 2pdr gun, 3 MG; armour 1–3½in; engine Continental R975-EC2 9-cylinder, 400hp air-cooled; 25mph; 19ft x 9ft 5in x 8ft 9in.

4. Cruiser Tank, Ram II: This version provided an up-to-date improved design and certain structural changes superseding the

Ram I during 1942. Equipped with a 6pdr gun and a Gyro-stabiliser for control of gun elevation, and splash beading around the turret and hatch cover. Many improvements and modifications were incorporated in the Ram II during production. These included the addition of a transmission oil cooler, elimination of the sponson doors, elimination of the machine-gun cupola, addition of a floor escape hatch, elimination of pistol ports in turret, and modification to the engine to allow the use of 80 octane fuel. Eighteen hundred and ninety-nine were produced in Canada during 1942/43 most of which were shipped overseas. 65,000lbs; crew 5; 6pdr gun, 3 MG; armour 1–3½in; engine Continental R975-CI or R975-EC2 9-cylinder, 400hp air-cooled; 25mph; 19ft x 9ft 1in x 8ft 9in.

5. Ram Mk II Modified

6. Ram, Command/OP Tank: This vehicle was developed at the request of the Canadian Army Overseas and was used with success in action in N.W. Europe; eighty-four of these vehicles were produced at the Tank Arsenal, Montreal during 1943. Basically the Command version was similar to the Ram II but with certain changes to adapt it to this special role. The main armament was replaced by a dummy gun in a turret that was restricted to 90° traverse, the turret basket and gun-traversing gear were eliminated allowing sufficient room in the hull for the seating of the command staff as well as the installation of the tables. Additional wireless and line communication equipment was also provided, and provision was made for mounting artillery observation equipment, the rotating hatch was calibrated so that the hatch periscope could be used as a direction finder. Browning machine-guns were carried in the bow and on the turret hatch. 64,000lbs; crew 6; 2 MG; armour 1–3½in; engine Continental R975-CI 9-cylinder, 400hp air-cooled; 25mph; 19ft x 9ft 1in x 9ft.

Ram AVRE: Two trial vehicles were converted for assault engineer use in 1943. The type was not adopted.

7. CRUISER TANK, GRIZZLY I
The Grizzly was the Canadian-built version of the US Medium Tank M4AI ('Sherman II') and conformed almost completely to the specifications of that vehicle, but with certain revisions to conform with British and Canadian standards. These included the fitting of a turret 2in Smoke Mortar, the installing of a No 19 wireless set in the turret bulge and other items of equipment. Only one turret hatch was provided on the Grizzly. 67,000lbs; crew 5; 75mm gun, 3 MG; armour 1–3in; engine Continental Radial R975-CI 9-cylinder, 400hp air-cooled; 19.3mph; 20ft 1in x 8ft 8in x 9ft 10in.

British and American types used by Canadian tank units 1940–45: See relevant sections for further details. M4 Medium Tank (Sherman) various models, mainly M4AI, M4A2, M4A4; Light Tanks, M3 and M5 series (various models); Churchill I, III, IV V, VII and AVRE; Cruiser Tank, Cromwell.

CZECHOSLOVAKIA

INTRODUCTION

When Czechoslovakia was separated from the former empire of Austria-Hungary, and established as an independent state on October 1918 she already possessed a large armament concern with a world-wide reputation, namely the Skoda Company of Pilsen. Originally Skoda had specialised in gun manufacture but soon expanded their activities to include aircraft and automobile construction. In 1927 the CKD (Ceskomoravska Kolben Danek) concern resulted from the amalgamation of four companies, one of which was the Praga automobile factory. A widely known company, Tatra, was another experienced motor car manufacturer. With such an industrial background, supplemented by iron works of repute, Czechoslovakia was well placed to produce tanks of her own.

For the first few years the Czechs bought tanks from abroad, seven Renault FTs being purchased from France. By the mid twenties Skoda had started design and production work on armoured cars for the Czech Army, and they were soon joined by the Tatra automobile factory. After working in Sweden for a few years, the German tank designed J. Vollmer came to Czechoslovakia where he designed the wheel-and-track tank KH50. Prototypes were built in 1925 by Skoda in collaboration with Tatra. The basic design led to the KH60 in 1928–9 and the KH70 in 1930, further development of the wheel-and-track concept being abandoned in 1934.

The widespread publicity which the Vickers Carden-Loyd two-man tankettes received during the early thirties was echoed in Czechoslovakia. Demonstration samples were obtained from Vickers-Armstrongs and were extensively tested. On their basis, CKD/Praga developed their own P-I version and this small vehicle was accepted into service as the T33 (T standing for 'Tancik', 'Tankette').

The Czech tankettes were furiously decried by their users but nevertheless the order was maintained and even expanded for 'economic' reasons. A short time later, Skoda also proposed a similar vehicle they had designed as a private venture, the S-I (T-I/MU-4) tankette. The Skoda vehicle offered the advantage of a more powerful engine giving a higher top speed than the P-I (T33), but as the contract had already been awarded to CKD, the Skoda model was not adopted. It was however sent to Yugoslavia where it competed with the Polish-built TK-3 tankette. The S-I was recognised as the better vehicle but the order placed with Skoda by the Yugoslavian government was not for the S-I itself as expected, but for a 47mm gun armed development model designated S-Id.

Stimulated by the official order for their P-I tankette, CKD/Praga then went on to produce an actual light tank, the P-II. It was a 7.5ton machine armed with a 37mm gun and its successful trials led to its acceptance as the Czech Army's LT34 (LT 'Lehky Tank' or 'Light Tank'). Once again, CKD had beaten Skoda in having their own vehicles ordered by the Czech Army.

In 1935, however, the Skoda company introduced their promising S-IIa/T.II design for an 8ton light tank armed with a 37mm gun and the end of the year brought a substantial order for it. With CKD as co-contractor,

Skoda placed their S-IIa/T.II tank in production under the official designation of LT35. Although a sound design basically, the LT35 was plagued by teething troubles and production difficulties throughout its life. Nevertheless (and unfortunately) it became the most widely-produced armoured vehicle of the Skoda company and the most numerous tank of the Czech Army. Later the S-IIa, having primarily acquitted itself as a light tank, was developed further as the S-IIc; it was then redesignated into medium tank prototypes such as the S-IIb, S-IIr (T-21) and S.IIs. None of these variants matured to the production stage.

In the meantime CKD/Praga was also involved in the design and early production stage of two light tanks: the 4ton AH-IV (armed with machine-guns) and the 8ton (LT)TNH (armed with 37mm gun). These machines embodied a Wilson type power train and were based upon a common running gear including four large road wheels resisted by semi-elliptic leaf springs. Both the AH-IV and the (LT)TNH represented a significant advance over the former models and were the subject of continuous adaptations to meet specific requirements of the company's foreign customers.

In 1937 a special board was appointed with the task of testing new armoured vehicles and selecting the best production orders on behalf of the Czech Army. In the light tank field Skoda submitted only three refined samples of their S-IIa design while CKD offered their TNH, LTL (an export version of the former) and a rebuilt LT34 (P-II). All the Praga models performed very well, the key to their success laying in the fact they had a very good performance as well as being easy to service and maintain. The Czech Army then placed an order for the TNHP which became designated LT38, the first deliveries being scheduled for the end of 1938. As the Czech Army also had need of a medium tank armed with a 47mm gun, the board put in competition the Skoda S-IIb with the Praga V-8-H. Neither of them were satisfactory on trials, but while the S-IIb was a total failure, the V-8-H showed some promise. Owing to the pressure of events outside Czechoslovakia, the V-8-H was ordered as the ST.39 (ST standing for 'Stredni Tank' or 'Medium Tank'). In order to hasten deliveries, a joint production programme was negotiated again between CKD/Praga and Skoda.

From 1935 onwards, Skoda and CKD had also become highly competitive in the tank export business. Skoda had sold tanks to Rumania (S-IIa) and to Yugoslavia (S-Id) while many foreign countries had awarded orders to CKD/Praga who, by 1939, were able to offer commercially eight alternative designs of their two basic AH-IV and (LT)TNH types. Between 1935 and 1939 CKD export contracts totalled 346 machines, orders having been placed by Latvia (LTL), Persia (AH-IV, TNH). Peru (LTP), Rumania (R-I), Sweden (AH-IV-Sv TNH-Sv) and Switzerland (LTH). After the invasion of Czechoslovakia in March 1939, the Germans took over all the LT38 (TNHP) machines being constructed by virtue of outstanding Czech contracts as well as some originally intended for sales abroad (TNH-Sv).

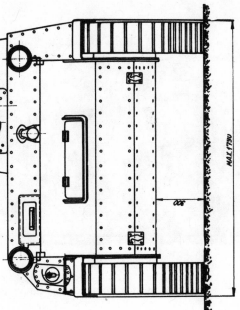

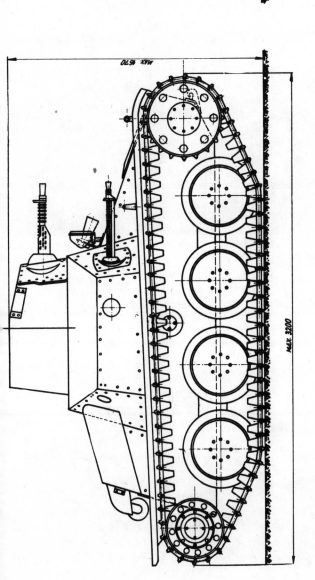

Abmasse : Länge   3200
Breite   1790
Höhe   1670

Betriebsstoffen 3500 kg.

Abstand des niedrigsten Punktes von der Erde 360 mm
Gewicht des kompl. bewaffneten und ausger-ústeten Wagens mit.

Spezif. Druck der Raupe auf weichen Boden 0·46 kg/cm²
Geschwindigkeit auf der Strasse maxim. 44·5 km/Stunde.
Geschwindigkeit in weichen Terrain 15–30 km/Stunde.
Minimalgeschw. nach vorne 2·6 km/Stunde und dabei eine maxim.

Zugkraft von 2800 kg.

Bei 9 km/Stunde eine Zugkraft von 790 kg.
Überschreitbarkeit von Gräben mit scharfen Kanten 1·3 m
Steigfähigkeit auf Abhängen mit zusammenhaltendem Boden 45°
Durchwaten von Furten mit hartem Grund: 0·9 m
Munitionsvorrat : 3000 Schuss für die Maschinengewehre.
Besatzung   : 2 Mann – 1 Schütze und 1 Lenker.

One of Ceskomoravska Kolben Danek's drawings of the Light Tank AH IV, dated 12 May 1936.

4. Wheel-and-track Tank KH.70: Last development of the KH series with an engine up-rated to 70hp. The wheel-and-track changing method was improved in this version. Four prototypes were built in 1930 and were used by the Czech Army as driver training vehicles up to 1936.

I, 2. WHEEL-AND-TRACK TANK KH.50

Wheel-and-track (Kolohousenka) light tank designed by the German engineer J. Vollmer and built by Skoda in collaboration with Tatra. Two prototypes were purchased in 1925 but they were rejected by the Czech Army after service evaluation. 6.8tons; crew 2; I 37mm gun or I MG; armour I3mm; engine I gasoline, 4-cylinders, 50hp; 7.5mph on tracks, 2I.7mph on wheels; I4ft 9in x 7ft 6½in x 7ft 9¾in.

5. TANKETTE, S-I (T-I/MU-4) (SKODA)

Two-man tankette designed by Skoda to compete with the CKD/Praga P-I vehicle. All welded construction. Front drive. Rejected by the Czech Army, it was demonstrated in Yugoslavia in 1938. 2.3tons; crew 2; 2 7.92mm MG; armour 5.5mm; engine I Skoda gasoline 4-cylinders, 40hp air-cooled; 28mph.

3. Wheel-and-track Tank KH.60: Improved KH.50 with an engine up-rated to 60hp and a slightly heavier armour. Built in 1928–29.

6. Tankette, (Skoda) S-Id: Two-man heavy tankette evolved from the Skoda S-I design. Front drive. Manufactured in 1938 for Yugoslavia; later it was also used by Rumania; 4.5tons; crew 2; I 47mm gun, I 7.92mm MG; armour I5mm; engine I Skoda gasoline 6-cylinders, 60hp air-cooled; 28mph; 8ft 6in x 6ft x 4ft 6in.

7. LIGHT TANK LT-35 (SKODA S-IIa/T-II)

Very advanced for its time, this Skoda light tank design featured a compressed air-assisted steering and gear shifting device. Notwithstanding very painful trials, it was accepted as the LT-35 by the Czech army and ordered in large quantities, but its career was dogged by a spate of troubles because its mechanical complication. After the German invasion of Czechoslovakia, the existing LT-35s were taken over and used by Germany as the 'PzKpfw. 35(t)' and the production was continued. The use of these Skoda vehicles on the Eastern front led to a redesign of the power train with a mechanical steering system. In 1936–37, the S-IIa/T-II) had been exported to Rumania which received more from Germany after 1940. 10.5tons; crew 4; 1 37mm gun, 2 7.92mm MG; armour 25mm; engine 1 Skoda gasoline 6-cylinders, 120hp liquid-cooled; 21.1mph; 16ft 1in x 7ft 0½in x 7ft 3in.

8. In Rumanian Service.

Medium Tank (Skoda) S-IIb: Medium tank evolved from the Skoda S-II basic design. Only one pilot model was built. Evaluation trials held in 1938 proved it was very unreliable and the design was not accepted.

Medium Tank (Skoda) S-IIr/T-21: Medium tank evolved from the Skoda S-II basic design in 1936–38 and produced in prototype form only. After some modifications, it was produced in Hungary as the '40' M TURAN' from late 1941 onwards. 16tons; 1 47mm gun, 2 7.92mm MG.

LIGHT TANK (SKODA) S-III

The last specification for a wheel-and-track tank laid down in 1933 by the Czech MoD was soon revised toward a full track design. Skoda went on to introduce, in mock-up form, a threefold design. Two alternatives were for turretless vehicles (self-propelled guns), the third one being for a 37mm gun turreted tank. One prototype was built by Skoda and purchased by the Czech Army.

9. TANKETTE T-33 (CKD/PRAGA P-I)

Evolved from the Vickers-Armstrongs two-man tankettes, of which samples had been demonstrated in Czechoslovakia, the CKD/Praga P-I had two light machine-guns. Although the Army had criticised its design for its poor riding qualities and other defects, seventy samples were ordered as the T-33. They were still in service with the border guard units in 1939. 2.5tons; crew 2; 2 7.92mm MG; armour 12mm; engine 1 Praga gasoline 4-cylinders, 31hp liquid-cooled; 21.75mph.

10. LIGHT TANK LT-34 (CKD/PRAGA P-II)

First Czech-built tank ordered in quantity, the CKD/Praga P-II was a successful design from the point of view of easy maintenance, but it was too noisy and tiring to drive. It was accepted as the Czech Army's LT-34 light tank and fifty machines were ordered. In 1938, the LT-34s were reworked and fitted with the same 125hp engine and gearbox as the LT-38 (TNHP) light tank. After the German occupation, they were given to Rumania. Front driven vehicle. 7.5tons; crew 4; 1 37mm gun, 2 7.92mm MG; armour 15mm; engine 1 Praga, gasoline 62hp, liquid-cooled; 21.1mph. 13ft 3in x 6ft 8in x 6ft.

15. AMPHIBIOUS LIGHT TANK (CKD/Praga) F-IV-HE

In 1937, CKD/Praga produced a pilot model for an amphibious tank which was tried up to 1939. It was taken over by the Germans and tested by them. One-man turret. 6tons; crew 3; 1 MG; engine 1 Praga gasoline 4-cylinders, 120hp liquid-cooled; 28mph on roads, 3.5mph in water.

11, 12. Small Tank (CKD/Praga) R-1: Scaled down version of the (LT)TNH design sold to Rumania. Thirty-five vehicles were delivered in 1936–37. Very similar to the AH-IV, it had no cupola on top of the turret and a less powerful engine. 4tons; crew 2; 2 MG; armour 12mm; engine 1 Praga gasoline 6-cylinders, 60hp liquid-cooled; 28mph; 10ft 6in x 5ft 6in x 5ft 11¾in.

13. Small Tank (CKD/Praga) AH-IV: Scaled-down version of the in 1935–36. It had many interchangeable components and spares with the (LT)TNH series of tanks. One-man turret housing one machine-gun; another gun was located in the bow, offset to the right. 4tons; crew 2; 2 MG; armour 15mm; 1 Praga gasoline 6-cylinders, 50hp liquid-cooled; 24.9mph; 11ft 2in x 5ft 10½ x 6ft 2in.

16. Light Tank (CKD/Praga) TNH: Export version of the (LT)TNH design built for Iran (Persia) in 1935–37. Adapted for desert use. Circular turret with a cupola on top and prominent bow machine-gun plate. 8.5tons; crew 3/4; 1 37mm gun, 2 MG; armour 25mm; engine 1 Praga gasoline, 100hp liquid-cooled; 26.1mph; 14ft 9½in x 6ft 8¾in.

14. Small Tank (CKD/Praga) AH-IV-Sv: Scaled-down version of the (LT)TNH series designed for Sweden where fifty vehicles were built under licence by Jungner with Volvo engines. It was armed with twin Browning machine-guns in the turret which was surmounted by a small cupola. Known as the 'Strv m/37' in Swedish service. 4.5tons; crew 2; 2 8mm MG; armour 15mm; engine 1 Volvo gasoline 80hp, liquid-cooled; 29.8mph.

17. TNH Prototype.

18. TNH with modified armament.

Light Tank (CKD/Praga) TNH-Sv: Export version of the (LT)TNH design built for Sweden. Tanks on order for Sweden were still on the production line when the Germans invaded Czechoslovakia and took them over. Later, Germany sold a manufacturing licence to the Scania Vabis company which built these tanks for the Swedish Army under the designation of 'Strv m/4l' with a Bofors 37mm gun and Scania Vabis engine. 10.5tons; crew 3/4; 1 37mm gun, 2 8mm MG; engine contemplated: 1 gasoline, 125hp liquid-cooled.

19. **Light Tank (CKD/Praga) LTH:** Export version of the (LT)TNH series designed for Switzerland. Twenty-four vehicles were built under licence in 1939–39; they had both a Swiss-made gun and diesel engine. Designated as 'Pz.39' in Swiss service. 7.5tons; crew 3; 1 24mm (Oerlikon) cannon, 2 MG; armour 32mm; engine 1 Saurer Arbon, diesel 125hp; 28mph; 14ft 1½in x 6ft 7in x 6ft 3in.

20. **Pz.39** (LTH in Swiss service)

21. **Light Tank (CKD/Praga) LTP:** Export version of the (LT)TNH design built for Peru. Twenty-four vehicles were delivered in 1938. Armed with a Skoda gun. 7.5tons; crew 3; 1 37mm (Skoda) gun, two MG; engine 1 Praga gasoline 125hp, liquid-cooled; 28mph.

22, 23 Light Tank (CKD/Praga) LTL: Export version of the (LT) TNH design built for Latvia. Twenty-one vehicles were delivered in 1938–40. Armed with either a 37mm gun or a 20mm (Oerlikon) cannon. 7.2tons; crew 3; I 37mm gun or I 20mm cannon, 2 MG; armour 25mm; engine I Praga gasoline 125hp, liquid-cooled; 33.6mph.

24. LIGHT TANK LT-38 (CKD/PRAGA TNHP)

The TNHP stemmed from a basic design common with the AH/(LT)TNH series and it profited from experience gained with these export models. It shared with them several mechanical components and used a similar suspension. The TNHP was armed with a 37mm Skoda gun and two machine-guns of the model 7.92mm ZB vz/37, from which the British Besa machine-gun was developed. It also embodied a front drive and a Praga-Wilson pre-selector five-speed gearbox. Chosen as the standard light tank of the Czech Army, after the LT–35, the TNHP was redesignated LT–38. Its production continued up to 1942 on behalf of Germany, under the designation 'PzKpfw. 38 (t)', with a Praga EPA (125hp), then EPA/AC (150hp) motor. 9tons; crew 3/4; I 37mm gun, 2 7.92mm MG; armour 25mm; engine I Praga gasoline, 125hp liquid-cooled; 26.1mph; 15ft 3in x 7ft x 7ft 2in.

25. MEDIUM TANK ST-39 (CKD/Praga V-8-H) (above, first prototype)

Medium tank introduced by CKD/Praga as a competitor for the Skoda S-IIB. It was accepted by the Czech Army as the ST-39 and a joint production programme for 300 vehicles of this type was negotiated between CKD/Praga and Skoda. Only prototypes had been delivered when the Germans invaded Czechoslovakia. 16.5tons; crew 4; I 47mm gun, 2 7.92mm MG; armour 50mm; engine I Praga gasoline 8-cylinders, 240hp liquid-cooled; 28mph. 17ft 2½in x 7ft 4½in x 7ft 6½in.

26. Second Prototype.

FRANCE

INTRODUCTION

While Colonel E. D. Swinton was putting his proposals to the War Office in England, the French Colonel J. E. Estienne, having seen trials with a Holt caterpillar tractor, was also proposing the development of a 'cuirassé terreste' (land battleship). He was successful in getting agreement in principle quite quickly from General Joffre, the C-in-C of the French Army. In 1916, the Schneider works undertook the construction of an armoured tracked vehicle named after the works. The Schneider tank weighed 13tons and was armed with a 75mm gun and two machine-guns. An order for 400 tanks was signed on 25th February 1916.

Meanwhile, on 8 April 1916, the Direction du Service Automobile (DSA), jealous because it had not been consulted, placed an order with the FAMH company (Saint Chamond) for 400 tanks of a type which had been hastily designed by Colonel Rimailho. The Saint Chamond tank was a bit heavier than the Schneider, a trifle faster and better armed. Its special feature was an electric transmission, a very advanced idea for the time. Unfortunately, in the field the Saint Chamond was less successful than the Schneider because its suspension was inadequate in rough going.

The new French armoured force began to get organised in August 1916, and on 30 September, Colonel Estienne was promoted to the rank of Brigadier and appointed Army Commander of the Assault Artillery. The Schneider and Saint Chamond tanks were formed into small units of 'AS' or Artillerie Spécialé organised into 'groupements'. Training centres for the Assault Artillery were established first at the Trou d'Enfer Fort, near Marly, then at Cercottes and at Champlieu. In March 1917 13 groups of Schneider tanks and 2 groups of Saint Chamond tanks were under training.

Meanwhile General Estienne had not lost interest in promoting the development of tanks. With his support, Louis Renault, the industrialist, designed a light tank which was by far the most remarkable AFV of the war. The prototype, called FT, was different from every other tank in that it had a 360degree turret. Eventually a gun tank and a wireless tank were developed on the same chassis, and the Renault tank was built in very great numbers by four firms. General Estienne had also recommended the building of a heavy breakthrough tank to be ready for the coming offensive in 1919. The design of this vehicle was undertaken by Savatier and Jammy of the FCM company, prototypes A and 1B being followed by the 1A and 2C. The 2C weighed 68tons, had a 75mm gun and four machine-guns, and it was powered by two motors. 300 machines of this type were ordered, but delays in development, a shortage of skilled manpower and of basic materials prevented the carrying out of this order. Meanwhile the French Army acquired 90 Mark V* tanks from England. The development of the 2C continued into the twenties and the order was reduced to 10.

As in England, the French armoured force — Assault Artillery or Special Artillery — encountered resistance, and even its very existence was in jeopardy several times, especially after the stalemate of the Nivelle offensive in 1917. Nevertheless General Estienne kept it alive against all odds, and the Assault Artillery became a major factor in the final victory of 1918.

In spite of the cancellation of most of the outstanding orders, the Armistice left France with a lot of material that was defective because of over-hasty production. General Estienne started studying new equipment as well as the development of a method of employment of an independent armoured force. This time his ideas were not accepted, and in 1920 tanks were reassigned to the Infantry.

The first programme for tank development, laid down in 1921, provided for the study of a heavy breakthrough tank and also for the search for a successor to the Renault FT in the form of a battle tank to accompany infantry. While the final touches were being put to the (FCM) 2C, General Estienne, now 'Inspecteur des Chars', was studying a 'Char de bataille' (Battle Tank). Five prototypes were ordered from different engineering firms: Renault/Schneider, FCM, FAMH (Saint Chamond) and Delaunay-Belleville. The final result of these studies, in 1925, was the creation of an outstanding vehicle — the Char B. Three prototypes 'Chars B', called 'Tracteurs 30' for security reasons, were ordered in 1926 and manufactured in 1929–30.

As the French Army had no less than 3,737 Renault FT tanks in 1921, there was no question of scrapping as obsolete such a large number of vehicles. Attempts were made to modernise the vehicles by eliminating defects and improving their performance. The most spectacular modifications were those tried between 1924 and 1927, when the original suspension and tracks were replaced using new Citroën-Kégresse running gears and continuous rubber tracks, the first model having a friction drive for its tracks, the second having applied metal shoes on the rubber band. Field trials during the Riff War in Morocco were not conclusive.

In 1926, the War Ministry published a new tank programme providing for three types of vehicle: a light tank, a battle tank and a heavy tank. The Renault Works, continuing its drive for a successor to the FT, produced the NC.1 (NC.27), a few dozen of which were bought by Japan. The improved version which followed it, the NC.2 (NC.31) did not go into quantity production and was also rejected by the French Army. These two vehicles were a step forward technically speaking in that they were the first in France (or indeed in the world) to use the Cleveland differentials for steering. Samples of both the NC.1 and NC.2 types were sent to Denmark, Greece, Portugal, Sweden and Yugoslavia for trials.

In spite of the relative failure of the NC.1 and NC.2, Renault continued with the development of the same basic vehicles, and in 1930 produced the DI, which was the first French tank with a 47mm gun. Unfortunately this vehicle had a lot of faults which earned it a bad reputation.

The political climate at that time did not favour tank development. The Disarmament Conferences condemned heavy tanks as 'offensive weapons'. In 1930, France sacified her 90 remaining outdated and worn-out Mark V* tanks at the altar of the Geneva Conference. Generally speaking, the French General Staff remained faithful to its policy of limiting the role of tanks to infantry support, and the economic crisis then ravaging France prevented the mass production of the new vehicles developed.

Nevertheless new ideas were emerging on the deployment of large moto-mechanised forces. In 1931, the infantry established an experimental unit, the 'Détachement mécanique de combat' (mechanised fighting unit). Other trials were carried out in 1932 with a 'Détachement d'engins blindés' (armoured vehicles unit). These experimental units were the embryos for the DCR of 1940. The creation of an independent armoured force had been advocated since 1934 by Charles de Gaulle in his book 'Vers l'Armée de métier'. In this book, the author expressed his views on the twin idea of a professional army that was also a mechanised army of shock troops. This was an idea that brought him trouble. Presented to the political authorities by Paul Reynaud, the ideas of Charles de Gaulle were anathema to an opposition who considered that a professional army was 'anti-republican' and who were against armoured divisions because they were 'offensive weapons'.

Little by little, the French cavalry was also becoming mechanised. In 1931 and 1932 new programmes were prepared defining 3 types of 'auto-mitrailleuses':
1: Auto-mitrailleuse de découverte (AMD): distant reconnaissance wheeled armoured cars.
2: Auto-mitrailleuse de reconnaissance (AMR): cross-country reconnaissance, machine-gun armed light tank.
3: Auto-mitrailleuse de combat (AMC): tracked vehicle, more heavily armed and armoured, capable of fighting.

In response to this programme, Renault produced two fast tracked vehicles — the AMR-33 (VM) and the AMR-35 (ZT) — and two peacetime tracked combat vehicles — the AMC-34 (YR) and the AMC-35 (ACGI).

In 1931, the Cavalry put forward a proposal for a mechanised force called 'Détachement mécanique de sûreté' (mechanised security unit) and then experimented with a 'Division de cavalerie de type mixte' (mixed cavalry division) in 1932. This contained mechanised elements, motorised elements and horsed elements. Next year again, after some hesitation, the Cavalry at last formed a large mechanised unit (having two tank battalions) which would eventually become a 'Division Légère Mécanique' (Light Mechanised Division) containing a reconnaissance regiment, an armoured brigade, a regiment of motorised infantry and a regiment of towed artillery.

In 1934, manufacture started of the D2, a slightly faster and more heavily armoured vehicle than the DI, for service with the infantry. Following a new 1933 specification for light tanks, it was decided in 1935 to re-classify the DI and D2 as medium tanks. That year was a very important one for the development of French armoured forces: firstly the I.ére Division Légère Mécanique (DLM) became definitively established from 1 July onwards. In addition, the BI tank went, if only rather slowly, into quantity production. It was also the year when the 1933 programme light infantry tank R-35 was adopted by the army and built by Renault. Finally in 1935, two cavalry tanks were also accepted — the H-35 light tank by Hotchkiss, and the S-35 medium tank that had been studied and produced by SOMUA within the AMC programme of 1934.

In June 1936 France still had only 194 modern tanks. These were 160 DI, 17 D2 and 17 BI tanks. During the same year, the French army approved a new infantry tank, the diesel powered FCM-36. Meanwhile, General Gamelin laid down and got accepted a four-year rearmament plan on 7 September 1936. This plan foresaw the formation of three 'divisions légères mécaniques' (DLM) with S-35 and H-35 tanks, of two 'divisions cuirassées de réserve' (DCR) with B tanks (12 battalions) and fifty battalions of R-35 and FCM-36 light tanks to accompany infantry. The next four years were spent in establishing this force. In August 1936 the French government partially nationalised the larger industrial concerns including Schneider, Hotchkiss and Renault, in order to achieve its programme. A part of Renault became the AMX (Atelier de Construction d'Issy-les-Moulineaux) which soon expanded into another works at Satory. This state-run factory was principally engaged in the production of B tanks, R-35 tanks and R-31 tankettes. It also carried out design studies for the AMX-38, AMX-R-40 and for self-propelled guns. In spite of these measures, the inadequacies of French industry together with social troubles delayed the achievement and completion of the armament programme, with the result that the first 500 R-35 tanks, ordered in 1935 and 1936, were not completed until April 1938, while the 400 H-35 tanks ordered at the same time were not all delivered until October 1938.

At the end of 1937, it was decided to form the DCRs with four battalions of B tanks instead of six, so that there would be three divisions instead of two. However a decision of the Supreme War Council intervened next year and delayed the formation of the first two DCRs until October 1939.

When Poland was invaded by Germany on 1 September 1939, the French army had 1,670 light tanks R-35 and H-35, 100 light tanks FCM-36, 261 fast medium tanks S-35, 213 medium tanks DI and D2, 172 heavy tanks BI and BI-bis and 407 cavalry 'auto-mitrailleuses'. The French army still had some old vehicles, notably about 1,600 light tanks (Renault) FT and 6 heavy tanks (FCM) 2C. Of the total, several hundred tanks, old and new, were stationed in North Africa, the Near East, Indo-China and Madagascar. In France, the order of battle of the French army only contained four large armoured units: these included two 'divisions légères mécaniques'. The third, which was formed in August 1939, did not become operational until February 1940. There was also an embryonic training armoured division, with four battalions of B tanks, known as the 'Groupement de chars de Nancy'. On 2 September Gamelin ordered the creation of two 'demi-brigades cuirassées' (armoured half-brigades) which became the nuclei of the first two 'divisions cuirassées de réserve' (DCR). These were formed on 2 January 1940 on the basis of two battalions of B tanks and two battalions of H tanks. A third DCR was formed on 16 March 1940, but this was still not operational by 10 May 1940.

After eight months of war, the number of tanks in service had appreciably grown. When the real war started in May 1940, there were 2,691 light tanks R-35 (R-40) and H-35 (H-39), 100 light tanks FCM-36, 384 heavy tanks BI and BI-bis, 416 fast medium tanks S-35 and 864 cavalry 'auto-mitrailleuses', to which should be added the DIs (in North Africa), as well as the D2, the FT and the old 2Cs.

After the fall of France, the German army amassed a lot of captured material which it put to its own use. The chassis of type H and FCM light tanks, and of heavy B tanks were the basis for self-propelled guns. R tanks without turrets were used as tracked tractors. R-35 and S.35 tanks were sent to Italy and Romania.

In spite of the German occupation, some French military engineers and technicians worked in secret on the development of a new heavy tank based on the old B tank, but this vehicle, the ARL 44, was not to become a reality until after the war. In 1945, the roles were reversed with the French army using some captured PzKpfw V PANTHERs in their units.

Glossary of French Abbreviations

AMC	Auto-mitrailleuse de Combat
AMR	Auto-mitrailleuse de Reconnaissance
AMX	Atelier de construction d'Issy-les-Moulineaux
APX	Atelier de construction de Puteaux
ARE	Atelier de construction de Roanne
ARL	Atelier de construction de Rueil
bis	Derivative
DEFA	Direction des Etudes et Fabrications d'Armement
FAMH	Forges et Aciéries de la Marine et d'Homécourt (Saint Chamond)
FCM	Forges et Chantiers de la Méditerranée
SAUR	Société Anonyme des Usines Renault
SEAM	Société d'Etudes et d'Applications Mécaniques
SOFAM	Société de Fabrications d'Armement et de Moteurs
SOMUA	Société d'Outillage, de Mécanique et d'Usinage d'Artillerie.
STA	Section Technique Automobile

Schneider CA on the Western Front, 1917.

Chars Hotchkiss H.35 advance, 1940.

Renault tanks in French Somaliland, 1940.

I. CHAR D'ASSAULT, SCHNEIDER CA.I

This first French tank was designed by Eugène Brillé of the Schneider company, in collaboration with Colonel (later General) J. E. Estienne, and was based upon a Holt tracked tractor. The first machine was delivered in September 1916 and took the designation of CA.I. It carried a short barrelled 75mm gun in a right front sponson giving it a very limited traverse. While contemporary British tanks had a rigid suspension, the Schneider tank 'rode' over vertical coil springs. A nosepiece acted as a wire cutter. Double doors at the rear gave access into the vehicle and a ventilator was fitted through the roof. 400 machines were built. The Schneider tank was first committed to battle at Berry-au-Bac on 14 April 1917. 13.5tons; crew 6; 75mm gun and 2 8mm MG; armour 11.4mm; engine (Schneider, gasoline, 4-cylinders), 55hp, liquid-cooled; 3.7mph; 19.8ft x 6.6ft x 7.9ft.

2. **Schneider CA.I, late production:** Enlarged and better protected fuel tanks with improved roof ventilation.

Schneider Char de Ravitaillement: 1918 modification to some vehicles with gun removed and replaced by extra door for use as supply tank.

Char d'Assault, Schneider CA.2: Improved model with traversing turret and 47mm gun in front roof replacing hull-mounted gun. Built 1917 as prototype but not put into production. Used for training only.

Char d'Assault, Schneider CA.3: Projected improved model with twin roof cupolas and MG in nose; longer rear hull. Never built, though 50 were ordered.
Other users: Germany (captured vehicles, not used in combat); Italy (few only, not used in combat); USA (few only as supply tanks).

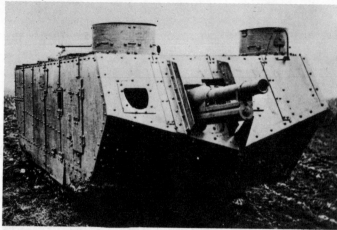

3. CHAR d'ASSAULT, SAINT CHAMOND

Evolved from a trial machine built early in 1916 by connecting two Holt tractor chassis. The Saint Chamond tank was designed by Colonel Rimailho and built by the FAMH (Saint Chamond) company, under the parentage of the STA. The early production type was armed with a Saint Chamond TR commercial gun. The original version had a flat top with two cylindrical cupolas in front or four such cupolas on the four corners at the hull. It had a spring type suspension similar to that of the Schneider. One Panhard petrol motor powered the tank through a Crochat-Collardeau electric transmission: a dynamo, operated by the power plant, supplied current to an electric motor for each track. Duplicate controls were provided at either end. The FAMH delivered 400 Saint Chamond tanks which saw action for the first time on 5 May 1917. Some tanks of this type, sent to Russia after the Revolution, were captured and used by the Red Army. 23tons; crew 9; 75mm gun and 4 8mm MG; armour 11.5mm; engine (1 Panhard, gasoline, 4-cylinders), 90hp, liquid-cooled; 5.3mph; 28.96ft x 8.75ft x 7.75ft.

4. **Char d'Assault, St Chamond (improved model):** After the first 165 tanks had been produced, the 75mm Saint Chamond TR gun was replaced by the regular 75mm Model 1897 field gun.

5. Further modifications followed: sloping roof was substituted for the flat one and later production had only one flat-sided cupola for the driver. Raised forward end of the hull ensured greater room. The hull was uparmoured to 17mm against German 'SmK' piercing bullet and original narrow tracks were replaced by wider ones.

Char d'Assault, St Chamond (experimental): One vehicle fitted with 'dumb' track unit under nose to improve trench-crossing.

Char St Chamond de Ravitaillement: Vehicle with guns removed as supply tank.
Other users: Germany (few captured vehicles, not used in combat); USA (few only as supply tanks).

6. CHAR-MITRAILLEUSE, RENAULT FT SERIES (above, prototype)

Conceived by General Estienne as a light infantry accompanying tank, and designed by Messrs Renault and Serre, the Renault FT (Faible Tonnage) prototype undertook trials at the Champlieu Camp in February 1917. In March 1917, Renault received a first order for 150 machines. It was the first tank in the world with an all-round traverse turret. A small number of the first production models were equipped with moulded steel turrets, but due to manufacturing difficulties an eight-sided riveted turret was designed, this was again changed on the Renault FT·18 to a cast steel type. Renault, Berliet, SOMUA and Delaunay-Belleville received an order for 1,000 machines, while the Miris Steel Company, of Sheffield, and other English steel works supplied the armour plate. Suspension was achieved by leaf springs combined with a vertical coil which tensioned the upper track run. Front idlers were of steel-rimmed laminated wood. The Renault FT first appeared in battle on 31 May 1918 at the Forest of Retz. During the thirties, the new 7.5mm model 31 machine-gun superseded the 8mm Hotchkiss in the vehicles that remained in service. 6.5tons; crew 2; 1 8mm MG; armour 6–22mm; engine 1 Renault gasoline, 4-cylinder, 35hp, liquid-cooled; 4.8mph; 13.25ft (excluding ditching tail) x 5.67ft x 7ft.

7. Char-Mitrailleuse Renault FT17, Moulded turret

8. Char-Mitrailleuse Renault FT17, Angled riveted turret

9. Char-Mitrailleuse Renault FT18, Cast turret

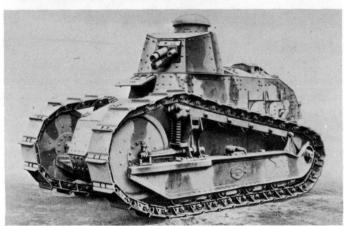

10. Char-canon FT17: The 37mm Puteaux gun appeared in both, angled riveted and cast turret versions; production orders for the 37mm gun versions totalled 1,830 vehicles. Both machine-gun and cannon armed Renaults were supplied to Belgium, Brazil, Canada, China, Czechoslovakia, Finland, Holland, Japan KO-GATA SENS HA), Poland, Russia (captured), Spain and the USA.

11. Char-canon FT18: Many FT tanks still existed in France in May

1940 and the Germans captured a large number and used them for internal security purpose (see German section). Some FT turrets were incorporated as observation cupolas into the Atlantic Wall pillboxes. 6.7tons; 1 37mm gun; other details as basic vehicle.

14. **Char démineur, Renault FT17:** The Renault FT was tested with two ploughshares mounted forward and held on arms hinged on the front idler axles. This became one of the earliest minesweeping tanks.

12. **Char-canon, Renault BS:** This version mounted a short-barrelled 75mm gun in a seven-sided riveted turret. The escape hatch was offset to the left side and a turret bustle projected at the rear to allow space for gun recoil. An order for 970 units was delayed and none was ready before the Armistice. Only a few were completed and some saw action in North Africa between the wars. The Allies encountered a few Renault BS when they landed there in 1942 during Operation Torch. 7.2tons; 1 75mm gun; other details as basic vehicle.

13. **Char fascine, Renault FT18:** An adaptation of the standard Renault FT with a front cradle for carrying fascines which could be dropped into wide trenches from within the tank.

15. **Char projecteur, Renault FT:** A variant of the FT designed for police use against civil disturbances after the war. The turret carried a high tubular metal quadripod mast fitted at the top with two searchlights which could be rotated and aimed downwards in any direction.

19. Renault FT18 Kégresse-Hinstin (1925) Rear rollers eliminated

6. Char Renault TSF: Command tank (TSF stood for 'Télégraph Sans Fil') with turret replaced by box-like superstructure. Many in service between the wars.
Other users: Britain (1918, command role only in small numbers); Germany (1,560 Renault FT tanks were still in service with the French in 1940; vehicles then captured by the Germans were used by occupation forces in France and North Africa to 1945 and 1942 respectively); Italy (1918–20, as 'stop gap' while Italian version was built — see Italian section); Soviet Russia (1919–24, captured from White Russians); Spain (1920–40); USA (1918–9, forming the main equipment of US tank battalions on the Western Front, pending proposed production of a US built version — see USA section); also, variously from 1919 until c.1940: Belgium, Brazil, China, Czechoslovakia, Finland, Japan, Netherlands.

20. Renault FT with Kégresse suspension, under tests with the US Army

17. Renault FT in British service, 1918. The British used these vehicles for command and liaison work and in most cases the gun was removed as shown here.

21. Renault Kégresse-Hinstin M26/27: This was a further development of the Kégresse suspension and featured a modified trackwork with one return roller. The continuous rubber band track was strengthened with metal pads. While the front ditching rollers had been discarded, the rear ones were retained. 6.4tons; 10mph; 15.75ft x 5.95ft x 8.5ft; other details as previous vehicles.

18. RENAULT FT KEGRESSE-HINSTIN M24/25
This development, tested in 1924–25, was an attempt to modernise the Renault tank by making it faster and quieter by means of a new Citroën-Kégresse running gear and continuous rubber band tracks. Front and rear rollers increased trench crossing capability. Some saw action in Morocco in 1925. This running gear attracted the interest of the US Ordnance Department who acquired one vehicle for tests. 6.5tons; crew 2; 1 37mm gun or 1 8mm MG; armour 6–22mm; engine (1 Renault, gasoline, 4-cylinders), 35hp, liquid-cooled; 7.5mph; 16.41ft x 5.95ft x 7.01ft.

22. CHAR NC1 (NC27) LIGHT TANK
Designed for use by infantry, the NC was an outgrowth of the

Renault FT with an up-armoured hull. It was suspended by a triple coil spring column suspension combined with six vertical hydro-pneumatic shock absorbers and ran on three four-roller bogies and an independent front roller per side. The Cleveland controlled differential steering system was used for the first time on a French tank. Also known as the NC.27 (1927), the NCI was not adopted by the French Army; production models were however, sold to Japan where it was designated OTSU-GATA SENSHA (Tank Type B), and Yugoslavia. Other users: Japan (see above), Yugoslavia. 8tons; crew 2; I 37mm gun or I MG; armour 30mm; engine (I Renault, gasoline, 4 cylinders) 60hp, liquid-cooled; IImph; 14.48ft x 5.58ft x 7ft.

23. CHAR NC2 (NC3I) LIGHT TANK
Similar to the NCI but fitted with a more powerful engine, new radiator and heavier tracks. Also designated NC3I (1931). Supplied to Greek Army. 9.5tons; crew 2; 2 7.5mm MG; armour 8–34mm; engine Renault gasoline, 4-cylinder 75hp, liquid-cooled; 12.5mph; 14.67ft x 5.17ft x 7.17ft.

24. CHAR LEGER PEUGEOT
This light tank was built in prototype form by the Peugeot company in 1918–9. Unlike the Renault FT, it featured its engine in front while the fighting compartment was at the rear. It had an upper hull combined with a fixed turret. 6tons; crew 2; I 37mm gun and I MG; engine I Peugeot, 4-cylinders, liquid-cooled.

25. CHAR DELAUNAY-BELLEVILLE MEDIUM TANK
This tank was an outgrowth of the Renault FT built in prototy form by the Delaunay-Belleville company in 1918–20. It embodi some very advanced design features such as two Williams-Jann hydraulic transmissions (one for either track) which were interc nected to a gun-laying device located in the turret, so the ta could be steered by laying the gun on its target. 13tons; crew I 37mm gun in turret and 2 8mm MG in hull front; armour 16m engine (I Renault, gasoline) 100 hp, liquid-cooled; 12mph; 16.48ft 6.95ft x 8.33ft.

26. CHAR IA HEAVY TANK
By July 1916, a team headed by Messrs Jammy and Savatier unde took studies for a heavy 'break-through' tank, or 'Char Lourd', the FCM establishment of La Seyne, near Toulon. A pilot mod was ordered on 20 October 1916. Two alternative types of tran mission were planned: one mechanical and one electric. The pil model was not ready before December 1917. On trials the tank pe ormed well but turning was difficult. So the development w ıot continued and interest was switched to the 2C type wi petrol-electric transmission. 4Itons; crew 7; 105mm gun, 2 8m MG; armour 35mm (max); engine (I Renault, gasoline, V-I2) 240h liquid-cooled; 3.72mph; 27.34ft x 9.33ft x 6.5ft.

27. CHAR 2C HEAVY TANK
The Char 2C was a heavy 'breakthrough' tank designed by FC and selected for the large scale offensive planned for 1919. Thre hundred of these tanks were requested but industrial, technolog cal and workmanship difficulties delayed the production. The te tanks produced prior to the Armistice of November 1918 did n become operational before 1921, having received two Merced 6-cylinder engines of 180hp each, formerly built by Germany f their airships and taken over by France as war reparations. Lat two 250hp Maybach motors were substituted. These power plan supplied drive to rear sprockets through petrol-electric transmissio with one generator and one electric motor per track. Manned a crew of 12, the 2C — world's first multi-turret tank — ran on suspension of 24 double roller wheels in six bogies suspended b flat springs. The turrets featured stroboscope vision devices. 1940 the surviving six machines of that type were destroyed their railway flat cars by German air attacks. 68tons; crew I 75mm gun in front turret, 4 8mm MG (one in front, one on eac side, one in rear turret); armour 45mm(max); engines (2 Merced gasoline, 6-cylinders) 2 180hp, liquid-cooled; 33.66ft x 9.66ft 13.17ft.

31. CHAR FAMH, LIGHT TANK
Small lightweight assault tank with 75mm gun in hull front, skirted suspension and tracks which were similar to those of the NC2. Cylindrical turret with stroboscopic vision cupola. Built by Schneider in 1924 as a commercial venture for overseas sales but not taken up.

28. Char 2C-bis Heavy Tank: In 1926, FCM modified one 2C as the 2C-bis, by fitting it with new engines, a short barrelled 155mm gun, and a heavier protection. I 155mm gun 4 8mm MG; engines 2 Sautter-Harlé, gasoline, 2 250hp. Other details as Char 2C.

29. CHAR SEAM (PONIATOWSKI-PETROLEO-ELECTRIQUE)
Experimental tank developed by the Société d'Etudes et d'Applications Mécaniques and fitted with petrol-electric transmission. Unarmed.

32. CHAR AMPHIBIE (SCHNEIDER-LAURENT AMPHIBIOUS TANK)
The Schneider-Laurent amphibious and wheel-and-track tank was a 1928 private venture of the Schneider company. The change from wheels to tracks could be done in three minutes without the crew dismounting from the vehicle. This tank featured a 'turtle' type upper hull of riveted construction and the trackwork was fully covered by skirting plates. The turret was fitted with a searchlight atop. 10tons; crew 3; I 37mm gun, I MG (not fitted); armour 15mm; engine (gasoline, 8-cylinders) 100hp, liquid-cooled; 28mph on wheels, 18.6mph on tracks, 10mph in water; 19.67ft x 7.17ft x 8ft (on wheels).

30. CHAR CITROEN (PI03) LIGHT TANK
This prototype tank, designed and built by Citroën, featured an upper hull of riveted construction with some castings in front. The running gear had three two-wheel bogies and two return rollers each side. Vertical casings enclosed the springing system. Both drive sprocket and idler wheel were flanged and toothed the central line of track guide horns. Armament was one machine-gun housed in an all-round traverse turret. No data available.

33. AUTO-MITRAILLEUSE AMPHIBIE, DP2 (AMPHIBIOUS TANK)
In 1935, the Société de Construction de Locomotives Batignolle-Chatillon, in collaboration with Hispano-Suiza and the Société des Propulseurs Hydrauliques, produced a pilot model for an amphibious tracked vehicle. It featured a very low running gear of four two-wheel bogies and one large side pontoon overhanging the tracks each side. The prototype sank on its maiden trip in water; development continued but the design did not go beyond the experimental stage. 12tons; crew 3; I MG; armour 15mm; engine (I Hispano-Suiza, gasoline V-12) 228hp, liquid-cooled; 24.8mph on land, 4mph in water.

AMR 33 (RENAULT TYPE VM) LIGHT TANK PROTOTYPE

In the basis of the 1931 programme for cavalry full-tracked armoured cars, Renault designed their VM vehicle in 1932. An order was placed for five pilot models which differed mainly by their suspension system. Variants with leaf springs or rubber springs were tried. Details as for production AMR 33.

34. AMR 33 (Renault Type VM) Experimental vehicle with scissors suspension.

35. AMR 33 (Renault Type VM) Experimental vehicle with leaf-spring suspension.

36. AMR 33 (RENAULT TYPE VM) LIGHT TANK (above, early production model)

One of the Renault VM pilot models was officially standardised as the Auto-mitrailleuse de Reconnaissance Renault, modèle 1933, after a few modifications. The running gear was composed of four rubber-tyred road wheels mounted on bell crank 'scissors' type articulations with horizontal rubber springing. Although armed with a single rifle calibre machine-gun, this tracked vehicle was noteworthy as being fast on road and as having good performance cross-country. This type was widely used by cavalry regiments and reconnaissance troops. 5tons; crew 2; 1 7.5mm MG; armour 13mm (max); engine (1 Reinastella, gasoline, 8-cylinders) 84hp, liquid-cooled; 40.4mph; 11.5ft x 5.25ft x 5.66ft.

37. AMR 33 (Renault Type VM)

38. AMR 35 (RENAULT TYPE ZT) LIGHT TANK (above, with 7.5mm machine-gun)

The Renault ZT soon followed the VM and was officially designated Auto-mitrailleuse de Reconnaissance Renault, modèle 1935. It carried various armament: either a 7.5mm M.31 machine-gun or a 13.2mm Hotchkiss heavy air-cooled machine-gun or even a 25mm Hotchkiss anti-tank gun. Like the VM, both hull and turret were of riveted construction. Although a little slower and less versatile than the VM, the ZT was credited with better crew comfort and better vision devices, with an easier accessibility to the engine compartment and a simpler suspension. It quickly superseded the AMR 33; 200 were built. 6.5tons; crew 2; 1 7.5mm MG or 1 13.2mm MG or 1 25mm cannon; armour 13mm (max); engine (1 Renault, gasoline, 4-cylinders) 85hp, liquid-cooled; 34.3mph; 12.6ft x 5.34ft x 6.18ft.

39. AMR 35 with 13.2mm gun.

40. AMR 35 with 25mm gun.

43. AMC 34 Pilot model with Renault FTI8 turret and 37mm gun

4I. AMC 34 (RENAULT YR) LIGHT TANK

The Auto-mitrailleuse de Combat Renault, modèle 1934, was a fast full-tracked combat car designed by Renault for use with the French mechanised cavalry. The pilot model was fitted with a Renault FT turret but the production model vehicles had a new turret housing a short barrelled 25mm gun and one machine-gun. In service 1935–40. The suspension was a much strengthened version of the type used on the AMR 33. In effect this was an uparmoured version of the AMR 33. I0.8tons; crew 3; I 25mm gun and coaxial 7.5mm MG; armour 20mm (max); engine (I Renault, gasoline, 4-cylinders) I20hp, liquid-cooled; 25mph; I3.08ft x 6.76ft x 7.5Ift.

44. AMC 35 (Renault Type ACGI) Prototype vehicle

AMC 35 (Renault ACGI) Light Tank: The AMC 35 followed the unsatisfactory AMC 34 and was built by Renault who built the early production models. The vehicle made use of a bell crank scissors suspension system with horizontal rubber springing. The tracks were of the outside guided type, and were driven by front sprockets. The hull was of riveted construction with rolled steel plates. Late production vehicles were built by AMX. Some of these vehicles were purchased some time prior to World War II by Belgium, where they were equipped with a re-designed turret and armed wih a 47mm anti-tank gun and a I3.2mm Hotchkiss machine-gun. I4.5tons; crew 3; I 47mm gun and coaxial 7.5mm MG; armour 25mm; engine (I Renault, gasoline, 4-cylinder) I80hp, liquid-cooled; 25mph; I4.58ft x 6.92ft x 7.67ft. Note: A variant of the AMC 35 had a long barrel 25mm Hotchkiss anti-tank gun in place of the short barrel 47mm gun.

42. AMC 34 Prototype vehicle

45. AMC 35 with 47mm gun.

46. AMC 35 with 25mm gun.

49. CHAR LEGER H-39 (HOTCHKISS) LIGHT TANK
This was a development of the H-35 fitted with the new engine and a long barrelled 37mm gun. This variant was officially designated: Char Léger Hotchkiss, modèle 1939-H. At first the longer gun was mounted by priority on platoon leader tanks and later was extended to other vehicles. The H-39 was used by Germany in Russian and Mediterranean theatres of war and by the Free French Forces. Some vehicles of this type were being used by the Israelis as late as 1956. See German section for vehicle in German service. Details as for H-35 and H-38, except for different gun.

47. CHAR LEGER H-35 (HOTCHKISS) LIGHT TANK
The H-35 was a cavalry tank designed and built by Hotchkiss from 1936 onwards. At first, the French infantry branch considered it unsuitable for them but adopted it later. The suspension included three 'scissors' articulations with horizontal coil springs on each side. Steering was controlled by means of a Cleveland differential and the tracks were driven by front sprockets. A one-man APXR.I turret housed a short-barrelled 37mm gun and one MG. The Hotchkiss 1935 motor had a 3.48 litre capacity. This type was in service until 1940 and thereafter captured vehicles were extensively used by the Germans. 10.6tons; crew 2; 1 37mm gun and coaxial 7.5mm MG; armour 40mm; engine (1 Hotchkiss, gasoline, 6-cylinders) 75hp, liquid-cooled; 17mph; 13.83ft x 6.08ft x 7ft.

50. CHAR LEGER R-35 (RENAULT TYPE ZM) LIGHT TANK
The R-35 was a light infantry support tank designed by Renault to meet the 1933 programme. Its 37mm short barrelled gun was housed in a one-man turret with hand traverse only. It was steerable through a Cletrac geared differential and brakes. It was fitted with 'scissors' horizontal coil spring suspension. The R-35 was the most numerous French tank in 1940, about 2,000 being built. Foreign sales were made to Poland, Turkey, Romania and Yugoslavia (see appropriate section). The Germans used captured vehicles with some modifications and converted many others to artillery tractors. They also supplied other R-35s to Italy (see German and Italian sections for further details). 10tons; crew 2; 1 37mm gun and coaxial 7.5mm MG; armour 40mm (max); engine (1 Renault, gasoline, 4-cylinders) 82hp, liquid-cooled; 12.5mph; 13.16ft x 6.08ft x 6.83ft.

48. CHAR LEGER H-38 (HOTCHKISS) LIGHT TANK
Subsequently the H-35 tank was engined with the higher capacity (5.976 litres) Hotchkiss 1938 power plant, developing 120hp at 2,800rpm. As a result the vehicle was faster (22.1mph/36kph). This variant was distinguishable by a higher rear deck but was otherwise externally similar to the H-35. 12tons; engine (1 Hotchkiss 1938, gasoline, 6-cylinders) 120hp, liquid-cooled; other details as for H-35.

51. Prototype for R-35: Showing basic hull shape, original twin MG armament, and lack of cupola.

52. Char Léger R-35 fascine carrier: This was a standard vehicle fitted with a high girder frame for transporting and dropping fascines. The turret and gun were retained. A few vehicles of this sort were in use in 1940.

53. Char Léger R-35 Avec Tourelle FCM–36: Experimental installation of the FCM welded turret.

54. Char Léger R-35 Avec Nouveau Tourelle: Experimental installation of cast FCM type turret on modified R-35 chassis.

Char Léger R-40: The late production model of the R-35 was re-designated as R-40 and equipped with the long-barrelled 37mm gun. Details as for R-35.

55. Char Léger AMX R-40: This was a development of the R-35 fitted with an AMX running gear giving better performance over rough terrain. Twelve small road rollers on each side were suspended by means of six vertical coil springs which acted from three working beams pivoting on their centre. 12.5tons; crew 2; 1 37mm gun, 1 MG; 12.5mph; 13ft 9in x 6ft 2in x 7ft 2in.

56. CHAR LEGER FCM-36 INFANTRY TANK
Designed for the purpose of accompanying infantry, the FCM-36 was the first French diesel-engined tank: its Berliet 8.4 litres, 4-stroke, water-cooled power plant was built under licence from the British firm of Ricardo. It was also noteworthy as being built with welded armour in both hull and turret. Protected by skirting plates with mud chutes on their upper parts, the suspension included nine bogie wheels (four paired and mounted on pivoting arms and one independent adjusting roller) per side, suspended by spiral springs combined with guide rods and rubber shock absorbers. At first, a contract for 100 machines was placed in 1936; another order for a further 100 units was cancelled owing to the prohibitive price asked for by the builder. The FCM was in service in 1940 when many were captured and later used by the Germans. 12tons; crew 2; 1 37mm gun and coaxial 7.5mm MG; armour 40mm (max); engine Berliet, diesel, 4-cylinder, 91hp, liquid-cooled; 15mph; 14.58ft x 7ft x 7.17ft.

57. The original FCM-36 prototype: Showing turret shape and extra side armour.

58. CHAR DI INFANTRY TANK

The DI was an infantry medium tank designed by Renault to meet the 1926 defence programme. It came into service from 1931 onwards and was one of the first tanks in the world with a cast turret. It was also the first French tank to carry a 47mm anti-tank gun. The DI had 14 small road wheels per side with a suspension system similar to that on the NC, consisting of three vertical coil springs and hydro-pneumatic shock absorbers. The running gear was protected by skirting plates and the hull was of riveted construction. Power drive was transmitted to the rear sprockets through a six speed gearbox and steering was effected by means of a Cleveland controlled differential. The DI was equipped with a wireless set with a large triangular aerial behind the turret. It was well fitted with vision devices. Recognised as underpowered and prone to mechanical breakdowns, it became an unpopular tank which was mainly used in North Africa. It was in service until 1940. 13tons; crew 3; 1 47mm gun and coaxial 7.5mm MG plus 1 7.5mm MG (fixed) in front hull; armour 35mm (max); engine (1 Renault, gasoline, 4 cylinders) 65hp, liquid-cooled; 11.3mph; 18.94ft x 7.08ft x 7.84ft.

61. CHAR D2 INFANTRY TANK

The D2 was a medium infantry tank developed from the DI to provide heavier protection and more horsepower. The pilot model appeared in 1932 and Renault began deliveries in 1934. Two prototypes were engined with diesel motors but this was not continued. The D2 had a cast APXI type turret and the triple coil spring column suspension with hydro-pneumatic shock absorbers similar to those on the NC and DI. Transmission was of the mechanical type with five forward and one reverse speeds and multi-plate clutch. The drive was applied to rear sprockets and steering was by Cleveland controlled differential. The order for these vehicles was reduced to only 50 in 1936, the new SOMUA tanks being preferred instead. 18.5tons; crew 3; 1 47mm gun and coaxial 7.5mm MG or 1 7.5mm MG (fixed) in front hull; armour 20–40mm; engine (1 Renault, gasoline, 6-cylinders) 150hp, liquid-cooled; 14mph; 17.9ft x 8.75ft x 7.25ft.

59. Char NC 31 Modifié: This was a NC 31 tank modified as a development vehicle for the Char D1 series.

62. Char D2 (Prototype): Early development vehicle for the Char D2 series equipped with Renault FT18 turret.

60. Char DI (Type ST2): Reworked model of the DI, equipped with the Renault FT18 cast turret and 37mm gun.

63. Char D2 (Prototype): Prototype vehicle for the Char D2 series with cast APX type turret.

64. CHAR B HEAVY TANK (above, pilot model built by FCM)

At the request of General Estienne and on the basis of previous studies worked out by Renault, Schneider, FAMH, FCM and Delaunay-Belleville, a new battle tank was developed under the code designation of 'Tractor 30'. In 1929–30, three pilot models were built by Renault and FCM: later they became designated 'Char B (BI)'. These three pilot models were extensively reworked and modified for tests and the first one, re-engined and uparmoured, became the early prototype for the BI-ter in 1937. 25tons; crew 4; I 75mm gun, in low front hull position, 2 7.5mm MG (fixed), in low front hull position, 2 7.5mm MG (flexible), in turret; armour 40mm (max); engine (I Renault, gasoline, 6-cylinders) 180hp, liquid-cooled; 12.5mph.

65. CHAR BI HEAVY TANK

The Char BI was the production version of the Char B; its production began in 1935 and a small number were built before it was continued as the more powerful BI-bis. It was more heavily armed, having a semi-automatic 47mm gun in an APXI turret instead of the machine-guns. Steering was through a double differential combined with a hydrostatic unit — the Naeder — in the steering drive which gave it an infinite number of turning radii, so the 75mm gun could easily be lined up to its target. The BI ran on a Holt suspension improved by FCM and fully covered by skirting. Suspension was by leaf and coil springs acting on vertical articulations and completed by bumper pads. Overall tracks of the sole plate type were toothed by rear driving sprockets and could be adjusted from inside the tank. The BI was very advanced in design: it had self-sealing petrol tanks, many lubrication points connected by pipes to grouped lubricators, a fireproof bulkhead, a gyroscopic compass, an electric starter and a floor escape hatch was used for the disposal of empty cases. The BI had a badly distributed crew which had to be composed of well-trained specialists. The Char BI layout influenced the British A20 design of 1939. 30tons; crew 4; I 75mm gun, in low front hull position, I 7.5mm MG, fixed, in low front hull position, I 47mm gun and coaxial 7.5mm MG in turret; armour 40mm (max); engine (I Renault, gasoline, 6-cylinders) 180hp, liquid-cooled; 17.2mph; 20.92ft x 8.17ft x 9.21ft.

66. CHAR BI-BIS HEAVY TANK

The BI-bis was the main battle tank of the French Army in 1940. Evolved from the BI, it was uparmoured to 60mm and fitted with a new APX4 turret and gun. At first, the early production machines were powered by a 250hp engine: they were later re-engined with a 300hp aircraft motor. The late production machines had greater range thanks to auxiliary fuel tanks designed by either ARL or FCM. The BI-bis was built from 1937 onwards by Renault, FAMH Saint-Chamond, Schneider and FCM under the parentage of the ARL. In 1939, the AMX became also involved into production of this tank. It was considered as very powerful but costly to produce. 32tons; crew 4; I 75mm gun, in low front hull position, I 7.5mm MG, fixed, in low front hull position, I 47mm gun and coaxial 7.5mm MG in turret; armour 60mm (max); engine (I Renault, gasoline, 6-cylinders) 180hp, liquid-cooled; 17.2mph; 20.94ft x 8.19ft x 9.17ft.

67. CHAR BI-TER HEAVY TANK

This tank was a BI-bis development which did not go beyond the prototype stage. Preliminary studies started in 1935 with the BI pilot model 101 as a basis. The BI-ter had to be uparmoured to 70mm and to be powered by a Renault V-12 engine developing 400hp but the very few pilot models produced had a Renault engine (type BI-bis) uprated to 310hp. The 75mm gun was provided with a right and left traverse. A shorter BDR transmission gear was planned resulting in a roomier fighting compartment. The upper track returns ran under cast steel tunnels and the side armour was suitably sloped. 36tons; crew 5; I 75mm gun, in low front hull position, I 7.5mm MG, fixed, in low front hull position, I 47mm gun and coaxial 7.5mm MG in turret; armour 70mm; engine I Renault (petrol, 6-cylinders) 310hp, liquid-cooled; 16.5mph; 20.8ft x 8.94ft x 9.5ft.

68. CHAR S-35 (SOMUA) MEDIUM TANK

This cavalry medium tank was one of the finest armoured fighting vehicles of its day and was the first in the world with all-cast hull and turret construction. At first, it was designated as 'AMC SOMUA, type AC3' but it was redesignated later as 'Char SOMUA, modèle 1935-S'. Powered by a V-8 gasoline engine, the S-35 was steered by means of a mechanically operated double overlapping differential system. The turret had an electric power traverse. The tank ran over nine road wheels per side, suspended by combined coiled and semi-elliptic leaf springing, protected by skirting plates. Captured S-35 were used by both German and Italian armies. About 500 were built. 20tons; crew 3; 1 47mm gun and coaxial 7.5mm MG; armour 40mm (max); engine (1 SOMUA, gasoline, V-8 cylinders) 190hp, liquid-cooled; 25mph; 17.33ft x 6.94ft x 8.58ft.

69. Char S-35 (SOMUA) prototype vehicle.

70. CHAR AMX-38 LIGHT TANK
Designed by AMX, this medium tank did not reach operational

status. It was an advanced design fitted with a gas filtration plant and a wireless set. The motive power, provided by a diesel engine, was transmitted to the drive sprockets through Wilson-Talbot gears. The trackwork, fully covered by skirting plates, included 16 bogie wheels and 4 return rollers per side. One or two production vehicles were ready when war started in 1939 but the events of 1940 terminated production completely. 16tons; 1 47mm gun and coaxial 7.5mm MG; armour 60mm (max); engine (1 Aster, diesel, 4-cylinders) 150hp, liquid-cooled; 15mph; 16.94ft x 5.93ft x 7.25ft.

71. CHAR DE TRANSITION ARL-44 HEAVY TANK
The design of this tank started clandestinely when France was still under German occupation. On the basis of the BI-bis, the ARL conducted the studies of a new heavy tank which, as a step forward to more modern design, was christened as 'Char de Transition ARL-44'. The tank carried a long barrelled gun housed in a Schneider turret powered by a Simca traversing gear. The trackwork was protected by skirting plates. The production was carried out by both FAMH and Renault under the parentage of the ARL. This tank made its one and only public appearance at the National Day Parade on 14 July 1951. 45tons; crew 5; 1 90mm gun and 2 7.5mm MG; engine 1 Maybach, gasoline; 23.1mph; 34.5ft x 11.6ft x 10.5ft.

GERMANY

INTRODUCTION

The German War Department received an idea for the type of vehicle later known as a tank well before the start of World War I. This vehicle, called a Motorgeschütz (Motor gun), was designed by an Austrian Army Officer, Gunther Burstyn, in 1911. The Austrian War Office proved uninterested in the project but the publication of an enthusiastic magazine article led the German War Office to make enquiries. However, they rejected the design when they saw it, on the grounds that it might infringe patents for agricultural tractors. The Motorgeschütz looked well ahead for its time and would have had a traversing turret and long steering arms and wheels as well as a tracked chassis. Interest soon waned for this project but in 1913 another enthusiast, Friedrich Goebel, demonstrated an armoured cross-country vehicle which was unpowered and moved on pivoted legs like a child's walking toy. Lack of control was an inherent drawback and the Testing Commission asked for a powered example. This adopted a single Pedrail-type track unit but lacked steering; it was called the 'Landpanzerkreuzer'. The whole project was eventually dropped as impractical, however, and Goebel meanwhile designed a larger (118ft long version) of the Landkreuzer. This again was not proceeded with.

Though agents in Britain passed the information to Germany that 'Landships' were being built, no official attempts to build tanks were made in Germany until after the appearance of the first British tanks in action in September 1916. Even then there were attempts to play down the importance of the tank in order to maintain the morale of the troops in the front line. Various tank designs were offered to the War Department by commercial undertakings but none were adopted. Among there were the Treffas-Wagen, a tricycle 'big wheel' machine and a couple of Orion machine tractors, basically agricultural tractors with armoured bodies.

A major step forward however, was the Bremer Marien Wagen, basically a 4ton Daimler truck with the back wheels replaced by tracked units. In October 1916 this was modified by having its front wheels replaced by tracked units. By March 1917 the vehicle had been given an armoured body, with plans to fit guns later, and thus became Germany's first armoured vehicle. It was not a true tank design however, being really just a tracked motor-lorry. On trials it proved unsuccessful with much track shedding and poor traction. It was not taken up though un-armoured versions of the same vehicle were later used as supply carriers.

The first real German tank was the well-known A7V named after the abbreviation for the German War Department motor vehicle section. This section formed a committee late in 1916, composed of motor industry chiefs and army officers, to procure a standard tank for the German Army. Modified Holt tractor suspension units were proposed by the vehicle's designer, Joseph Vollmer, as these were cheap and simple, with a well-proven springing system. The A7V Tank was a big box-like vehicle which carried a heavy gun in the nose and had five machine-gun positions. It needed a crew of 18 and could be driven in either direction. The prototype was

successfully tested in March and April 1917 and plans were made to put the A7V into production (plus an unarmoured cargo version) though some redesign work was required.

Prevailing economic conditions in Germany, plus the need to concentrate on conventional arms output, meant that the A7V production was a slow and protracted affair. Less than 20 of the 100 vehicles ordered were actually delivered, several of these being cargo carriers rather than tanks. Production of the few that were completed took over a year owing to material shortages.

Meanwhile the small German tank arm was equipped entirely with captured British vehicles, Tanks Mk IV and V and Whippets. The first company of A7Vs was not formed until early 1918. The A7V proved unstable, and its poor tracks gave a poor trench-crossing performance.

An improved model was proposed by Vollmer, based on the British tank Mk IV. Originally an exact copy was planned but this would have been costly and time consuming. A compromise which used the engine and suspension of the A7V was arrived at simply by the adoption of the 'lozenge' shape body. The 57mm guns were carried in side sponsons exactly in the British manner. Several interesting further developments were planned based on the A7V/U but no production was achieved because of the deteriorating economic position, and only the prototype vehicles were built.

The biggest tank projected by the Germans in the World War I period was the mighty K-Wagen, a 42ft, 148ton 'landship' powered by two Daimler aero engines. It was designed to be broken into small sections for transport by rail. Joseph Vollmer (the A7V engineer) and Captain Wegner (the A7V army liaison officer), designed this vehicle. Two initial examples were still being built at the time of the Armistice and these were broken up by the Allies before they could be tested.

Vollmer was greatly in favour of building light tanks in large numbers rather than limited numbers of heavy tanks. He persuaded the A7V committee and the War Department to sponsor some Leichte Kampfwagen (Light Combat vehicles). These were built on Daimler car chassis, utilising the mechanical parts and with a strengthened front axle. LK.I had a small machine-gun turret, while LK.II had a limited traverse 57mm gun in a barbette. In June 1918 some 580 LK.IIs were ordered but again the order could not be fulfilled before the Armistice had brought the war to an end. A further design the LK.III was to be purpose-built, rather than an adaption of a motor car chassis, but this never left the drawing board. There were several other promising tank designs in the air meanwhile, including one each from Krupp, Daimler, and Oberschlesien Eisenwerk, but none of these were completed.

With the Armistice the German tank force was disbanded although at no time had it been large enough to pose a threat to the Allies. Despite the number of designs and prototypes produced, only the A7V saw service, the main operational tank force being composed of captured British tanks.

The Treaty of Versailles included terms banning tanks

in the postwar German Army. Nonetheless, ideas were kept alive by contact with Sweden, where a modified design based on the LK.II was put into production for the Swedish Army under German technical guidance. Later in the 1920s liaison was made with the Red Army, and secret training and testing facilities for new designs were made available at the Russian tank school in Kazan. Apart from a few armoured cars, (officially allowed for security police use), there was no official tank production until Hitler came to power in 1933. From 1926 to 1929 however, some experimental tanks were built secretly by major armament and engineering firms. A light tank was called the 'Leichte Traktor' (light tractor) and a heavy tank was called a 'Grosstraktor' (heavy tractor) the pretence being that these were agricultural or industrial vehicles in order to beat the Versailles Treaty ban.

Rearmament started secretly in 1932 and got into full stride in the next couple of years with Hitler and the Nazi Party in full control of the country. The Treaty limitations were openly flouted and aircraft, big guns, tanks, submarines, and other proscribed weapons went into production.

The Army took up the ideas of tank theorists like Fuller and Liddell Hart, and armoured (Panzer) Divisions were formed, three of them by 1935. To get them equipped quickly two light tank types were specially developed, the PzKpfw I and II. These were the mainstay of the German Panzer Divisions for the next few years while two larger 'medium' designs were developed, the PzKpfw III and IV. Two further designs of heavy tank, originally called NbFz (new design) were built in a small pre-production batch. These were similar to the British 16ton Tank and Russian T–28 types, both contemporary early 1930s designs, complete with small auxiliary turrets. About 1939 the two NbFz types were redesigned PzKpfw V and VI designations (not to be confused with the later Panther and Tiger vehicles).

Early in 1939 Czechoslovakia was annexed and all that country's tank force was passed over to the German Army. When war was declared in September 1939, there were still only limited numbers of PzKpfw III and IV, and Czech tanks, under their German designations of PzKpfw 38 (t) and PzKpfw 35 (t) were the most numerous types in service. It was not until late 1940 that the PzKpfw III and IV were in full service. Though it had originally been intended to phase out the earlier vehicles once the PzKpfw III and IV were in service, the need for armoured vehicles in quantity meant that the PzKpfw I and II plus the Czech types were still to be seen with second line units right up to 1945. In addition the basic chassis of these vehicles were used as the basis for a variety of self-propelled guns and tank destroyers through to 1945.

With the invasion of Russia in June 1941, the tenor of German tank development changed considerably. A certain amount of complacency had manifested itself after the superior showing of German armour in Poland, France and the initial Western Desert successes. The PzKfw III and IV were considered to be excellent and the early weeks of 'Barbarossa' the invasion of Russia

augured well, with the estimated annihilation or capture of over 20,000 obsolescent Russian tanks. Then in July 1941 the T–34 was encountered for the first time: by October 1941 is was being encountered in force. This superb vehicle rendered all existing German tanks virtually obsolete overnight. Compared to the PzKpfw III and IV it was superior in firepower, speed, shell-deflecting shape, suspension, armour thickness, and manoeuverability.

The German Ordnance Department, at the suggestion of Guderian, appointed a commission to recommend new measures to combat the T–34. This led initially to the development of the Tiger I (PzKpfw VI). It was based on some earlier (1937–40) prototypes and designs, but it was then revised starting in October 1941, to include immensely thick armour and an 88mm gun based on the successful high velocity flak/anti-tank gun of the same calibre. prototypes were ready by March 1942 — such was the speed of development. The armour and firepower were superior to any other tank at the time and it was a formidable weapon despite its low speed and initially poor reputation for reliability.

The first German tank to be directly and totally designed as a result of the T–34 Commission's findings was the PzKpfw Panther. This closely duplicated the shape and layout of the T-34 — in particular the shaped armour and high velocity 75mm gun. It was designed by January 1942 and a prototype was ready by May. The Panther was in service by mid 1943, with top priority for production. (The several production improvements in both the Tiger and Panther, plus the 'rival' prototypes for each requirement, are recorded in more detail in the reference section which follows).

Meanwhile quite successful efforts were made to improve the fighting qualities of the PzKpfw III and IV, with more powerful guns and extemporised, but serviceable, extra armour. The PzKpfw IV remained in production until 1945, the most numerous of all German World War II tanks, while PzKpfw III production was terminated in 1944. The chassis of both models were used extensively for self-propelled guns and tank destroyers.

The final phase of German tank development prior to 1945 saw efforts to produce even bigger tanks with more armour and greater firepower. The Königstiger, or Tiger II, was the only one of the new designs to see service. This huge vehicle of nearly 70tons weight, was a scaled-up design combining the gun and other features of the Tiger I and the shape and mechanical layout of the Panther. A more refined big tank of this type was the Panther II, projected but never built. The Königstiger enjoyed limited success, especially when it was first in action in 1944 and still enjoyed the advantage of surprise. However, such a large tank had tactical limitations imposed by its bulk and weight and smaller tanks were able to get the better of it. By 1944 the Allies were enjoying total air superiority over all the battlefields and this was another prime factor which helped to limit the effectiveness of German tanks in general and the super-heavy tanks in particular.

Finally there came a last generation of immense giant

tanks of which only the Maus saw completion and had advanced sufficiently for possible production. The vehicle was designed by Dr. Porsche, a noted automotive engineer who was involved closely in many World War II German tank projects. Maus weighed 188tons and was intended to carry a 150mm gun and a coaxial 75mm gun, its great weight forcing the crossing of rivers on the riverbed as no bridge could support it. By late 1944 however, German industry was in a desperate state, much disrupted and short of materials; Maus was never put into production, since such facilities as remained available were needed for conventional weapons production. Another giant tank in the same class was the Tiger-Maus or Lion (Löwe) which was to be built by Henschel as a further enlargement of the Tiger II. It was still in the project and design stage in 1945.

In 1943 meanwhile, the German Ordnance Department had begun to rationalise tank production to cut back on the variety of projects and designs which were proliferating. The plan was to produce a series of designs with common parts and mechanical features giving optimum changeability of components, thus greatly simplifying the spare parts and maintenance problems. The so-called 'E' series was to feature light, medium and battle tanks, as well as carriers and SP gun chassis. Largest of all was a heavy tank, the E.100, the only one of the 'E' series to be built. This was to be a 140ton giant tank, based on the Tiger II layout. Only the hull was completed by May 1945, and it proved to be the last of the giant tanks, and the last of the Third Reich's technically excellent, but tactically inferior designs.

Glossary of German Abbreviations

Ausf.	Model, mark
Bergepanzer	Armoured recovery vehicle
DB	Daimler-Benz
H	Henschel
K	Krupp
MAN	Maschinenfabrik Augsburg Nürnburg
P	Porsche
PzBefWg	Panzerbefehlswagen (command tank)
PzBeobWg	Panzerbeobachtswagen (armoured observation post)
PzKpfw	Panzerkampfwagen (armoured fighting vehicle, tank)
Sd Kfz	Sonder Kraftfahrzeug (special vehicle number —, ie: ordnance designation)
VK	Experimental model

A7V tanks on the Western Front, June 1918.

German dummy tanks on army manoeuvres, 1927.

A panzer division advances into Libya.

I. A7V STURMPANZERWAGEN

Designed by Joseph Vollmer early in 1917 under aegis of special committee formed by A7V Allegmeine-Kriegs-Department 7, Abteilung Verkehrswesen — General War Department 7, Traffic Section) to produce a tank for the German Army. Basis was lengthened track from Holt tractor, parts being obtained from Austria in the first instance. Prototype ran in April 1917; in service September 1917 and first used in action against British tanks in March 1918. Owing to steel shortages only about 20 were completed as tanks, with another 30 as unarmoured load carriers (Uberlandwagen). Powered by twin Daimler engines in centre with control position above; could be driven in either direction. Holt-type suspension. Box-like hull with one-piece sides in later vehicles. 30tons; crew 18; 57mm gun plus 6 MG; armour 15–30mm; engine (2 gasoline) 200hp; 8mph; 26.25ft x 10ft x 10.8ft. Other users: Poland (few captured vehicles, 1920).

2. A7V late production vehicle with one-piece hull sides.

3. A7V/U STURMPANZERWAGEN

Designed by the A7V committee to overcome inherent faults (instability, poor trench-crossing) of A7V Sturmpanzerwagen. It utilised existing parts but had sponsons and overall tracks U— Umlaufende Ketten—all-round tracks) in layout copied from British tanks. Twenty ordered, but only the prototype was actually completed. Like British tanks it had 57mm guns in side sponsons and four Maxim MGs. Holt-type suspension, twin Daimler engines. Superficial resemblance to British Mk IV but larger. Inferior performance to British tanks. 39tons; crew 7; 2 57 mm guns plus 4 MG; armour 20–30mm; engine (2 gasoline) 210hp; 7.5mph; 27.5ft x 15.48ft x 10.5ft.

A7V/U2: Projected version with smaller sponsons and MG in command cupola.

A7V/U3: Projected version with MG armament only. Neither the U2 or U3 versions were built.

4. K-WAGEN HEAVY TANK

Very heavy breakthrough tank intended for service in 1919 and weighing 148tons. Designed by Vollmer for A7V committee. Could be broken into four parts for rail transport. Designed and ordered in December 1917 but delayed by material shortages. Two under construction at Armistice in November 1918 were destroyed by the Allied Control Commission. The K-Wagen featured a massive box-like hull with roller-type tracks and sponsons for four 7.7cm guns. Power was from twin 650hp aero engines with electro-magnetic clutch transmission. Neither vehicle was (actually completed. 148tons; crew 22; 4 7.7cm guns plus 7 MG; armour 30mm; engine (2 gasoline) 1300hp; 42.58ft x 20ft x 9.42ft.

5. LK.I LIGHT TANK

Designed by Vollmer who advocated simple light tanks rather than heavy expensive tanks (LK — Leichte Kampfwagen). Utilised Daimler car chassis and existing axles for sprocket and idler wheels. Prototypes only, mid–1918. Followed usual automobile layout with engine at front and driving compartment behind. Light turret was fitted to take MG. 6.89tons; crew 3; 1 MG; armour 8mm; engine (gasoline) 60hp; 7.5mph; 18ft x 6.58ft x 8.18ft.

6. LK.II LIGHT TANK

Developed from LK.I prototype to meet specifications laid down by A7V committee. Based on LK.I but with thicker armour and 57mm gun in rear barbette. Two prototypes completed in June 1918 leading to production order for 580. None completed when war ended. Like the LK.I the LK.II was based on the Daimler automobile chassis layout with fixed barbette at rear. 8.75tons; crew 3; 57mm gun; armour 14mm; engine (gasoline) 60hp; 7.5mph; 16.75ft x 6.48ft x 8.18ft. Other users: LK.II design became the basis of the Swedish Strv m/21 in 1921-2.

LK.II with Machine Guns: Project for version of LK.II with MGs replacing 57mm gun and a traversing turret.

LK.III LIGHT TANK
Project for major redesign with layout reversed to place turret at front and engine at rear, utilising purpose-built parts instead of car chassis. 57mm gun in traversing turret with proposed alternative of 20mm Becker Flieger Kanone. 1,000 ordered but pilot model not completed by time of armistice.

PROJECTED TANKS 1918
Three further tank designs were projected but the Armistice of November 1918 brought all work on these to a halt. Most advanced was a Krupp light tank which had a crew of two and a shield for following infantry. With a length of 12ft 9in overall, a prototype was under construction at the war's end. Oberschlesien Eisenwerk had designed a heavy tank with traversing turret and 37mm gun, two prototypes of which had been ordered when the war ended. It was 22ft long and had sprung tracks and auxiliary MG turrets. Daimler had designed a Sturmwagen to meet similar specifications to the Krupp vehicle, again with an infantry shield at rear. No order for this was placed by the time of the Armistice.

7. BEUTEPANZERWAGEN IV (armed with 57mm Sokol guns)
Owing to the delayed production of home-built tanks, the main strength of the German tank arm in 1917–18 was made up of captured British tanks, mostly Mk IV, but also some Mk Vs. These vehicles were captured at Cambrai and elsewhere: for German service they were overhauled and rearmed with ex-Russian 57mm Sokol guns (as used in the A7V) in place of the British 6pdrs. Female tanks were armed with MG08 Maxims. (Beutepanzerwagen — 'captured armoured vehicle'). The picture above shows a Mk IV. For further details see the British section.

8. Beutepanzerwagen IV: Armed with MG08 Maxim machine-guns.

9. Beutepanzerwagen Mk A: One German company was equipped with captured ex-British Medium Mk A Whippet tanks. For further details see British section.

10. LEICHTE TRAKTOR VK.31 LIGHT TANK
Produced as one of a series of light tanks built secretly in Germany and tested at Kazan (USSR) in defiance of Versailles Treaty. Known under cover name of 'tractor'. Three prototypes each built by Rheinmetall and Krupp. Total of 289 ordered but these were cancelled in favour of later designs. Front engine, rear turret, as in LK.II of World War I. 9.5tons; 3.7cm gun; mild steel; 12mph. No other details known.

11. GROSSTRAKTOR I (DAIMLER-BENZ) HEAVY TANK
Built by Daimler-Benz to a secret German War Office contract, one of three test vehicles in the heavy tank class. Tested secretly at Kazan USSR. Two prototypes built. Slab sided vehicles with prominent mud chutes. Amphibious. 7.5cm gun plus 3 MG; mild steel; engine (gasoline) 300hp. No other details known.

12. Grosstraktor II (Rheinmetall) Heavy Tank: Built to the very same contract as Grosstraktor I but with less sophisticated suspension, simpler shape, and side access doors. Mild steel prototypes for trials only. Details generally as for Grosstraktor I.

13. Grosstraktor III (Krupp) Heavy Tank: Built to same requirements as Grosstraktor I and II but with many detail differences. Two prototypes only, mild steel. Rear turret with MG was specified for all three. Details generally as for Grosstraktor I.

14. LANDWIRTSCHAFTLICHER SCHLEPPER (La.S) (KRUPP L.K.A.I) Pz.Kpfw I prototype
Prototype for a light tank in the 5ton class to meet a Heereswaffenamt (War Department) requirement for the rearmed Reichswehr, 1933. Selected for construction from designs tendered by Rheinmetall, Daimler-Benz, MAN, Henschel, and Krupp, the L.K.A.I being the Krupp model. Designation La S meant 'agricultural tractor' to conceal true purpose. This small vehicle was based largely on the layout of the Carden Loyd Mk I tankette chassis (see British section), a sample of which was purchased as a gun carrier from Britain in 1932. Turret had twin coaxial MGs. Used for trials only. Crew 2; mild steel; engine (gasoline); 25mph.

15. PANZERKAMPFWAGEN I AUSF A (Sd Kfz 101) LIGHT TANK

Production vehicle derived from the Krupp L.K.A.I prototype. The Pz.Kpfw I Ausf A entered production in 1934 and the Pz.Kpfw I Ausf B in 1935. The B model was slightly longer, had an extra road wheel, and a slightly more powerful engine. The Pz.Kpfw I was mainly intended as a cheaply produced training vehicle for the newly formed German armoured divisions. They were, however, still in wide service in the early part of World War II. The Pz.Kpfw I was similar to the L.K.A.I but with smaller road wheels and leaf spring suspension equalised by external beams. Coil springs on loading wheels. 5.4tons (5.8tons); crew 2; 2 MG; armour 7–13 mm; engine (gasoline) 60hp (100hp); 25mph; 13.2ft (14.7ft) x 6.8ft x 5.6ft (figure in parentheses applies to Model B). Other users: Spain (Nationalist) 1937-9.

16. Pz.Kpfw I Ausf B

17. Kleiner Panzerbefehlswagen I (Sd Kfz 265): Modified vehicle based on Pz.Kpfw I Ausf B but with fixed superstructure and cupola. Commander's vehicle. Some Pz.Kpfw I Ausf A with fixed turrets were also used by unit commanders.

18. Pz.Kpfw Ib, Ladungsleger I: Conversion for use by assault engineers with gantry and platform for carrying and placing explosives in demolition work

19. Flammpanzer I: A small number of the Ausf A version were converted in the field by the Afrika Korps to the role of flame-throwers. The right machine gun was removed from the turret and replaced by the projector of the light portable infantry flame-thrower Model 40, the cylinders for fuel and compressed air was also installed inside the turret.

20. Pz.Kpfw I Ausf C (VK.60I): Prototype for an uparmoured version of the Pz.Kpfw I for the reconnaissance and airborne roles. Kraus-Maffei/Daimler-Benz design, 1939–40. Order for 40 vehicles never completed and the project was abandoned in 1941 after only the prototype was built. Had a 20mm gun and 7.92mm MG instead of the twin MGs of earlier models. Interleaved wheels with centre track guides. 8tons; armour 10–30mm; engine (gasoline) 150hp; 40mph. Other details as Pz.Kpfw I.

21. Pz.Kpfw I neuer Art verstärk (VK.I80I): Project put forward in December 1939 for vehicle based on Pz.Kpfw I but heavily armoured for infantry support role (neuer Art (verstärkt) — uparmoured new model). Prototype built in June 1940 but the project was later abandoned. Interleaved wheels, but suspension heavier than VK.60I. 18tons; armour 30–80mm; 15mph; 14.3ft x 8.6ft x 6.75ft. Other details as VK.60I and Pz.Kpfw I.

22. KRUPP L.K.A.II LIGHT TANK (Pz.Kpfw II Prototype)
Prototype by Krupp offered to the Heereswaffenamt to meet a requirement for a larger light tank in the 10ton class, promulgated in 1934. This vehicle was based closely on the original L.K.A.I prototype (see above) but enlarged and with a new turret having a 20mm gun as called for in the official specification. The design was not adopted however. Details generally as for L.K.A.I.

23. PANZERKAMPFWAGEN II AUSF al, a2, a3 (Sd Kfz 121) LIGHT TANK
Design by MAN (a rival was offered by Henschel) for a light tank in the 10ton class produced to meet the same requirement as the L.K.A.II. The MAN design was chosen for production and in 1935 the first 25 pre-production machines (Ausf al) were built. A further 25 with detail changes were designated a2 and a further 50 in 1936 were designated a3. Layout of all was similar with rear engine and front drive. They were externally similar but had internal detail changes in cooling and (in the a3) in the suspension. The equalising beam and paired bogies with equalising beam were features of the al and a2. There was a cast nose. 7.2tons; 20mm gun plus MG; armour 14.5mm; engine (gasoline) 130hp; 25mph; 15.8ft x 8.6ft x 6.75ft.

Pz.Kpfw II Ausf b: Improved 1936 model, externally similar to the Pz.Kpfw II Ausf a3 but with increased (30mm) front armour, uprated (140hp) engine, and new driving sprockets with geared front drive which was standardised for later models.

24. Pz.Kpfw II Ausf c: Much improved 1937 model with modified turret and full width front superstructure. This vehicle formed the basis for the subsequent definitive production models. About 2,000 were built and were used for training and for equipping the first panzer divisions. Major new feature was the distinctive suspension consisting of large diameter road wheels on elliptic springs. The superstructure was more angular than on earlier models. 8.8tons; crew 3; 20mm gun plus MG; armour 14.5–30mm; engine (gasoline) 140hp; 25mph; 15.8ft x 7.08ft x 6.6ft.

25. Pz.Kpfw II Ausf A (above), B, C: Main production versions of the Pz.Kpfw II series, developed from the earlier Ausf a, b, and c models, incorporating lessons learned from the Ausf c type. Widely used in early World War II period. Hull had an angled instead of rounded nose as had been featured in the Ausf c type. There were splash plates on the top and bottom of the mantlet. Ausf A had only a periscope for the commander but Ausf B and C had a centrally placed turret cupola which was distinctive. Thicker armour than Ausf c but otherwise similar layout. Variants included SP guns, not covered here. 9.5tons; crew 3; 20mm gun plus MG; armour 10–30mm; engine (gasoline) 140hp; 16ft x 7.08ft x 6.75ft.

26. Pz.Kpfw II Ausf B.

27. Pz.Kpfw II Ausf D, E: Produced by Daimler-Benz in 1939, these models were similar to previous vehicles but differed in having Famo/Christie-type suspension to give a top road speed of 35mph. However cross-country performance was poor and led to their early withdrawal. They were largely taken out of first line service in 1940 and converted for other roles. Some became flamethrowing tanks (see below) and others SP guns. 10tons; crew 3; 20mm gun plus MG; armour 10–30mm; engine (gasoline) 140hp; 35mph; 15.48ft x 7.48ft x 6.75ft.

28. Flammpanzer II: Of the Pz.Kpfw II Ausf D/E, some 95 were converted to flamethrowing tanks with twin flame projectors with **40yard** ranges.

29. Pz.Kpfw II Ausf F (above), G, J: Further improved version of the Ausf C uparmoured to give added protection from heavier anti-tank guns; 35mm frontal armour and 20mm on the sides. They were built in 1940–41. Appearance was similar to the Pz.Kpfw II Ausf C but with noticeably thicker armour and conical hub to the idler wheel as distinctive features. The Ausf G and J were externally similar to the Ausf F except for the addition of a stowage box on the turret rear. 9.5tons; armour 20–35mm. Other details as Pz.Kpfw II Ausf A-C.

30. Pz.Kpfw II Ausf A fitted with flotation equipment: Various models of the Pz.Kpfw II series (mainly A-C) were fitted with flotation equipment in the form of pontoons in late 1940 for the proposed invasion of Britain (Operation Sea Lion). A propeller powered from the main shaft via the gearbox provided propulsion in the water, giving up to 5 knots speed. The type was not used in operations. Details as for basic vehicle.

31. VK.160I (D) (Pz.Kpfw II n. A. verst): Contemporary project to the VK.180I, this time for a heavily armoured version of the Pz.Kpfw II. Built by Daimler-Benz using as a basis the chassis of a Pz.Kpfw II Ausf D. Built in 1940 and abandoned in 1940 when the light tank class was found to be outmoded. Vehicle had massive armour protection with 80mm at front and 50mm at sides. There was an escape hatch in each side and the wheels were interleaved. 16.5tons; armour 50–80mm; engine (gasoline) 140hp; 20mph. Other details as for Pz.Kpfw II Ausf D.

32. VK.1602 (D) Leopard (leicht): Produced in 1941 to meet a Waffenamt requirement for a battle reconnaissance tank, with sufficient armament to protect itself. Armed with a 5cm gun, it was based on the chassis of the VK.160I and VK.130I, but was less heavily armoured. It was cancelled in early 1942 in favour of the Puma armoured car which then became the main German type of reconnaissance vehicle. The chassis and superstructure were similar to the VK.130I but with wide open-topped turret and 5cm gun. the road wheels were interleaved.

33. VK.90I (Pz.Kpfw II n.A.): This was produced by Daimler-Benz to meet a 1938 requirement for a fast lightened version of the Pz.Kpfw II. It had a similar hull to the Pz.Kpfw II Ausf D but with overlapping bogie wheels and torsion bar suspension. 75 pre-production vehicles were ordered in 1940 but later cancelled. This tank was armed like other Pz.Kpfw IIs with a 20mm gun and 7.92mm MG but utilised a stabilised mount. 9.2tons; crew 3; 20mm gun plus MG; armour 14–30mm; engine (gasoline) 150hp; 32mph; dimensions as Pz.Kpfw II Ausf D.

VK.903: Third prototype of the VK.90I experimentally fitted with the turret from the VK.130I.

34. VK.130I (Pz.Kpfw II n.A.): Derived from the VK.160I, VK.1602 and VK.90I designs, this incorporated features of each in an attempt to produce a specialised armoured reconnaissance vehicle (Aufklärrungspanzer). Mild steel prototype was completed in April 1942. It was similar in appearance to the VK.90I but with interleaved bogie wheels and heavier armour. Weight 13tons. Other details as for VK.160I and Pz.Kpfw II Ausf D.

VK.1303: Third prototype of VK.130I type with modifications intended to reduce weight by a ton. This became the production prototype for the Luchs (Lynx). Trials only, 1943.

35. Pz.Kpfw II Ausf L (Sd Kfz 123) Luchs (Lynx): Production vehicle based on the VK.1303 prototype. Built from late 1942 it was in service in early 1943 and was used mainly as a reconnaissance vehicle (Aufklärungspanzer). Top speed was 38mph. Chassis was built by MAN, and hull and turret by Daimler-Benz. 100 were built with 20mm guns; a further 31 were completed with 50mm guns replacing the 20mm weapon. This was the final type of German light tank both in production and in service. Later vehicles had spaced armour at front. 11.8tons; crew 3; 20mm or 50mm gun and MG; armour 10–30mm; engine (gasoline) 180hp; 37.5mph; 15.4ft x 8.25ft x 7.08ft.

36. ZUGFUHRERWAGEN (Pz.Kpfw III PROTOTYPE) (above Krupp Prototype M.K.A.)
Produced under the 'concealed purpose' designation of Zugführer-wagen (ZW) (platoon commander's vehicle), this was a tank in the 15ton weight class intended to form the backbone of the panzer divisions being formed in the late 1930s. However, by 1942 the Pz.Kpfw III series had been eclipsed in importance by the Pz.Kpfw IV. The first ZW series prototypes were ordered in 1936 from Daimler-Benz, and Rheinmetall. The Daimler design was chosen for production in 1937 and first vehicles were in service in the same year. Models A–D were pre-production types with varying suspensions and other details to assess the best features for production vehicles. Model E was the first quantity production type. Superstructure and turret were virtually enlarged from the Pz.Kpfw II design. The Krupp prototype design (above) for the ZW requirement was not selected for production but features from it were used in the Pz.Kpfw IV design.

37. Pz.Kpfw III Ausf A: (Sd Kfz 141): Large road wheels, coil spring suspension, internal mantlet, 3.7cm gun, 'dustbin' cupola. Ten built 1937. 15tons; crew 5; 3.7cm gun and 3 MG; armour 10–14.5 mm; engine (gasoline) 230hp; 20mph; 18.9ft x 9.3ft x 7.75ft.

38. Pz.Kpfw III Ausf B: As Ausf A but with small road wheels

on elliptical spring suspension. Built 1937. Details as Ausf A except weight 18tons; height 8.4ft.

Pz.Kpfw III Ausf C. Similar to Ausf B but with extra leaf springs to give individual suspension to each wheel. Built 1938. Details as Ausf B.

39. Pz.Kpfw III Ausf D: As Ausf C but with thicker armour, new gearbox, and new cupola with shutter-type visor slots. 10 built 1938–9. Suspension as Ausf C. 19.3tons; crew 5; 3.7cm and 3 MG; armour 10–30mm; engine (gasoline) 320hp; 25mph; 18ft x 9.7ft x 8.08ft.

40. Pz.Kpfw III Ausf E: More powerful engine and new torsion bar suspension with six road wheels. Formed basis for subsequent production models. Total of 440 built, 1938–9. External mantlet on later vehicles with 5cm gun. Early vehicles had 3.7cm gun and internal mantlet as did Models A–D. Details as Ausf D except weight 20tons; 5cm gun (late vehicles) and 2 MG; engine (gasoline) 300hp.

41. Pz.Kpfw III Ausf F: Improved turret ventilation and 5cm L/42 gun from late 1940, though early vehicles had a 3.7cm gun. Stowage box on turret and rear smoke emitters. Built 1940–41. Picture shows the upgunned version. Details as Ausf E except weight 20.3tons; width 9.75ft.

42. Pz.Kpfw III Ausf G: As Ausf F but with new cupola with sliding vision shutters. Tropical version (Tp) had air filter on engine and dust deflector plate at rear. Early vehicles had 3.7cm gun most had 5cm as illustrated. Total of 450 built, 1940–41. Details as Ausf F.

43. Pz.Kpfw III Ausf H: Major production changes with wider tracks, new final drive, and new idler wheels and sprockets, all simplified to facilitate mass production. Later vehicles had extra armour. All had 5cm gun, some later rearmed with long calibre 5cm weapon. In production 1941. Spaced armour on hull front and mantlet in some vehicles. 26.6tons; crew 5; 5cm gun and 2 MG; armour 18–30+30mm; engine (gasoline) 300hp; 25mph; 18.33ft x 9.8ft x 8.33ft.

44. Pz.Kpfw III Ausf J: Thicker basic armour. Picture above shows short 5cm gun mounted; later vehicles had a longer L/60 5cm gun (below). Some vision slots in hull and turret eliminated to simplify production. Details as Ausf H except weight 22.3tons; armour 18–50mm.

45. Pz.Kpfw III Ausf J with long L/60 5cm gun.

46. Pz.Kpfw III Ausf L: Spaced frontal armour added and L/60 5cm gun fitted as standard when built. Built in 1942. Smoke dicharges on turret. Details as Ausf J except armour 18–50+20 mm. Some vehicles were tropicalised.

47. Pz.Kpfw III Ausf L fitted with skirt armour.

48. Pz.Kpfw III Ausf M: Basically similar to Ausf L but with hull vision ports and escape doors eliminated to simplify production. Optional skirt armour carried by some vehicles as shown above. Built in 1942. Some were rearmed with the 7.5cm gun as for Ausf N (below). Details as for Ausf L.

49. Pz.Kpfw III Ausf N (Sd Kfx 141/2): Version of Ausf M identical in all respects but fitted with short 7.5cm gun instead of 5cm gun. Acted in close-support role. Last production type; 666 built, some by conversion from Ausf L vehicles. 1942–3. Details as Ausf M.

50. Pz.Kpfw III Flammpanzer III (Sd Kfz 141/3): Ausf H or M converted to flamethrower tank by replacement of main armament with a flame projector; 100 built. Carried 1,000 litres of flame fuel. Other details as Ausf N and M.

51. Panzerkampfwagen III (Tauchfähig) (Submersible): Ausf E or F with air tubes and rubber seals to all orifices. Specially converted for projected Operation Sea Lion (invasion of Britain in 1940). Intended to leave landing barge and drive submerged along sea bed at a depth of 25ft. Not used in Sea Lion, but some of these vehicles were used in the Russian campaign during 1941 for the crossing of the River Bug. For this operation the flexible snorkel or air tubes were replaced by 10ft steel pipe and the exhaust fitted with one-way valves.

52. Panzerkampfwagen III (Tauchfähig)

53. Panzerbefehlswagen III Ausf D (Sd Kfz 266, 267, 268): This was the Pz.Kpfw III, Ausf D, converted to the role of command tank for tank unit commanders. Equipped with a dummy 3.7cm gun in a fixed turret with a prominent rail or loop aerial mounted over the rear deck behind the turret. The fighting compartment was altered to take various wireless equipment and map tables. Three versions existed of this vehicle, Sd Kfz 266, 267, 268. according to wireless equipment installed.

54. Pz.Bef.Wg. III Ausf E: Produced in 1940, this model was based on the chassis of the Pz.Kpfw III, Ausf E. Similar design to the Pz.Bef.Wg III, Ausf D.

55. Pz.Bef.Wg. III Ausf H: Produced in 1941, this was again based on the chassis of the Pz.Kpfw III, Ausf E, but reworked with additional 30mm armour plates and wider tracks. The dummy gun represented a short 5cm gun.

56. Pz.Bef.Wg. III Ausf K: This version appeared in 1942 and was an adaption of the normal combat tank converted to the role of command tank by the installation of extra wireless equipment in addition to that normally carried.

57. Panzerbeobachtungswagen III (Armoured Observation Vehicle) (Sd Kfz 143): Produced from 1942, the function of this vehicle was the control of German SP gunfire. Equipped with various wireless and observation equipment, like the Pz.Bef.Wg. a dummy gun was mounted, but in this case offset in the turret mantlet, a machine-gun being fixed in the centre.

58. Pz. Kpfw III with Famo Suspension: Experimental prototype

produced in 1942 with interleaved road wheels. Project cancelled after trials.

59. VK.2001 (BATAILLONSFUHRERWAGEN) Pz.Kpfw IV PROTOTYPE (above, Rheinmetall-Borsig prototype)
Ordered under the 'concealed purpose' name of 'batallion commander's vehicle', this was the forerunner of the Pz.Kpfw series. Intended as a support tank for smaller vehicles, it was in the 20 ton class and, in 1934, Krupp, Daimler-Benz and Rheinmetall-Borsig received prototype orders. Production orders eventually went to Krupp. Features of this vehicle included a squared-off superstructure with simple 'box bogie' spring suspension. It was unarmed. Prominent side skirts with mud chutes originally extended outside the idler but were later cut back.

VK.2001(K) AND VK.2002 (MAN) PROTOTYPES
Rival designs produced in 1935 to meet the same BW class requirement as the VK.2001(Rh.B) (see above). The VK.2001(K) project was awarded the production contract in 1936 and formed the basis for the subsequent Pz.Kpfw IV series. Vehicles had interleaved road wheels and 75mm guns. Much modified with new simpler suspension and features from the VK.2001(Rh) prior to production.

60. PANZERKAMPFWAGEN IV AUSF A (Sd Kfz 161)
In production in 1937 based on the Krupp VK.2001 prototype but much modified. The later Pz.Kpfw IV models became the major German service type, eclipsing all others and being produced in greater numbers (8,500) than other types. The Model A was the initial production type and entered service in 1937. It had a 'dustbin' cupola and 35 were built. Features common to all Pz.Kpfw IV variants were the small bogie wheels in pairs, prominent rear air intakes, four return rollers, cupola projecting through back of turret, and a short 75mm gun with prominent serial deflector. The basic Pz.Kpfw IV was a very sound and dependable design, lending itself to much further improvement and conversion to self-propelled guns at a later date. 17.3tons; crew 5; 75mm gun and 2 MG; armour 8–30mm; engine (gasoline) 250hp; 18.5mph; 18.7ft x 9.3ft x 8.6ft. Other users: Spain (1939–c1964); Syria (1945–c1968); USSR (captured vehicles, 1942–5).

61. **Pz.Kpfw IV Ausf B:** Second production type with straight-fronted superstructure (it was 'recessed' in the Ausf A). There was several other detail changes; 42 were built, 1937–8. Cupola was modified. 17.7tons; engine (gasoline) 320hp; length 19.7ft. Other details as Ausf A.

62. **Pz.Kpfw IV Ausf C:** Similar to Ausf B but with armoured sleeve to turret MG and small detail changes. Details as Ausf B except engine (petrol) 300hp.

63. **Pz.Kpfw IV Ausf D:** More powerful engine and 'stepped' front to superstructure. Changes included new mantlet and new pattern tracks. Introduced in 1940. Details as Ausf C except height 8.9ft.

64. **Pz.Kpfw IV Ausf E:** As Ausf D but with cupola moved forward and other detail changes, 1940. Details as Ausf D except weight 21tons; 21mph. 150 built.

65. **Pz.Kpfw IV Ausf F:** Major changes including armour increase from 30 to 50mm, straight front superstructure, and wider tracks. Details as Ausf E except weight 22.3tons; produced in 1941. Later called Pz.Kpfw IV Ausf FI when new upgunned version was produced.

66. **PANZERKAMPFWAGEN IV AUSF F2 to J (Sd Kfz 161/1, 161/2)**
The most important of the Pz.Kpfw IV production series providing the backbone of the German panzer divisions during the latter half of World War II. They were both up-gunned and up-armoured compared with the early models and a major improvement on the original Pz.Kpfw IV design. The principal change was the fitting of the L/43 and (later) the L/48 long barrelled 7.5cm gun in place of the short low-velocity 7.5cm gun of early models. The new gun gave the Pz.Kpfw IV a new lease of life and bought it near parity in hitting power with later Russian and American types. Numerically these were the most important German tanks and they were never fully superseded by later designs like the Panther. Final models had the added refinement of spaced armour and side skirt armour.

Pz.Kpfw IV Ausf F2: Like the Ausf FI but fitted with the new long 7.5cm L/43 gun. Used in Western Desert with considerable success, 1942, and a major production type. 23.6tons; crew 5; 7.5 cm gun and 2 MG; armour 10–50mm; engine (gasoline) 300hp; 25mph; 22.08ft x 9.6ft x 8.9ft.

67. **Pz.Kpfw IV, Ausf G:** As for Ausf F2 but with improved armour including thicker superstructure top. Some vehicles had spaced armour and side skirts fitted. Details as Pz.Kpfw IV, Ausf F2.

68. Pz.Kpfw IV Ausf G with armoured skirts.

69. Pz.Kpfw IV, Ausf H: As for the F2 but with various modifications, that included 7.5cm L/48 gun, new turret hatch cover, new type of drive sprocket spaced armour and armoured skirts. Details as Ausf G except weight 25tons; 23.5mph; 23.33ft x 11ft x 8.9ft.

70. Pz.Kpfw IV Ausf J: Final production model with many detail improvements and wire-mesh side skirts as an anti-bazooka device. Appeared in 1944. Extra armour protection included thicker superstructure top. Vehicle simplified by having hand traverse only for turret. Earlier models all had hand and power traverse. 25tons; crew 5; 7.5cm gun and 2 MG; armour 10–50mm; engine (gasoline) 300hp; 23.5mph; 23.33ft x 11ft x 8.9ft.

71. PANZERKAMPFWAGEN NEUBAUFAHRZEUGE V HEAVY TANK
Ordered in 1934–5, the Pz.Kpfw NbFz was a Rheinmetall design with turret and guns by Rheinmetall (Model B) and Krupp (Model A). It was a heavy tank with a 'concealed purpose' name of NbFz ('new construction vehicle'). It had a chassis and suspension parts based closely on the VK.2001(Rh) medium tank (see above). NbFz Model A had coaxial 7.5cm and 3.7cm guns while NbFz Model B had 10.5cm and 3.7cm guns coaxial in a vertical

plane. The design was based in shape on the Grosstraktor of 1929 but with suspension from VK.2001. Like the Grosstraktor, these NbFz vehicles had auxiliary MG turrets (the same as the main turret on the Pz.Kpfw I), one in front and one at the rear. Only 8 mild steel prototypes were built and no production order was subsequently given. Used in the Norwegian campaign of 1940, these vehicles are believed to have been scrapped in 1941. The NbFz Models were at one time in 1940 designated Pz.Kpfw V and the NbFz Model B was designated Pz.Kpfw VI. The design completed the German 'family' of related tanks — light training tank (Pz.Kpfw I), light reconnaissance tank (Pz.Kpfw II), medium tank (Pz.Kpfw III), and support tank (Pz.Kpfw IV), with the NbFz becoming the heavy tank. As the latter were not adapted for production, however, the designations Pz.Kpfw V and VI were later used on the Tiger and Panther tanks of 1942–3. 35(36tons); crew 6; 75mm and 37mm guns (105 and 37mm guns) plus 3 MG; armour 10–70mm; engine (gasoline) 500hp; 22mph; 24ft x 10ft x 7.9ft (Details in parentheses refer to Model B).

72. Pz.Kpfw NbFz. VI

VK.6501 Pz.Kpfw VII HEAVY TANK
Experimental prototype for a heavy tank, two of which were being built in 1938–40 before the project was cancelled in favour of a lighter type the VK.3001. Also known as the SW ('assault tank'). Vehicle had interleaved road wheels, 7.5cm gun in main turret, and auxiliary MG turrets. It was not completed with armament however.

73. VK.3001(H) HEAVY TANK
Prototype design for a 'breakthrough' tank in the 30ton class, ordered from Henschel in 1940 as a continuation of a project shelved in 1938. Four prototypes were built but the project was superseded by the heavier VK.3601 and VK.4501 requirements in 1941–2. Prototypes completed March-October 1941. Similar in appearance to Pz.Kpfw IV but with interleaved road wheels. Simulated turret only. Two of these prototypes were subsequently completed as 12.8cm SP guns in 1942 and were used operationally on the Russian front. In this form they no longer followed tank configuration, however.

74. VK.3001(P) LEOPARD MEDIUM TANK
Porsche-built design in the 30ton class as an alternative to the VK.3001(H) (see above). Cancelled in 1942 when the VK.3001

requirement was dropped. Vehicle was externally similar to the VK.3001(H) but had more novel mechanical features including petrol-electric drive and longitudinal torsion bar suspension as later perpetuated on the Porsche Tiger design. Also known as the Porsche Type 100.

VK.3002(DB) PANTHER PROTOTYPE
Ordered from Daimler-Benz in November 1941 as an immediate production design able to meet the threat of the new Russian T–34. Total of 200 ordered but later cancelled when the MAN Panther design was adopted instead. Prototype vehicle built but uncompleted. This vehicle was very similar to the Soviet T–34 from which it was partially copied. Had transverse rear engine, rear drive, leaf spring suspension, all-steel resilient wheels, sloped hull, 75mm gun, and diesel engine, all very unconventional by German engineering standards.

PANZERKAMPFWAGEN V PANTHER (Sd Kfz 171) HEAVY TANK
This was designed by MAN to the VK.3002 requirement in competition with a Daimler-Benz design (above) as a new heavy tank able to combat the Russian T–34 on superior terms. It was judged to be better than the DB design. A priority order was placed in September 1942 and the first vehicle was produced in November 1942. The Panther was the best German tank of World War II. Features included interleaved road wheels with torsion bar suspension, well-sloped hull and turret; rear engine and front drive; 75mm high velocity gun. Very fast and manoeuvrable for its large size.

78. Panther Ausf G: 1944 production type with modified and improved hull shape, driver's vision port eliminated, and better vision devices including episcope for driver. Late (1945) models had all steel resilient wheels and cleaning gear stowage box across hull rear. Details as Ausf A except weight 44.8tons; armour 15–100mm; height 10ft.

75. Panther Ausf DI: Pre-Production vehicles with less powerful engine, thinner armour, and early model gun.

76. Panther Ausf D2: First production type with 'dustbin' type cupola, driver's vision port, and MG port, both in hull front. 43tons; crew 4; 7.5cm gun plus 2 MG; armour 15–80mm; engine (gasoline) 650hp; 28.5mph; 22.9ft x 11.45ft x 9.8ft.

79. Befehlspanzer Panther: Commander's model with extra radio sets and aerials. Details as Ausf D.

77. Panther Ausf A: Late 1943 production vehicle with ball mounting for hull MG and new pattern vision cupola. Details as Ausf D except weight 45.5tons; armour 15–110mm; engine 700hp; height 10.3ft.

80. Beobachtungspanzer Panther: Artillery observation officer's vehicle with fixed turret, wooden dummy gun, and ball-mounted MG in turret front.

VK.360I(H) HEAVY TANK

Project for a heavier 36ton tank based on the VK.300I requirement and suggested by Hitler (higher speed, thicker armour, and heavier gun). Prototype was completed in March 1942 but the project was ultimately replaced by the VK.450I. Similar to the VK.300I(H) but with large full-depth bogie wheels and elimination of return rollers. Suspension was later used on Henschel Tiger tank.

81. PANZERKAMPFWAGEN VI TIGER (P)

Porsche design to meet new requirement for heavy 45ton vehicle ordered in May 1941. Prototype ready in April 1942. Not accepted for service in this form, the rival Henschel design being preferred. Petrol electric drive, longitudinal torsion bar suspension, over-hanging side panniers, and flat cylindrical turret. After cancellation of this vehicle as a battle tank, the 90 hulls of the initial order, which had already been laid down, were converted to large Panzerjäger under the designation PzJg Tiger(P) Ferdinand (later Elefant). 8.8cm gun and 2 MG; engine (petrol-electric).

82. PANZERKAMPFWAGEN VI, TIGER AUSF E (Sd Kfz 181)

Henschel design to meet VK.450I requirement, built in competition with VK.450I(P) (Porsche Tiger). Proved much superior to the Porsche design and was adopted for production. Heaviest tank in the world at the time of its introduction. Interleaved road wheels with outer run of wheels removable to allow normal wide battle tracks to be replaced by narrow travelling tracks. Over-hanging side panniers, mortised interlocking armour construction and same turret as Porsche Tiger. Early production vehicles were equipped for deep wading with snorts and rubber sealing. Late production vehicles had all steel resilient wheels instead of rubber-tyred wheels. These vehicles also had simpler cooling and a vision cupola replacing the original 'dustbin' type. For unit commanders there was a Befehlspanzer Tiger fitted with extra radios. 55tons; crew 5; 8.8cm gun and 2 MG; armour 26–100mm; engine (gasoline) 700hp; 23.5mph; 20.7ft x 12.45ft x 9.5ft.

83. Pz.Kpfw VI equipped for deep wading

84. Bergepanzer Tiger: Recovery vehicle based on gun tank. Gun removed, turret traversed and fixed, and winch fitted on turret roof.

85. Late production Tiger E with steel resilient wheels.

86. Pz.Kpfw VI, TIGER II AUSF B (KONIGSTIGER) (Sd Kfz 182)
Henschel design to VK.4502 requirement calling for a replacement for the Tiger (Tiger Ausf E). Prototype was completed in November 1943 with first production models appearing in November 1944. Delay was caused by design changes to standardise parts with other tanks (eg, Tiger Ausf E, Panther, and projected Panther II); there was also disruption by enemy action. A total of 484 Tiger

Ausf B vehicles were completed by the end of World War II in May 1945. This was the heaviest operational tank of the Second World War but its extreme size and weight proved a severe tactical limitation. The Tiger Ausf B had sloped hull armour and many components in common with the Panther. It was proposed to rationalise production with the projected Panther II (Panther Ausf F), though this latter vehicle was not ready for production by the end of the war and was not built. The Tiger Ausf B had a massive turret with 8.8cm gun; interleaved all-steel resilient road wheels were standard. In addition to the VK.4502(H) which became the Tiger Ausf B (also called the 'Königstiger' – King Tiger – or Tiger II) and was designed and built by Henschel, a rival design (the VK.4502(P)) was offered by Porsche to meet the same requirement. Like other Porsche designs, this had petrol-electric drive. It was not accepted, but turrets for the anticipated order for 50 initial production vehicles were built and these were subsequently used on the first 50 Henschel-built Tiger Ausf B tanks. The Porsche turrets were distinguished by a bulging cupola and curved turret front. The Henschel turret on subsequent vehicles had smooth sides and a conical mantlet. 69.7tons; crew 5; 8.8cm gun plus 3 MG; armour 25–150mm; engine (gasoline) 700hp; 23.5mph; 24.24ft x 12.5ft x 10.26ft.

87. Early production Tiger II Ausf B, with Porsche turret.

88. PANZERKAMPFWAGEN MAUS HEAVY TANK

Super-heavy tank designed in 1943 by Porsche with Hitler's approval. Weighed 180tons and was intended to out-gun and out-last any known Allied tank. Armed with 12.8cm gun and with frontal armour of 240mm (9½in). Originally known under code name of 'Mammut' (Mammoth). Six vehicles ordered but not completed. Prototype built by November 1943 and tested Winter 1943–4. Construction was of flat rolled plate armour mortised and welded. Petrol or diesel engine of 1200hp allowed for in design, built by Daimler. Suspension was on 48 partly interleaved road wheels in four wheel bogies, each bogie being set on a longitudinal torsion bar. Vehicle was fully submersible (with snort breathing tube) for crossing rivers since it was too heavy for normal bridges. 180–188tons; crew 6; 1 15cm gun, 1 7.5cm gun, 2 MG; armour 50–240mm; engine (petrol/electric or diesel) 1200hp; 12.5mph.

89. PANZERKAMPFWAGEN E.100 HEAVY TANK

Produced by Henschel to a Heereswaffenamt requirement for a super-heavy tank in competition with the Maus. Largest of a projected E series (E=Entwicklungtypen=standard type) but the only E.100 series prototype was uncompleted at the end of World War II. Weighed 137tons (light) with 250mm (9½in) frontal armour on turret. Interleaved road wheels and basic hull shape similar to King Tiger but with addition of heavy armour side skirts which were removable by jibs carried on the vehicle. 137–140tons; crew 6; 15cm gun, 7.5cm gun and 2 MG armour 50–250mm; engine (V-12) 1200hp; 25mph; 34.16ft x 14.9ft x 11.08ft.

FOREIGN TYPES IN GERMAN SERVICE 1939–45

Foreign tanks used by the German Army were mainly types designed and produced in countries under German occupation, chiefly, Czechoslovakia and France, very little use was made of Russian, British or American tanks that were captured, these being used locally and not issued as standard equipment. The most important of the vehicles that were taken into German service as standard equipment were the Czech Skoda(S–IIa) LT.35 which was designated Pz.Kpfw 35(t) and the Praga(TNH)LT.38 that became the Pz.Kpfw 38(t). These two vehicles were absorbed into the German Armoured Divisions and used in France in 1940 and the early Russian campaigns. Production of the Pz.Kpfw 38(t) was continued till 1942, and was still in service at the end of the war as a chassis for self-propelled artillery. Though no-other foreign tank was used on such a scale, use was made of certain French types such as the Renault AMC35 and R.35, Hotchkiss H.35 and H.39, the SOMUA S35, the Char BI and FCM the Germans modifying certain vehicles by removing the dome type cupola top and fitting split hatch covers. Due to the one-man turrets that these tanks were equipped with, they were considered unsatisfactory for front line combat and were at first used for training and policing. (Polizei-Panzerkampfwagen) limited use being made with them in Norway, Russia and the Balkans. But later with the shortage of tanks some regular armoured divisions were equipped with them. All captured material received a 'fremdengeräte' (Foreign Eqiupment) number which was for tanks the 700 series. This was followed in brackets by the initial letter of the country of origin. (a) amerikanisch — American; (b) belgisch — Belgian; (e) english — 'English' (British); (f) französisch — French; (h) hollandisch — Dutch; (i) italienisch — Italian; (j) jugoslawisch — Yugoslavian; (p) polnisch — Polish; (r) russisch — Russian; (t) tschechisch — Czechoslovakian. For example Panzerkampfwagen 35-H 734(f).

90. Pz.Kpfw 35(t)

91. Pz.Kpfw 38(t)

92. Pz.Bef.Wg.38(t)

93. Pz.Kpfw 7TP(p)

94. Pz.Kpfw 35-S 739(f)

95. Pz.Kpfw I8R 730(f): armed with the 7.5mm MG.

96. Pz.Kpfw 35R 73I(f)

97. Pz.Kpfw 38-H 734(f)

98. Pz.Kpfw 39-H 735(f)

101. Pz.Kpfw M 4-748(e)

99. Pz.Kpfw BI Flamm(f): conversion of the Char BI-bis(740) to flamethrower.

102. Pz.Kpfw T34-747(r)

100. Infanterie Panzerkampfwagen Mk II 748(e)

103. Pz.Kpfw L/3-35-731(i)

GREAT BRITAIN

INTRODUCTION

Britain was the first country to commit tanks to combat in World War I, though development of tracked fighting vehicles was being carried out concurrently by France, quite independently of the British.

The idea for an 'armoured landship' — the concept which was soon to be known as a tank — originated from several quarters. In 1912 an Australian engineer named de Mole sent the British War Office plans for a tracked fighting vehicle not unlike, in shape, the vehicles which later evolved. De Mole's idea was not taken up however, and it was the stalemate in the fighting on the Western Front which gave the final impetus to the development of 'landships'. The machine-gun was the dominant infantry weapon in 1914 and against it infantry advances were decimated. The need for an armoured carrier which could transport infantry and machine-guns in an advance on the enemy trenches, with immunity from machine-gun fire, was taken up in several quarters.

Colonel Ernest Swinton, a staff officer on the Western Front in 1914–15, saw American Holt Caterpillar tractors being used to tow guns across country and suggested a version with an armoured body for service as a machine-gun carrier. After a peremptory trial the somewhat intransigent British War Office dropped the idea. Meanwhile the Royal Naval Air Service had raised some armoured car squadrons in Belgium in August 1914 to patrol and protect their advanced airfields. Under Captain (Later Sir) Murray Sueter, they suggested an extension of the armoured car idea to embrace an 'armoured landship' on a tracked chassis, to attack enemy trenches. An alternative to the RNAS idea was a 'Big Wheel Machine' with 40ft diameter wheels in tricycle arrangement and big guns carried between the front wheels.

Winston Churchill, then First Lord of the Admiralty, accordingly set up a 'Landship Committee', under the Chief of Naval Construction, to investigate the ideas. Subsequently they also sponsored the building of prototype vehicles and the establishment of a trials unit. Pedrail, Killen-Strait and Bullock Commercial tracked units were investigated, the latter being chosen as the basis for a prototype. In the event, by September 1915, only lengthened Bullock tracks were utilised in the resulting Lincoln Machine No 1 better known as 'Little Willie', the first practical tank. This was designed by William Tritton, head of the Foster Engineering Works at Lincoln, and Major W. G. Wilson, an eminent prewar automobile engineer. Little Willie had low set short tracks and a high box-like hull. It proved to be top-heavy and the tracks were insufficiently long to enable it to clear enemy trenches.

This was realised even while the vehicle was being built and Tritton and Wilson accordingly produced a new design with the all-round tracks giving rise to the familiar lozenge shape of early British tanks. In actual fact the lower run of the tracks represented the ground contact arc of a 40ft diameter wheel so utilising the major feature of the otherwise impractical 'Big Wheel Machine'.

The new prototype, 'Mother' or 'Big Willie', was extremely successful when tested in early 1916 and orders were placed for 100 production vehicles, although some senior military officers, notably Lord Kitchener, were sceptical of their tactical value.

The men who had played a prominent part in the evolution of the 'Landship', in particular Colonel Swinton, were keen to amass a large armoured force and then unleash it on the enemy in a big surprise attack. However, these hopes were dashed when the few available tanks known as Mark Is, were used prematurely, with only limited success at Flers-Courcelette, on 15 September 1916, to bolster the flagging Somme offensive. The tanks potential was realised however, and big orders were placed. Tanks Mark II, III and IV, were based on 'Mother' and Mark I, with only limited changes.

They had a tractor engine and were complicated to control, needing a chain of several men to work the controls and change gears. On the earliest vehicles a wheeled truck assisted steering but this was vulnerable and was soon discarded.

The first really big tank action was at Cambrai in November 1917, when a huge tank attack proved one of the most successful of all.

A big step forward in tank design came in 1918 with the Mark V, which featured a new purpose-built long-stroke tank engine, the Ricardo, and the new Wilson epicyclic gearbox, which made it possible for one man to control the vehicle single-handed.

The next major heavy tank design to enter production in 1918–19 was the Mark VIII, which was involved in a grandiose plan to be the 'International' tank for simultaneous service with the British, American and French. A factory was to be built in France to turn these out, but the Armistice of 1918 scotched these plans and production was terminated. Only 100 Mk VIII tanks were to see service, with the American Army from 1919 onwards.

To give increased carrying capacity, a lengthened version of the Mk V was extemporised in the field, the Mark V, and a production of this Mark V was also built.

A major tank offensive in 1918 at Amiens proved the value of the tank once and for all, but ambitious plans for tank offensives in 1919 were cut short by the Armistice.

Other British tank development in the early years was centred on the 'Cavalry' or fast tank, designed for the pursuit rather than for attacking enemy defences. The Medium Mk A of 1916, a twin-engined vehicle, also called the Whippet, was the principal type evolved, its planned successors, the Medium B and C being too late for war service.

Various ambitious types were being evolved for service in 1919. A very fast tank, the Medium Mk D and modified variants, showed great promise: it had an aero engine and flexible 'snake' tracks, offering a very high performance. Escalating development costs however, led to its abandonment in the early 1920s. The Tank Mk IX also suffered from the end of hostilities. This was the first real armoured tracked carrier, able to transport men and stores. Bridge laying and mineclearing special variants of the Tank Mk V** were developed, but only a few were in service.

The next twenty years were a time of severe financial stringency and indecision at higher command levels. To make the best of limited funds some young armoured service officers developed the one- and two-man tankettes, the Morris-Martel and Crossley-Martel taking their names from Colonel (later General Sir Gifford) Q. Martel, the designer. From the inexpensive tankette came the line of development which led to the machine-gun and infantry carriers which were famous in World War II. A second line of development, by Carden-Loyd and Vickers (who took over Carden-Loyd in 1930) led to the series of light two- or three-man tanks which were the most numerous British type by 1939. The Light Tank Mk I appeared in 1929 and developed through to the Light Tank Mk VI by 1939. These vehicles, only lightly armed and armoured, were adequate only for reconnaissance, but owing to the tank shortage of 1939–40 they were often used in battle — a rôle for which they were not suited.

In 1923 the Vickers Medium Tank Mark I appeared; this was the first British tank with a 360degree traversing turret to be adopted by the British Army. Originally classified as a light tank, this was later changed to medium when the small light tanks were introduced. The Medium Mk I and its successor, Medium Mk II, formed the backbone of the Army's tank strength until 1938, by which time they were obsolete. Excellent designs, they appeared in many forms and subvariants.

Vickers, the pre-eminent British tank manufacturer, designed and produced numerous models during the 1930s and sold scores of tanks commercially to other nations. Vickers export light tanks were very similar to the designs built for the British Army but with modifications and in many cases with slightly heavier armament. The most successful of these export models was the vehicle known as the 6ton Tank; manufactured with two alternative armament layouts, this vehicle was sold to many countries with variations in the armament. Though it was not taken into British service, the basic design was adopted by other countries — Russia where it evolved into the T–26 series, and Poland who developed it as the 7 TP. Another Vickers Commercial design that became the progenitor for a series of foreign-built tanks was the Medium C, samples of which were sold to Japan, who developed from it a standard indigenous design, the Type 89 Medium Tank.

Between the wars the Army was small, but ideas were developed by tank enthusiasts often at odds with the War Office. In 1926–27 the Experimental Mechanised Force was formed and was the forerunner of the armoured divisions of World War II. Captain Basil Liddell Hart and General J. F. C. Fuller were the two leading armoured warfare theorists of the period, and their writings and ideas were studied closely by (among others) the Germans. When Germany rearmed the in the 1930s, armoured divisions were given priority in equipment, while in Britain, there were more economies.

Two multi-turreted designs, the Independent of 1926 and the 16ton series of 1928–30, did not go beyond proto-type stage, and during the 1930s the new designs were based more on economical than tactical considerations. Official doctrine saw tanks as analogous to ships at sea: tanks which fought other tanks were called 'Cruiser Tanks' — these were fast and with moderate armour; tanks which supported and made 'holes' for the infantry, were called 'Infantry Tanks' — they had machine-gun armament at first and heavy armour; the light tanks had a scouting rôle. Within these categories new tank designs were evolved during the 1930s. The A9 and A10 were the Cruisers Mark I and II. The A11 and the A12, were the Infantry Tanks, Mark I and II, the famous 'Matildas'. These types were all in service in 1940.

In 1937 British Staff Officers in Russia saw the Christie-based, BT fast tanks in service — vehicles with a very much superior performance to any British tank. This led to the purchase of a vehicle from Christie's Company in America, and from this was developed the A13 series. The Christie suspension then became the standard for subsequent Word War II designs of Cruiser Tank.

Early experience with tanks in Europe in 1940, showed that the armour was too thin on British tanks. New designs in the pipeline, the Covenanter and Crusader, were better armoured. After the British withdrawal from Dunkirk in 1940, Britain was extremely short of tanks. The new designs included the Churchill and Valentine in the Infantry Tank category, plus the new Cruiser Tanks in the Centaur and Cromwell series. The British had standardised on the 2pdr gun prewar, while German types were fitted with a more powerful 50mm, later 75mm weapon, so in 1941 there was a rush to replace the 2pdr with the 6pdr. However, a shortcoming of the British pre-war designs was the lack of development potential. Bigger guns needed bigger turrets, so that considerable redesign was necessary to bring new models for existing tanks into service with 6pdr guns. By 1942, when these designs were ready, the German tanks had been further upgunned and there was a need for British tanks with 17pdr guns. These large weapons necessitated new designs altogether — the Challenger and the Black Prince, redesigns of the Cromwell and Churchill respectively. The Challenger was unsuccessful and the Black Prince too late for war service.

Meanwhile the shortcomings of British designs had been made up by the supply of American M3 and M4 Medium tanks under Lend-Lease, the first arriving when the British fortunes were at a low ebb in the Western Desert, in summer of 1942. The M4 Sherman tank from its arrival at El Alamein to the end of the war formed the basis of British armour. American M3 Light tanks and later derivatives were also supplied. The M3 and M4 Medium Tanks (Grant, Lee and Sherman) had 75mm guns which were more than a match for the German tank guns and could fire both armour-piercing and high-explosive rounds. Previous British tank guns could fire only AP rounds so could not provide their own support fire, a crucial requirement against anti-tank guns which previously had taken a big toll of British tanks. A British design of 75mm gun was developed in 1943 and this equipped the main service models of the Cromwell and Churchill in 1944. The 17pdr gun, the most powerful of the British wartime anti-tank guns, was meanwhile fitted to the American Shermans in British service, a compromise which produced one of the most effective tanks of the war years.

This 17pdr version of the Sherman was called the Firefly. An enlarged version of the Cromwell with a reduced version of the 17pdr gun, the 77mm gun, was also in service in 1944; this was the Comet, which also saw much postwar service.

All the lessons of the war years were incorporated in a new design of tank, the A41, which was produced in 1944. The A41 as built had a 17pdr gun, powerful secondary armament, and a wide, well-shaped chassis on a good suspension, and was well armoured.

This gave a big development potential in the A41. Arbitary rules on dimensions (intended to make vehicles suitable for rail transport) were at last revised to enable a really big turret ring to be fitted. The small size of the turret ring had been a limitation on installing larger guns in many earlier designs. Ironically however, the war was over before the first few A41s could see combat. As with the Centurion, however, the A41 formed the backbone of Britain's tank forces for the next twenty years.

British Tank Designation System
In the period of World War I, tanks were designated simply by mark numbers, for example 'Tank Mk I'. The terms 'male' and 'female' indicated gun armament in the former and machine-gun armament in the latter: 'hermaphrodite' was used in cases of mixed armament. Modifications to the basic designs, which were relatively infrequent, were denoted by the addition to the basic designation of a number of stars — 'Tank Mk V**', or Tank Mk V with two modifications. When the medium tanks appeared, the different models were indicated by letters of the alphabet, 'Tank Medium Mk A'. Some names — 'Whippet' and 'Hornet' for example — were semi-official and somewhat loosely used. From 1920 the Army used a somewhat similar form of designation, although the types changed. Sub-letters were used to indicate modified variants of the basic pattern: 'Light Tank Mk VIIc'. The manufacturer's name frequently appeared in everyday usage ('Vickers' Light Tank Mk II'), but this was in no way officially sanctioned. In addition to the foregoing systems, each design emanating from a War Office requirement received an ordnance designation in the A-series, starting in 1926 with the A1 'Independent'. Prototypes or design variants had an E-suffix to denote stages of development or modification, thus: A14E2. The early light tanks were designated in a separate L-series. In some cases the A-series prefix was incorporated into the army terminology, for example 'Cruiser Tank A13 Mk I', which was also the 'Cruiser Tank Mk III'. By 1940 designs were being produced at a fast-growing rate and names were therefore added to certain designs to prevent undue confusion. Thus the 'Cruiser Tank Mk V' later became known as the 'Cruiser Tank Mk V, Covenanter'. Sub-variants further added to the confusion, leading to such designations as the 'Cruiser Tank Mk V, Covenanter Mk III'. By 1942 the old system of type marks was displaced by that of type names; hence the 'Cruiser Tank Mk VIII, Cromwell Mk II' became the 'Cruiser Tank, Cromwell Mk II'.

MK 1 Tank advancing on the Western Front 1916.

Infantry Tanks MK II (Matilda) at Tobruk.

Churchill Crocodiles advancing for the assault on Brest, September 1944.

I. No I LINCOLN MACHINE

Also known as the Tritton Machine, this was the first true tank design to emanate from the work of the Land Ship Committee. Designed by Mr Tritton of William Foster and Company Ltd, and Lieutenant Wilson, RNAS, construction was begun on 12 August, 1915, utilising Bullock tracks which had been brought from America. It was otherwise built almost entirely of existing standard components, the engine and transmission being those of the Foster-Daimler tractor. The hull, made of boiler plate, was designed to take a centrally mounted turret with a 2pdr gun, but this was not fitted: instead a dummy turret was carried. Steering was accomplished by braking on the appropriate track and/or using the tail steering wheels. The performance of the Tritton machine was limited largely by the inadequacy of the tracks which gave continual trouble. 14tons; crew 4–6; engine (Foster-Daimler gasoline) 105hp; 3½mph; length 26.5ft.

2. LITTLE WILLIE

To meet revised War Office requirements for a vehicle to be able to cross a 5ft trench and surmount 4.5ft parapets. (The Lincoln Machine being limited to 4ft trench crossing, while the maximum height it could surmount was no more than 2ft), the vehicle was rebuilt using the original hull and engine, but was fitted with a new track frame and many of the component parts were specially made instead of being standard factory parts. It was decided by Tritton and Lieutenant Wilson to design a new type of track to replace the type being used on the No I Lincoln or Tritton Machine. After experimenting unsuccessfully with tracks made with various material that included Balata belting and flat wire rope fitted with teeth to engage on the drive sprocket a track was devised by Tritton consisting of cast steel plates riveted to links which incorporated guides to engage on the inside of the track frame. This proved successful and became the pattern of track construction used on all subsequent British World War I tanks until Mk VIII. The rear steering wheels were retained but the simulated turret was removed. Little Willie, as it became known was completed early in December 1915 but was already outmoded by a new design that was being developed. Details as for No I Lincoln Machine.

3. MOTHER

This was a new improved design by Tritton and Wilson which retained the rectangular box-like hull shape as used on the No. I and Little Willie machines, but incorporated new track frames, which took the track round the overall height of the vehicle. The shape of the frames was such that the lower run of the track in contact with the ground approximated in shape and radius to a 60ft diameter wheel. This would allow the vehicle to cross a 5ft wide trench or run up a 4.5ft vertical parapet, thus meeting the revised War Office requirements. To lower the centre of gravity, the idea of a traversing turret mounted on the hull was abandoned and guns were mounted in sponsons on the vehicles side. Two 6pdr naval guns were fitted since suitable weapons were not at the time available to the army. First trial run took place in January 1916 this was followed by demonstrations before generals and members of the Government. This led to a War Office order for 40 machines, later changed to 100. During its development period this prototype machine was known as the 'Wilson Machine', 'Centipede', 'Big Willie', or 'Mother'. 28tons; crew 8; 2 6pdr guns plus 4 MG; armour mild steel; engine (Daimler-Foster, gasoline) 105hp; 3.7mph; 32.5ft x 13.75ft x 8ft.

4. TANK MK I (above, Male)

Orders for 100 (later 150) vehicles, patterned on Mother were placed in February 1916 and basic design was identical to the Mother prototype except that armour was used instead of boiler plate. There was a raised cupola on the hull front for the driver and for the commander, and a dismountable sponson on each side carried the main armament in limited traverse mounts. Fitted with a pair of rear wheels to act as an aid for steering and to increase the vehicle's length for trench crossing. These proved unsuccessful during combat conditions and were discarded from November 1916. Another external feature on the Mk I was the bomb-roof made of chicken wire on a wood or metal frame, fitted over the hull top. Two versions of the Mk I were built, the Male tank armed with two 6pdr guns to attack enemy guns, fortifications and defences, and the Female version equipped with machine guns to give covering fire to the Male tank against infantry attacks or for mopping up. The Female sponson was slightly larger than the Male. The Mk I took part in the battles of the Somme in 1916 and Arras in 1917. 28tons (Male), 27tons (Female); crew 8; Male: 2 6pdr plus 4 MG; Female: 5 MG; armour 6–12mm; 32.5ft x 13.75ft (Male), 14.33ft (Female) x 8ft. Other details as Mother.

5. Tank Mk I Female

Mk I Tank Tender: Mk I tank converted to carry stores or troops by the removal of the sponsons and replacing them with mild steel boxes to increase cargo space. Fitted with a special attachment, these supply tanks were able to tow three sledges containing stores; first used in April 1917 after conversion.

6. Mk I Wireless Tank: This conversion consisted of a Mk I Female with the armament and mounts removed from the sponsons and replaced with wireless and office equipment. A pole mast was erected on the nose with aerials; first used at Cambrai in November 1917.

7. TANK MK II (above, Male) AND MK III

The Mks II and III were practically identical to the Mk I, but with modifications derived from the experience of the recent tank fighting. Improvements incorporated in these two machines, included the fitting of wider track shoes at every sixth link, slightly increased armour in the Mk III and a raised manhole hatch on top of the vehicles. Late production Mk III Males were armed with the short 6 pdr gun and the Female with a small sponson as fitted to the Mk IV. The first of each type was produced in January 1917, the Mk II by W. Foster and Company Ltd and the Mk III by the Metropolitan Carriage and Waggon Company Ltd. Fifty of each mark were built. Details as for Mk I.

8. Mk II Female

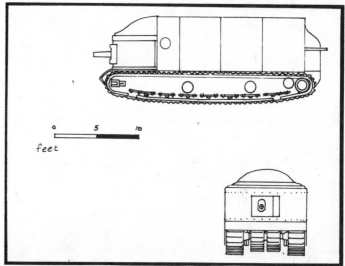

feet

9. FLYING ELEPHANT

This was a projected heavy tank developed (from July 1916) to withstand field gun fire by being constructed with frontal armour of 3in thickness and with side armour of 2in. The tracks were driven by two 105hp Daimler engines, mounted together on a common crankcase. As an aid to prevent bellying in soft ground, auxiliary twin tracks were fitted under the bottom rear half of the vehicle clearing the ground by 6in. When required they could be coupled to the main track and be brought into operation. The main armament, a 6pdr gun was carried in a large steel cupola mounted on the front of the vehicle, above the tracks. Designed by Tritton, the vehicle was near completion at W. Foster and Company Ltd when the project was cancelled in December 1916 in favour of production of more tanks of the Mk I type. 90–100tons; crew 8; 6pdr gun plus 6 MG; armour 50–75mm; engine (2 Daimler-Foster) 210hp; 26.75ft x 9.84ft x 10ft.

EXPERIMENTAL VERSIONS OF MK I AND MK IV TANKS

Early in 1917 trials took place on five experimental vehicles to determine the best form of transmission and control to incorporate in the new designs of tank then contemplated (ie Mk V etc). Vehicles tested were a Mk IV with Westinghouse Petrol-Electric drive, a Mk IV with petrol-electric drive copied from the French St Chamond tank, a Mk IV with Daimler Petrol-Electric drive, a Mk I with Williams-Janney hydraulic steering, a Mk I with Wilkins

Multiple Clutch and a Mk I with Wilson planetary transmission and epicyclic gearbox. The last of these was the most successful and was incorporated in the Mk V. The Williams-Janney equipment was used in the Mk VII tank and for the hydraulic operation of the jib in the Mk V** (RE Tank).

10. TANK MK IV (above, Male)

Design of the Mk IV was begun in October 1916, the first tank of this type being produced in March 1917. The type was used at the battles of Messines, Third Ypres and First Cambrai then was gradually superseded in 1918 by the Mk V. Similar in appearance to. the previous marks, it was an improved model incorporating lessons learned from combat experience. The sponsons were hinged to swing back into the interior of the machine when entraining on rail flats, the male sponsons were reduced in size and the bottom was modified to reduce the tendency to foul rough ground. The female sponsons were similarly altered. To make it possible to swing the male turret inwards the 6pdr gun was reduced in length to 23 calibres. On both versions the Vickers and Hotchkiss machine-guns were replaced by Lewis guns to bring the tank machine-guns in line with the Infantry (The Lewis guns were later replaced with modified Hotchkiss MGs). The Mk IV was provided with armour of special steel that was proof against the German armour piercing or 'K' bullets. Danger from fire was reduced by placing the petrol tanks outside and at the rear of the vehicle in an armoured container. Steel spuds were introduced to provide better traction on difficult ground, these were generally bolted on to every third, fifth or ninth track plate. A silencer was fitted to the exhaust pipe, and internal improvements were made for the crew with a new cooling and ventilating system and better means of escape. Details as for Mk I except 26.4ft x 12.84ft (Male), 10.5ft (Female) x 8.17ft. Other users: Germany (captured vehicles).

11. Tank Mk IV Female

12. Mk IV Supply Tank:
A large number of Mk IV tanks surplus to requirements were converted to supply or tank tenders by replacing the normal gun sponsons with mild steel boxes. A boosted Daimler engine was fitted giving 125hp. Ordered in July 1917, these vehicles carried forward small-arms ammunition, bombs or shells, and when returning brought back wounded men. Armed with one Lewis gun.

13. Mk IV Tadpole Tank:
To increase their trench crossing ability, a number of Male and Female Mk IV and Mk V tanks were modified by extending the rear section. This device, known as the Tadpole Tail, was evolved during 1917, and consisted of a pair of mild steel horns attached to the rear of the vehicle by metal straps and rivets and braced with diagonal stays thereby increasing the length of the vehicle by 9ft. This necessitated extension of the track by the fitting of 28 extra track shoes and an extension to the drive. One experimental Tadpole version was fitted with a platform built between the rear horns, on the bracing stays. This was used to mount a 6in mortar, firing forward.

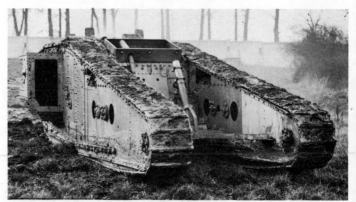

14. Mk IV Tadpole Tank with 6in Mortar

15. Mk IV Hermaphrodite:
With the appearance of German tanks in the field it was realised that the Female tank was at a disadvantage being armed only with machine-guns. This led to a number of Mk IV and Mk V Female tanks having a sponson replaced with the Male type armed with a 6pdr gun.

Mk IV Fascine Tank: To overcome the extra-wide trenches of the Hindenburg Line, a device known as the fascine was developed. This was an adaptation of the army fascine, and consisted of bundles of brushwood 10ft long by 4ft 6in wide, bound together with chains. These were carried on the unditching rails over the cab, and when required were released by the driver. Similar devices later introduced were the hexagonal shaped wooden crib and the steel crib.

16. Crane Tank (Salvage Tank): This equipment was mostly used in the tank workshops and several variants existed. One was a normal fighting tank with the guns removed and fitted with a rigged jib between the front horns complete with blocks and hand tackle. Another version had permanently fitted equipment. This consisted of a front rigged jib with the lifting power provided by a hand-operated winch mounted on the hull at the rear of the tank. The winch was provided with two platforms for the operators to stand on.

17. Mk IV with experimental unditching gear: Apart from steel spuds fitted to the tracks, other methods were evolved to enable tanks to extract themselves from bogged ground and other similar situations. These included torpedo-shaped spars which could be fastened to each track by chains, providing a purchase for the vehicle. These were replaced by an unditching beam which consisted of a baulk of timber weighing nearly half a ton, longer than the overall width of the tank hull. When required, it was fastened to the tracks by clips and chains. Movement of the track brought the beam forward over rails fixed to the hull top, passing it under the vehicle and providing a leverage for the vehicle to move forward. As these methods exposed the crew when engaged in attaching these devices to the tracks an experimental special unditching beam was devised in England during 1917. This could be connected and disconnected from inside the vehicle without exposing the crew. For this method the beam was permanently connected to two chains which passed all around the tank and could be connected to a main sprocket by a dog clutch operated from inside the machine. This vehicle was used for some years for experimental work but the idea was not adopted.

18. TANK MK V (above, Male)
The design of this vehicle was begun in October 1917, the first model being produced by the Metropolitan Carriage and Waggon Company in January 1918. The introduction of this model brought major improvements in all round speed, ease of manoeuvre, and better observation. Apart from the new Wilson planetary transmission which put the driving and control under one man, the Mk V had a more powerful engine specially designed for tanks by Ricardo. Slightly thicker armour was used on this vehicle, while the addition of an improved rear turret provided excellent all-round vision and rendered possible the fitting of the unditching beam to the tracks from the inside of the machine. The removal of the large differential gear as fitted to the earlier models, made possible the fitting of a machine-gun in the rear of the tank, and also allowed for large entrance doors in the back portion of the roof. Variants of the Mk V included a Hermaphrodite version, Mk V Carrier with sliding doors replacing the gun sponsons, and a Mk V with a Tadpole tail. There was also an experimental Mk V fitted with 'Snake' flexible tracks, which were being tested for the Medium Mk D project. 29tons (Male) or 28tons (Female); crew 8; 2 6pdr plus 4 MG (Male) or 6 MG (Female); armour 6–12mm; engine (Ricardo gasoline) 150hp; 4.6mph; 26.4ft x 12.84ft (Male), 10.5ft (Female) x 8.68ft. Other users: Estonia (1919), Germany (captured vehicles); Russia (White, taken over by Reds, 1918–19).

19. Mk V Male Tadpole

20. MK V with 'Snake' Flexible Tracks

21. Mk V with Unditching Spars

22. TANK MK V* (above, Male)

The design of the Mk V*, evolved by Tank Workshops in France, was begun in February 1918, the first machine being built by the Metropolitan Carriage and Waggon Company in May, 1918. This machine was 6ft longer than the Mk V to enable it to carry stores or up to 25 troops, and to increase its trench crossing capabilities to 13ft. This was achieved by lengthening the standard Mk V by inserting three extra panels on either side between the sponson and the gear housing. The Mk V* proved a more satisfactory extemporisation than the Tadpole tail. It was recognised as a major step forward in design owing to its increased versatility. 33tons (Male) or 32tons (Female); length 32.4ft; all other details as Mk V. Other users: France and America (few vehicles each).

23. Tank Mk V* Female

24. TANK MK V** (above, Male)

This vehicle differed in appearance to the Mk V* being designed as a new machine with many modifications. The major visual

difference was the commander's cupola which was brought forward behind the driver's position. A more powerful engine, the Ricardo 225hp, was fitted in this version. Design work on the Mk V** was started in May 1918, the first pilot model being built by Metropolitan Carriage and Waggon Company in December 1918. A small batch of these machines was completed after the war. 35tons (Male) or 34tons (Female); engine (Ricardo gasoline) 225hp; height 9ft; all other details as Mk V*.

25. Tank Mk V** (RE Tank) bridge carrier: A Mk V** converted to carry 20ft tank bridge which was slung from a jib carried at the front of the vehicle. Jib was hinged and could be moved hydraulically to lower and raise the bridge for positioning or recovery. Vehicle was intended to equip bridging companies formed in late 1918. After the Armistice a small bridging unit was retained.

26. Tank Mk V** (RE Tank) with anti-mine roller: This was the same vehicle as the bridging tank but with the bridge removed and a heavy roller slung from, and dragged by, the front jib which was dropped to its lowest position. A Mk IV tank was also converted experimentally to carry anti-mine rollers, slung from horizontal girders attached to the hull front.

27. TANK MK V***

This was built in mock-up form only and was a further modification of the Mk V, designed in 1918.

28. TANK MK VI

Designed as a lighter and faster tank than the Mk V the design of this version was radically different from that of the earlier tanks. The main armament, a 6pdr gun, was mounted in front, low down between the horns. Four MGs were carried in a fixed turret and two MGs in two small side sponsons. Designed and built in mock-up form only early in 1917, it was originally planned to supply 600 of these vehicles to the US Tank Corps. With the cancellation of the design, however, American interest turned to the Mk VIII tank.

29. TANK MK VII

The design of this model was begun in December 1917, the pilot model being completed by Messrs Brown Bros, Edinburgh, in July 1918. It was similar in outline to the Mk V but with an increased tail, lengthened by 3ft for better trench crossing. This machine was fitted with the 150hp Ricardo engine coupled to two Williams-Janney hydraulic gears, one to each track to improve its handling characteristics. Only one machine was built. An electric starter for the engine was used for the first time on this vehicle. 33tons; 4mph; 29.4ft x 8.58ft; all other details as Mk V.

30. TANK MK VIII

Designed in late 1917 by the newly-formed Mechanical Warfare Dept to incorporate all lessons learned from tank combat experience. It included some of the following features: the 300hp Ricardo engine was placed in a separate compartment from the fighting compartment partitioned by a bulkhead; ventilating fans prevented fumes or heat from entering the fighting area; the sponsons were hinged and mounted on roller bearings so that they could be moved by hand from within the machine; the main turret was fitted with a commander's cupola. The first machine was produced by the North British Locomotive Company in October, 1918. Also known as the 'Liberty', the 'International' or 'Allied' tank, this vehicle was selected for Anglo-American production and for Allied use under the terms of the Anglo-US agreement. 1,500 were to be built in a specially built factory in France, but these plans were not realised due to delay and then cessation of hostilities. 100 of these machines were later assembled in America during 1919–20 with the parts that had already been produced, to become the standard American heavy tank until 1930. A Mk VIII* with an overall length of 44ft was designed but not produced. It was planned to build some Mk VIIIs for France but this project was cancelled at the Armistice. 37tons; crew 12; 2 6pdr guns plus 7 MG; armour 6–16mm; engine (Ricardo [UK] or Liberty [USA] gasoline) 300hp; 6.5mph; 34.16ft x 12.33ft x 10.25ft. Other users: America (see American section).

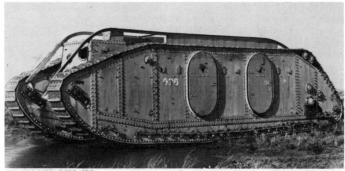

31. TANK MK IX

The design of the Mk IX, an infantry supply tank, was projected in September 1917, and the first machine was produced by Armstrong Whitworth in June 1918. It was specially designed to carry infantry (50 men) or supplies (10tons). A maximum cargo space 3ft 6in by 5ft 5in was achieved in the centre of the vehicle by moving the transmission gears to the rear of the machine and the engine well forward. The engine gear box and epicyclic gears were similar to those of the Mk V and the crew reduced to four. While this class of vehicle was being developed, the role of supply tank was undertaken by the adaptation of fighting types as they became obsolescent. Some machines of Mk I, II and IV and most of the Gun Carriers were modified as supply tanks. Though 200 of the Mk IX were ordered, only 3 were produced at the time of the Armistice and only 23 were completed altogether. Fitted with side doors but underpowered, it was called 'The Pig'. 27tons; crew 4; 1 MG; armour 6–10mm; engine (Ricardo gasoline) 150hp; 3.35mph; 31.95ft x 8.25ft x 8.66ft.

32. Tank Mk IX Amphibious (Duck): In 1919 a Mk IX was modified for trials as an amphibious tank, being fitted with a raised cab, flotation chambers (ex naval 'camels') and modified exhaust. Propulsion power was provided by a motor at the rear, hinged paddles or flaps were attached at intervals on the track.

33. TANK MEDIUM MK A (WHIPPET)

The first of the lighter or medium tanks was the Mk A, also known as the Whippet or Tritton Chaser. Evolved from an early design by Tritton, this machine was developed as a fast cavalry or pursuit tank to exploit opportunities of break-through created by the heavy tanks. The first machine was produced by Fosters in October 1917: in shape and design it differed from its predecessors, the fighting compartment, a fixed barbette, being situated at the rear and the engines and fuel tank at the front. The low tracks were driven by separate engines, each with its complete gear box and transmission. Steering was effected by a steering column which controlled a throttle on each engine in such a way that when one engine was accelerated the other was retarded. By means of a separate lever both engines could be controlled individually. Ventilation of the fighting compartment was effected by a fan on the transmission of each engine which forced air into the cab. 14tons; crew 3; 3 or 4 MG; armour 5–14mm; engine (2 Tylor) 90hp; 8.3mph; 20ft x 8.58ft x 9ft. Other users: Germany (captured vehicles) Japan (purchased 1922).

34. Whippet Prototype

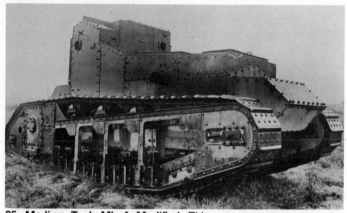

35. Medium Tank Mk A Modified: This was an early attempt by Major Johnson to evolve a high speed tank. During 1917 a Medium A was modified at the Central Workshops by fitting the vehicle with sprung tracks, the road rollers being on leaf springs. In 1918, the vehicle was again modified at No 3 Advanced workshops, by alteration of the superstructure and the installation of a Mk V transmission and Rolls Royce Eagle engine. When tested, speeds of over 20mph were attained.

36. MEDIUM MK B (WHIPPET)
Designed by Major Wilson, the first machine was produced by the Metropolitan Carriage Waggon and Finance Company in September 1918. In general shape this version reverted back to the rhomboidal design and all-round track of the previous heavy

tanks. Mounted on the front of the hull was a large fixed turret. Like the Mk VIII this vehicle had the engine in a separate compartment divided by a bulkhead from the crew. No side sponsons were fitted, the side doors being provided with revolver ports and ball mounts for MGs. Similar ball mounts were also fitted in the turret. An order for 450 Mk B's was given in mid 1918 but the Armistice led to the cancellation of the order after 45 vehicles had been completed. Seventeen of these were sent to Russia during 1919 with the British Mission, some of them later falling into the hands of the Red Army. Others were used for training at Bovington during 1919–21. An experimental Male version was also built, fitted with a 2pdr gun in a revolving turret. The Mk B was a cramped design which saw little service. 18tons; crew 4; 4 MG; armour 6–14mm; engine (Ricardo gasoline) 100hp; 6.1mph; 22.75ft x 8.84ft x 8.5ft. Other users: USSR.

37. MEDIUM MK C
Known as the Hornet, this version was regarded as the best overall British tank design of the 1918 period. Designed by Tritton at Foster's at the end of 1917 it incorporated the experience of the tank crews who had been consulted. In general layout the Hornet resembled the Medium Mk B in that it had a rear engine, overall tracks and a raised forward fighting compartment fitted with ball mounts for five MGs. Mounted on top of the fixed turret was a rotating cupola for the commander. Also provided was improved ventilation and better navigational and control aids; communication between the crew was by voice tube. Designed with sub-assemblies to facilitate mass-production, 450 were ordered and production was started in September 1918. Only 48 were completed as contracts were cancelled after the Armistice. Those that were delivered formed the main equipment of the Tank Corps until 1923 when they were replaced by the Vickers Medium Tank. An experimental Male version was built mounting a short 6pdr gun in the front of the turret. 20tons; crew 4; 4 MG; armour 6–12mm; engine (Ricardo) 150hp; 7.9mph; 26ft x 8.33ft x 9.5ft.

38. MEDIUM D (above, wooden mock-up)
This was the last British tank design of World War I, and was

designed by Lieutenant-Colonel Johnson as a first pursuit medium tank to meet Tank Corps requirements for 1919 on the Western Front where a tank offensive on a large scale was planned. For this roll a maximum speed of 20mph, range of 200miles and a weight limit of no more than 20tons was specified. Design work was started during October 1918, and by the time of the Armistice a full size wooden mock-up was constructed. With the advent of the Armistice production of tanks was stopped except for the few Medium 'Cs' then under construction and the Medium D that was being developed. By mid 1920 the first 'D' type vehicle was completed. This was fitted with wire rope suspension and tracks with articulated plates, that had been designed by Johnson to combine the springing needed for high speed with the minimum of extra weight (a prototype suspension and track having already been tested on a Mk V). The fighting compartment, consisted of a large fixed turret fitted for 3 ball-mounted machine-guns, at the front of the vehicle, in which the two gunners were positioned forward of the driver who sat at the rear in a small conning tower. The engine, a Siddeley Puma 240hp aero engine was situated at the rear. The track outline of the vehicle was lower at the front than the rear, to provide better forward vision. A Male version of the Medium D was also projected and was to be armed with a short (23 calibre) 6pdr gun. Though planned as the postwar equipment for the Tank Corps, the Medium D, owing to mechanical trouble, was superseded by the Vickers Medium Tank that appeared in 1922. 20tons; crew 3; 3 MG; armour 8–10mm; engine (Armstrong Siddeley Puma) 240hp; 23mph; 30ft x 7ft 5in x 9ft 2½in.

39. Medium D Modified: This version incorporated design changes to meet Tank Corps requirements among which were side escape hatch and the fitting of a second cupola for the commander. The role of commander had also been the function of the driver on the Medium D.

40. Medium D**: In answer to War Office requirements for an amphibious tank, a Medium D was modified to make it amphibious and water trials took place at Christchurch during 1921.

41. LIGHT INFANTRY TANK
In 1921 Johnson designed a slightly smaller vehicle closely based on the Medium D, designed to provide machine-gun support for infantry attacks. This was a 17.5ton vehicle, 22ft 3in long and was fitted with a 100hp Hall Scott aero engine. This vehicle was fitted with the Johnson Snake Track. This track was completely flexible in all directions; each track plate was fixed to a hollow tubular backbone which was joined to the next link by a spherical joint protected by mud seals. Speeds of over 30mph were achieved and the vehicle was very manoeuverable. The vehicle was also amphibious, the tracks supplying the propulsive power in water.

42. LIGHT TROPICAL TANK
Produced by the Tank Design Dept in 1921 under Lieutenant-Colonel Johnson, this vehicle was intended for Colonial use. The engine and the driver were placed forward, side by side in the hull and two machine-gun turrets were sited diagonally on the hull at the rear of the vehicle. The vehicle was equipped with Johnson Snake Tracks, and was powered by a 45hp Tylor engine giving a speed of 15mph. The weight of the tank was 5.5tons.

43. SUPPLY TANK
Designed as a companion vehicle to the Tropical Tank to which it was basically similar, this had a large open cargo compartment at the rear instead of the machine-gun turrets. These vehicles did not enter production, but were used in army trials and exercises in the early 1920s.

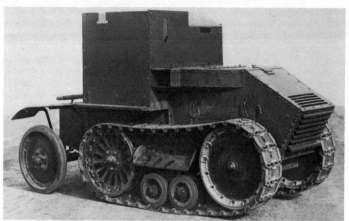

46. Morris-Martel Two-Man Tankette: 2.75tons; crew 2; I light MG; engine I6hp Morris 4-cylinder water-cooled; I0mph, I5mph road; 9.I0ft x 4.7ft x 5.6ft.

44. MORRIS-MARTEL TANKETTE (above, Martel Prototype)

The idea of armoured mobility for the foot soldier had first been suggested by the French General Estienne in 1915, who envisaged the employment en masse of skirmishers mounted in small armoured cross-country vehicles to replace the infantryman. This French project had later culminated in the Renault FT light tank. After World War I, this idea was again revived by Colonel (later Major-General) J. F. C. Fuller, and several British Army officers became interested. One of them, Major (later Lieutenant-General) Sir Gifford Le. Q. Martel undertook during 1925 to construct a machine at his own expense. The vehicle was built in Major Martel's garage and was made entirely of ordinary commercial motor components, the engine being taken from an old Maxwell car and the back axle from a Ford lorry. The tracks were specially made by the Roadless Traction Company, and the body was a mock-up in wood. As a result of a demonstration given by Martel with his home-made machine the War Office authorised the building of four factory machines and Morris Commercial Motors undertook to construct them. Except for the tracks and armour they were also made with commercial components and were fitted with a I6hp Morris engine. The weight of these machines was a little over 2tons. The first was delivered in March 1926, followed by three others, one of which was a Two-Man version. The One-Man Tank concept was later dropped as it was found that one man could not handle the machine-gun and control the vehicle at the same time. Eight of the Two-Man type were ordered in 1927, to be used as Scout machines with the Experimental Mechanical Force then being formed. One two-man machine was tested with single rear wheel steering.

Martel Prototype Tankette: Crew I; armour nil; engine motor car; 6mph, 20mph road; 8.0ft x 4½ft x 5ft.

47. CROSSLEY-MARTEL ONE-MAN TANKETTE

During 1927 an experimental version of the One-Man Tankette was built by Crossley Motors Ltd. This vehicle was of different design to the Martel model, having the I4hp Crossley engine at the rear and the fighting compartment to the front of the vehicle. It was fitted with the Citroen-Kegresse suspension and was tested with various rubber tracks. I.8tons; crew I; I light MG; armour 0.4in; engine I4hp Crossley; I8.6mph; I0ft x 4ft 9in x 5ft 4in.

45. Morris-Martel One-Man Tankette: 2.2tons; crew I; I light MG; engine 6hp Morris 4-cylinder water-cooled; I0mph, I5mph road; 9.I0ft x 3.4ft x 4.I0ft.

48. CARDEN-LOYD ONE-MAN TANKETTE

Due to the publicity received from the trials of the Martel prototype of the firm of Carden-Loyd Tractors Ltd, who had also constructed a cheap light tracked vehicle and exhibited it at Kensington during 1925, approached the War Office for recognition of their enterprise. The War Office recommended an order for an experimental machine. This was a single seater machine with a box type hull, there being no cover for the head and shoulders of the driver. The engine was situated at the rear and the suspension consisted of 14 small road wheels each side attached to a frame sprung on coil springs.

49. Carden-Loyd Mk I: The next model to appear was known as the Carden-Loyd Mk I, this was similar in design but was now fitted with a small 3-sided shield and armed with a light automatic gun.

50. Carden-Loyd Mk I*: This was a modified version of the Mk I, and was converted to the wheel and track principle, having two large pneumatic tyred wheels, one either side of the vehicle and a small steerable wheel at the rear. The wheels could be lowered for road running, replacing the tracks. 1.6tons; crew 1; 1 light MG; armour 6–9mm; engine 14hp, Ford model T.W/c; 31mph on wheels, 15mph on tracks; 10ft 5in x 4ft 6in x 4ft 10in.

51. Carden-Loyd Mk II: Mk II was similar to Mk I, but with a new suspension consisting of four 10in soft rubber bogies per side, replacing the 14 small road wheels.

Carden-Loyd Mk III: The Mk III version was the Mk II fitted with the wheel and track device as used on the Mk I*.

52. Carden-Loyd Two-Man Tankette: During 1926, as interest in the One-Man Tankettes had begun to wane, Carden-Loyd built a Two-Man machine, lower and wider to accommodate a second man. No designation was assigned to this machine.

53. Carden-Loyd Mk IV: This was the second version of a Two-Man machine to be built, it was fitted with a six-sided body for better protection, and a suspension similar to that of the Mk II. The suspension was later modified with the addition of five return rollers each side and the vehicle was armed with at 0.5 Vickers machine-gun.

54. Carden-Loyd Mk V: Late in 1926 the War Office ordered from Carden-Loyd eight modified vehicles to be used in conjunction with the eight Morris-Martel tankette in the role of scout machines with the experimental force. Similar in construction to the Mk IV, this version was fitted with a tricycle wheel and track device. 1.13tons; crew 2; 1 .303 Vickers MG; armour 6–9mm; engine 22.5hp, Ford model T 4-cylinder water-cooled; 31mph on wheels, 22mph on tracks; 9ft 11in x 6ft 6in x 3ft 4in.

55. Carden-Loyd Mk VI:

Designed for the role of a machine gun carrier, the Mk VI appeared in 1928. It was built by Vickers-Armstrong Ltd who had at this period absorbed the firm of Carden-Loyd. The body was similar in design to that of the Mks IV and V but with improvements which included the protection of the front differential housing with an armoured cover, the fitting of full-length stowage bins on either side of the superstructure, and the adoption of a new track and suspension. In its role of machine-gun carrier the Vickers machine-gun could be dismounted from the front of the vehicle and remounted on a tripod that was normally carried on the front left side of the vehicle. The Mk VI besides being the predecessor of a long line of machine-gun carriers also had considerable influence on the design of the first light tanks of the British Army. Various versions of the Mk VI were exported abroad, where in some cases they were built under licence often developing into a considerably different design to the original machine. Examples of this were the Italian CV33 and CV35, the French UE, Russian T27, Polish TK3 and the Czechoslovakian MU4. 1.5tons; crew 2; 1 Vickers .303 MG or .5 MG; armour 6–9mm; engine 40hp Ford model T; 28mph; 8ft 1in x 5ft 7in x 4ft.

56. VICKERS TANKS No 1 (above) and No 2

These were built and tested, 1921–2, but the project was dropped after trials had proved the vehicles to be mechanically unreliable Similar in shape to the Medium B, these vehicles were fitted with a dome shaped turret with a commander's cupola in the centre, and were the first British tanks to have a turret with 360° traverse. The difference in the two models was in the armament; No 1 was armed with three ball-mounted Hotchkiss machine-guns in the domed turret, while No 2 mounted a 3pdr gun and had ball mounts for three Hotchkiss machine-guns, plus a mounting in the turret roof for an anti-aircraft machine-gun. 8.75tons; crew 5; 3 Hotchkiss .303 MG or 3 pdr QF gun and 4 Hotchkiss MG; armour .5in; engine 86hp, water-cooled; 15 mph.

57. Vickers Tank No 1 (Rear view)

58. A1E1 INDEPENDENT TANK

Built by Vickers-Armstrong Ltd in 1925 to a specification laid down by the General Staff, the A1E1 was developed as a fast multi-gunned tank able to operate independently instead of with the slow moving infantry. Due to the lack of funds this vehicle did not go into production. Only the pilot model was built, but lessons learnt from its development proved of great value in the construction of tanks that were to follow. The Independent differed from previous tanks, in that it had a long track base with the hull built up between the suspension assemblies. The top plates were only just above the top of the track. In the front, mounted on the top plates were the forward two auxiliary machine gun turrets with the driver's compartment between them, the driver being further forward than in any other previous design. Behind the driver's compartment was the main turret with an all-round traverse, an observation cupola with all-round vision was mounted offset on the main turret roof from which the commander was in direct communication with each member of the crew by the Laryngaphone system. Behind the main turret and either side of the tank were the two aft machine-gun turrets. An indicating device was arranged in each of the turrets as well as in the commander's cupola, by which he could direct fire on to any particular target. This vehicle inspired similar development of multi-turreted tanks in Russia and Germany. 31.5tons; crew 8; 1 3pdr QF gun and 4 .303 Vickers MG; armour 13–28mm; engine 398hp Armstrong-Siddeley V-12 air-cooled; 25ft 5in x 10ft 6in x 8ft 10in.

59. A1E1 Independent Tank.

60. VICKERS MEDIUM TANK MK I

Development of this vehicle was begun in 1922, and the first production models were delivered as Light Tank Mk I to the army during 1924. This was the first British service tank to have all-round traverse and geared elevation for the gun. Sprung suspension gave the Vickers tank higher speeds than had been possible with earlier designs. The armament consisted of a 3pdr QF gun and four Hotchkiss machine-guns mounted in the turret, and two Vickers .303 machine-guns carried in ball mounts either side of the hull. With the adoption of a lighter class of light tank into the service, the Light Tank Mk I was reclassified as Medium Tank Mk I, the designation by which it is best known. 11.7tons; crew 5; 1 3pdr QF gun, 4 Hotchkiss and 2 Vickers .303 MG; armour 6.5mm; engine 90hp air-cooled Armstrong-Siddeley V-8; 15mph; 17ft 6in x 9ft 1½in x 9ft 3in.

61. Medium Tank Mk IA: Produced in 1924 by Vickers-Armstrong Ltd as Light Tank Mk IA and later re-designated Medium Tank Mk IA, this model was similar to the Medium Mk I but with various modifications which included an increase in armour thickness, a redesigned driver's cowl with flaps that opened to the left and right instead of folding backwards as on the Mk I, and a bevel in the rear of the turret for mounting a Hotchkiss machine-gun for the AA role. 11.9tons; crew 5; 1 3pdr QF gun, 4 Hotchkiss and 2 Vickers .303 MG; armour 6.5mm; engine 90hp air-cooled Armstrong-Siddeley V-8. 15mph; 17ft 6in x 9ft 1½in x 8ft 10½in.

Light Tank Mk IA Special (L) India: Two female versions were designed for use in India and produced in 1926 similar in design to the Mk IA, the difference being that four machine-guns in the turret constituted the main armament. Special efforts were made to improve the cooling of the fighting compartment by the extensive use of linings of asbestos and circulating fans. These vehicles were not reclassified as Medium Tanks.

62. Medium Tank Mk IA*: This was the basic Mk IA fitted with a co-axial Vickers .303 machine-gun instead of the Hotchkiss .303 MG. The turret was fitted with a commander's cupola. 11.9tons; crew 5; 1 3pdr QF gun, 3 Vickers .303 MG; armour 8–6.25mm; armour 6.5mm; 17ft 6in x 9ft 1½in x 9ft 10½in.

63. Medium Tank Mk I.C.S: Development of the Mk IA as a close-support weapon to accompany tanks and be capable of firing smoke. With this version the 3pdr QF gun was replaced by a 15pdr mortar.

64. Medium Tank Mk I Wheel-and-Track: Built by Vickers-Armstrong Ltd during 1926, this was a standard Mk I converted to wheel and track drive. The object was to provide increased road speed and reduce track wear on hard roads. Change from wheels to tracks was achieved by engine power in one minute. The design was not successful due to excessive pitching when running on wheels. 13.7tons; crew 5; 1 3pdr and 1 .303 Vickers MG; armour 8mm; 10mph on track, 20mph on wheels; height 9ft 6in on wheels, length 21ft wheels raised.

65. Medium Tank Mk I Wheel-and-track.

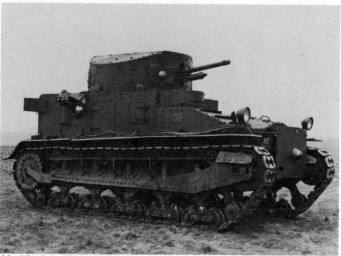

66. **Medium Tank Mk I (Ricardo C.I.):** This was an experimental installation of a 90hp 4-cylinder water-cooled Ricardo Diesel engine in a Medium Mk I.

67. MEDIUM TANK MK II

The Medium Mk I was followed in 1925 by an improved type, the Medium Mk II which possessed the following improvements: thicker armour but increased weight, the driver placed further forward giving a better vision, suspension protected by armoured skirting plates. Armament as for Mk IA. The Mk II was in service until 1939 and was then used for training. 13.2tons; crew 5; 1 3pdr QF, 4 Hotchkiss and 2 Vickers .303 MG; armour 8.25mm; engine 90hp air-cooled Armstrong-Siddeley V-8; 15mph; 17ft 6in x 9ft 1½in x 8ft 10in.

68. **Medium Tank Mk II*:** As for Mk II but with co-axial Vickers machine-gun in the turret, and the elimination of the Hotchkiss machine-guns, and the addition of a commander's cupola. 13.5tons; crew 5; 1 3pdr QF gun, 3 Vickers .303 MG; armour 8–6.25mm; engine 90hp air-cooled Armstrong-Siddeley V-8; 15mph; 17ft 6in x 9ft 1½in x 10ft.

69. **Medium Tank Mk II**:** During the year 1932, 44 Medium Mk IIs were converted by the installation of twin mountings for the 3pdr gun and a Vickers .303 machine-gun together with a commander's cupola on the turret roof. In addition to this, armoured containers for a wireless set were fitted to the backs of the turret. The converted vehicles were redesignated Mk II**.

70. **Medium Tank Mk IIA:** Medium Mk IIA was produced in 1930 by Vickers-Armstrong Ltd and 20 were built. The bevel was removed from the rear of the turret and a command cupola was fitted. The left ventilator was protected by an armoured box open at the top. The 3pdr gun and Vickers machine-gun were co-axial. The hull Vickers machine-gun ejected the empty cases to the outside of the tank. Other improvements included better suspension units with rearranged track return rollers.

Medium Tank Mk IIA*: Similar to Mk IIA, but fitted with an armoured wireless container.

71. Medium Tank Mk IIA.C.S: Similar to Mk IIA, but adapted to the close-support role by the fitting of a 3.7in howitzer. 14tons; crew 5; 1 3.7 Howitzer and 3 Vickers .303 MG; armour 8mm; engine 90hp air-cooled Armstrong-Siddeley V-8; 15mph; 17ft 6in x 9ft 1½in x 10ft.

72. Medium Tank Mk II (Tropical): Five Mk II tanks were specially modified and fitted to meet tropical conditions. They were sent to Egypt in 1928. The chief modifications were sun screens consisting of woven asbestos fitted outside the upper surfaces and sides of the tank with an air gap of 1–1.5in between the sheeting and the armour plate. The Rackham steering clutches and control levers were also insulated.

73. Medium Tank Mk II (Bridgecarrier): Developed during 1927, this Mk II was fitted with side brackets to carry bridge girders to construct a 18ft bridge. The bridging sections were assembled by the tank crew.

English Workman: Based on the Medium Mk IIA, this modified version was built in limited quantity for the Soviet Government during 1931 and was known to the Red Army as the 'English Workman'. (See Russian Section).

74. Medium Mk II Command Tank: Developed during 1931, this was a Mk II with a dummy gun in a fixed turret, in which were fitted two wireless sets. A wireless mast was carried on the right of the vehicle. Otherwise it was externally similar to the standard vehicle.

Medium Tank Mk II (Special): Delivered to Australia during 1929, these were modified Mk II Mediums differing in having a co-axial Vickers MG on the left of the 3pdr gun and a separate ball-mounted Vickers MG on the right.

75. MEDIUM TANK MK III

During 1930 it was decided to construct a new 16ton tank having certain features of the A6 series, and to be known as the Medium Mk III. Improvements to be embodied in this new design included the provision of a larger turret to take R/T and W/T and fitted with a commander's cupola, improvements in gun mountings, anti-gas protection, better accessibility, and new steering brake designs. Like the A6 series the Mk III was fitted with two auxiliary turrets mounting single .303in Vickers MGs. Only three pilot models were built, one by Vickers-Armstrong Ltd and two by the Royal Ordnance Factory. 16tons; crew 7; 1 3pdr QF gun and 3 Vickers .303 MG; armour 9–14mm; engine 180hp air-cooled Armstrong-Siddeley V-8; 30mph; 21ft 6in x 8ft 10in x 9ft 8in.

MEDIUM TANKS, A6 SERIES

These multi-turreted tanks were built by Vickers-Armstrong Ltd at the request of the British War Office, as an improved design of medium tank based on the Independent Tank. They were to replace the Medium Mk I and Mk II then in service. Three machines were built during 1928–30 and they were known as the 16 Tonners due to the weight limitations laid down in their specifications. This was exceeded in the actual vehicles when fully stowed. Though these machines did not go into production, due to drastic cuts in defence expenditure, they were used as test beds for experimental work with engines, gearboxes, suspension units, gunnery and other experimental work up to 1938.

76. A6EI

17.5tons; crew 7; 1 3pdr QF gun and 5 Vickers .303 MG; armour 9–14mm; engine 180hp air-cooled Armstrong-Siddeley V-8; 30mph; 21ft 6in x 8ft 9in x 9ft 2in.

77. A6E2

All data as for A6EI, but fitted with a 180hp Ricardo CI diesel engine this was later replaced with a 180hp Armstrong-Siddeley.

78. A6E3

All data as for A6EI, but with certain modifications. Main turret fitted with a single commander's cupola instead of two as fitted to A6EI and E2; the auxiliary turrets were redesigned and mounted single MG and the box bogie suspension was now converted to the Horstman type. During 1937 the A6E3 was fitted with a 500hp Thorneycroft RY 12 engine.

MEDIUM TANKS, A7 SERIES

Built in the Royal Ordnance Factory, Woolwich, the design work on the vehicles was started in 1929 by the Chief Superintendent of Design, and by the end of 1931 manufacture of the A7EI and A7E2 had been completed and initial trials carried out. Though the design of these two vehicles was good, various mechanical faults developed during the period of testing, and by the time that these had been rectified in 1936 the vehicles were out of date, being inadequate for the role of Medium Tanks.

79. A7EI

14tons; crew 5; 1 3pdr QF gun and 2 Vickers .303 MG; armour 9–14mm; engine 120hp air-cooled Armstrong-Siddeley; 25mph.

80. A7E2

All data as for A7EI, but differences in transmission and running gear. Turret later modified to mount 2pdr gun.

81. A7E3

During 1933 a parallel development was started on a third machine to be known as the A7E3. Experience gained with the development of the A6E3, A7E2 and the Medium Mk III was incorporated in the construction of this vehicle which was completed early in 1937.

Trials of the A7E3 took place during mid 1937 and proved unsuccessful due to various mechanical faults. Though the A7 series did not go into production, they were used as test beds for various experimental work with engines, transmissions and suspensions, the result of which was later incorporated in the development of Infantry Tank Mk II, the Matilda. 18.2tons; crew 5; 1 3pdr QF gun and 2 Vickers .303 MG; armour 14mm; engine Twin 252hp A.E.C. CI Diesels; 25mph; 22ft 6in x 8ft 11½in x 9ft 1in.

Vickers-Carden-Loyd Commercial Tanks: The following armoured vehicles were designed and produced during 1926–39 as private ventures for sale to foreign customers. Though some of these were tested by the British Army they were not adopted by them.

82. Medium Tank Mk 'C': Produced in 1926, this was a development of the Vickers Medium Tank, incorporating various new design features. Prototype vehicles were sold to Japan and Eire, the design being used as a basis for the development of the Japanese Type 89 light tank. 11.5tons; crew 5; 1 6pdr (57mm) gun, 4 Vickers .303 MG; armour 5–6mm; engine 132hp Sunbeam 6-cylinder water-cooled; 20mph; 18ft 4in x 8ft 4in x 7ft 11in.

83. Vickers-Wolseley Wheel and Track Tank: Built in 1927, this was an experimental vehicle, based on the Wolseley standard truck chassis and armoured by Vickers, it was an attempt to create a vehicle able to change from track to wheel drive, thereby combining high road speed with the ability to go cross country when required. It existed only as a prototype. 7.5tons; crew 4; 3 Vickers .303 MG; engine 120hp Wolseley 6-cylinder water-cooled; 15mph on tracks, 25mph on wheels; 16ft 8in x 7ft 3in x 7ft.

84. Vickers-Wolseley

85. 6ton Tank Mk 'E' (above, type 'A'): The Vickers 6ton Tank was designed in 1928 and models were produced for overseas sale up to 1939. They were sold to Bolivia, Bulgaria, China, Estonia, Finland, Greece, Japan, Poland, Portugal, Romania, Russia, Siam (Thailand). One machine was demonstrated in the United States in 1931. The 6ton tank influenced design in many countries, being either copied or built under licence. Examples of overseas-built versions include the Russian T26 series, the Polish 7TP series and American T1E4. Two versions of the 6ton Tank were produced. The first, known as Type 'A' suffered from the contemporary machine-gun complex, having two machine-gun turrets side by side; but it had some compensating features that included a fire-proof partition fitted between the engine and fighting compartment, a new type of improved suspension with a more durable short pitch track and was equipped with the Laryngaphone system. Later models were also fitted with the Marconi short wave radio SB-1A. The second variant, basically similar, had a two-man turret with a 47mm gun and a machine-gun and was known as type 'B'. Though not adopted by the British Army several machines were used during 1940 for training when some vehicles for foreign contracts were requisitioned. 7tons; crew 3; 2 Vickers .303 MG or 1 Vickers .303 and 1 .5 MG; armour 5–8–14mm; engine 80hp Armstrong-Siddeley 4-cylinder air-cooled; 22mph; 15ft x 7ft 11in x 6ft 10in.

86. Type 'B': 8tons; crew 3; 1 47mm gun and 1 Vickers .303 MG (Alternative MG — 1 7.92mm and/or 8mm RC); Bofors 37mm gun and 7.92mm MG fitted in Finland; armour 5–8–14mm; engine 80hp Armstrong-Siddeley 4-cylinder air-cooled; 22mph; 15ft x 7ft 11in x 7ft 2in.

87. 6Ton Tank Mk 'F': Supplied to China during 1935–6, this model was similar in construction to Type 'B' but was fitted with a modified turret with rear extension to house Marconi Type G2A Transmitting and Receiving Wireless equipment.

bious tank the T37 from this design. 2.17tons; crew 2; I Vickers .303 MG; armour IImm; engine 90hp Meadows EST 6-cylinder water-cooled; 3.72mph in water, 20 to 27mph on land; I3ft 4in x 6ft 9in x 6ft 2in.

88. Vickers Wheel and Track Tank (D3EI): Tested in 1928 under the British War Office designation, D3EI, this was a further attempt by Vickers-Armstrong Ltd to achieve a dual purpose vehicle combining wheel and track drive. The tracked running gear could be moved up and down by power take-off operating through bell cranks, the road wheels being rigidly fixed to the hull. 8.4tons; crew 3; 2 Vickers .303 MG; engine 90hp Armstrong-Siddeley air-cooled; I5mph on tracks, 45mph on wheels; I8ft x 8ft x 9ft.

89. D3EI on wheels

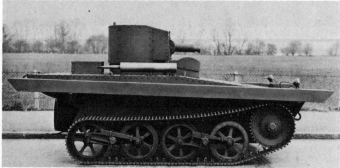

90. LIGHT AMPHIBIOUS TANKS A4EII/A4EI2 (above, A4EI2)
Two experimental tanks developed by Vickers-Armstrong in 1931–2. For the period of testing they were giving the War Office designation of A4EII and A4EI2, (they were also known as LIEI and LIE2). Each mounted a .303 Vickers MG in a rotating turret. A rudder and propeller were fitted at the rear of each vehicle for operating in the water, and balsa wood floats, encased in sheet metal were fitted in the form of track guards to give additional bouyancy to the water tight hull. The vehicle was steerable through the moveable propeller at the rear. Though these vehicles were not adopted by the British Army considerable foreign sales were made and examples were subsequently sold to China, Dutch East Indies, Thailand and the USSR who developed their own amphi-

91. A4EI2 rear view

92. PATROL TANKS, MK I (above) AND MK II
This vehicle was a turreted development of the Carden-Loyd Machine Gun Carrier Mk VI. Two versions were built in 1932. The first model was equipped with the normal leaf-spring carrier suspension, on the second version the leaf-spring was changed to double helical springs. Sold to Sweden, Denmark, Finland and Portugal. 2tons; crew 2; I .303 Vickers MG; armour 7–IImm; engine Meadows 6-cylinder 40hp; 30mph; 8ft 6in x 5ft 9in x 5ft 5in.

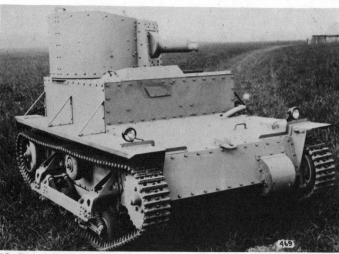

93. Patrol Tank Mk II

94. Light Tank Model 1933: During the mid-thirties the firm of Vickers-Armstrong Ltd built a series of light tanks for export, these were similar in design to the British Service tanks of that period which were also built by Vickers. The first of these was Model 1933 which bore a strong resemblance to Light Tank Mk IV, but was equipped with leaf-spring suspension and a cylindrical turret. Variants of this model were sold to Finland, Lithuania, and Latvia. 3.8tons; crew 2; 1 .303 Vickers MG; armour 7–9mm; engine 90hp Meadows EPT 6-cylinder water-cooled; 40mph; 11ft 10¾in x 6ft 2½in x 6ft 2in.

97. Light Tank, Model 1936: This was the model 1934 with a new hexagonal turret, reworked drivers hatch and other minor modifications. Supplied to China, Dutch East India. Also ordered by the Netherlands. Some tanks from this order were retained in England at the out-break of the war and used for training by the RAC where they were known as 'Dutchman'. 3.8tons; crew 2; 1 .303 Vickers MG; armour 7–9mm; engine 90hp Meadows EST 6-cylinder water-cooled; 40mph; 11ft 10¾in x 6ft 2½in x 6ft 2¼in.

95. Light Tank Model 1934: Similar to Model 1933, but fitted with coil spring suspension, they were supplied to Switzerland and Argentina. A batch of 42 equipped with high conical turrets was also delivered to Belgium where they were armed with the 13.2mm Hotchkiss machine gun and taken into service as the Tank leger, T15. 3.8tons; crew 2; 7.7mm or .303 Vickers MG; armour 7–9 mm; engine 90hp Meadows EST 6-cylinder water-cooled; 40mph; 11ft 10¾in x 6ft 2½in x 6ft 4in.

98. Model 1936 in service with the RAC

96. Model 1934, Belgium (T.15)

99. Light Tank, Model 1937: This was the model 1936 fitted with a specially designed turret to mount a 40mm QF anti-tank gun. 4tons; crew 2; 40mm QF Anti Tank gun or 20mm Oerlikon gun; armour 4–9mm; engine 90hp Meadows EST 6-cylinder water-cooled; 30mph; 11ft 10¾in x 6ft 2¼in.

100. Light Command Tank: Produced in 1938, this was a new design of vehicle having a modified type of Horstmann suspension and hull. The turret could be adapted to mount two Vickers .303 tank type MGs or one Vickers .303 and one Vickers 12.7mm tank type MGs or a 40mm QF gun, other weapons could be fitted to suit special requirements. A gunner's periscope was mounted on the turret roof. Ordered by the Belgian Army. 5tons; crew 3; armament alternative; armour 4–11mm; engine 90hp Meadows EST 6-cylinder water-cooled; 31mph; 13ft 8in x 6ft 9in x 6ft 7in.

101. LIGHT TANK A3EI
This was a three-man tank built during 1925 by the Royal Ordnance Factory, in an attempt to reduce the cost of manufacture by utilising a commercial type of engine, in this case an omnibus engine, and a cheap type of cast steel track. Based on a suspension similar to that of the Vickers Medium Tank, the A3EI mounted two small machine-gun turrets, one that was situated at the front of the vehicle, to the left of the drivers armoured hatch, and a second that was placed at the rear. This machine was later designated (1926) as Carrier, Machine Gun No I. 3tons; crew 3; 2 .303 Vickers MG; armour 6mm; engine 40hp AEC 4-cylinder water-cooled; 16mph; 17ft 6in x 9ft x 6ft.

102. LIGHT TANK A5EI (VICKERS THREE-MAN TANK)
One was built in 1930 as a three-man light tank, having a large two-man turret with co-axial .5 and .303 Vickers MG. The hull was similar to Light Tank Mk II with the track, sprocket idler and return-rollers as on Light Tank Mk I and Mk IA, but the suspension

consisted of two semicircular bogie units each side. Each unit consisted of four bogies in leaf spring pairs, comparable to that used on the Vickers 6ton Tank Mk 'E'. 4.5tons; crew 3; .5 and .303 Vickers MG; armour 4–6–9mm; engine 85hp Meadows EST 6-cylinder water-cooled; 30mph.

103. LIGHT TANK MK VII (A4EI)
This two-man light tank was built in 1929 and was a development of the Carden-Loyd Tankette series. Code named A4EI, the vehicle was armed with a Vickers .303 MG in a low bevel sided turret, the suspension consisted of four road wheels in leaf-spring pairs connected by an external girder side. Only one pilot model was built. 2.5tons; crew 2; I Vickers .303 MG; engine 59hp Meadows 6-cylinder; 35mph.

104. A4E4

LIGHT TANK MK VIII (A4E2-A4E5) LIGHT TANK MK I
This was the next design to follow the Carden-Loyd Mk VII and was considered sufficiently satisfactory for a small batch to be put into production in 1930, as Light Tank Mk I. Fitted with four road wheels, leaf-spring suspension, and three return rollers, and mounting a Vickers .303 MG in a cylindrical turret, this was the first light tank to be accepted into the British Army. These vehicles were designated A4E2 to A4E5 and were mainly used for various running trials and experiments. A4E2 was adapted as a self-propelled mount for twin .5 anti-aircraft MGs in an open circular mount, and A4E4 was later fitted with Horstman suspension. 4.8tons; crew 2; I Vickers .303 MG; armour 4–14mm; engine 58hp Meadows EPT 6-cylinder; 30mph; 13ft 2in x 6ft 1in x 5ft 7in.

105. A4E6

Light Tank Mk IA (A4E6-A4EI0): In October 1930 the first deliveries of the Mk IA materialised and running trials indicated that these vehicles were more satisfactory than the Mk I. Several models were built, these being designated A4E6 to A4EI0. They had more effectively sloped armour than the Mk I. On the A4E8 models, the coil spring Horstman suspension was introduced. Various experiments in armament were carried out, which included the fitting of a twin mounting taking both .5 and .303 Vickers MGs, the .303 being superimposed above the .5. This vehicle was designated A4EI0. During 1932 various experiments were conducted with two Mk IA machines. One was fitted with a Ricardo 65hp CI engine and the other with an improved form of laminated spring suspension with shortened track and without idler wheels. Four tanks of the Mk IA type were tested in India in 1931 and this led to subsequent orders by the Government of India for light tanks similar to those in current use in the British Army, but with slight modifications for local conditions. (Details as for Mk I).

LIGHT TANK MK II (A4EI3-A4EI5)

A total of 16 of these vehicles were produced in 1931. They were fitted with the Horstman coil spring suspension and had the same hull form as the Mk IA, but were fitted with a larger rectangular turret and a Rolls Royce engine instead of the Meadows type. The pilot models of this series were designated A4EI3 to A4EI5. Two of the Mk II series vehicles had close rivet construction to facilitate waterproofing and these were fitted with flotation units on either side and an outboard motor on the rear plate. Flotation trials were carried out at Portsmouth and Hayling Island. One of these amphibious vehicles was later fitted with experimental Horstman modified suspension adopted for the Light Tank Mk III. 4.25tons; crew 2; 1 Vickers .303 MG; armour 4–10mm; engine 66hp Rolls Royce 6-cylinder; 30mph; 11ft 9in x 6ft 3½in x 6ft 7½in.

106. A4E8

107. A4EI0

108. Light Tank Mk II

109, 110. Light Tank Mk II equipped with flotation units.

111. Light Tank Mk II with experimental Horstmann suspension.

112. Light Tank Mk IIA

LIGHT TANKS MK IIA AND MK IIB (A4EI6-A4EI7-A4EI8)

During 1931 it was decided that an improved Mk I would be
introduced and contracts for these were placed in June and July
respectively, 29 to be built by the Royal Ordnance Factory at
Woolwich, and 21 by Vickers-Armstrong Ltd. The 29 constructed
at Woolwich were later called Light Tanks Mk IIA and the 21
from Vickers-Armstrong Ltd, Light Tanks Mk IIB. In general the
Mk IIA was similar to Mk IIB, but there were certain differences
in design. The main differences was in connection with the fuel
supply, the Mk IIA being fitted with two tanks, one placed on the
right side track guard, and one on the rear sloping plate with
suitable armour protection. The Mk IIB was fitted with one large
capacity tank on the side. The suspension fitted to these vehicles
consisted of the Horstmann coil spring type as fitted on the
Mk II, but with only two return rollers. This suspension known
as the '2 pair spring' type was later replaced with the '4 pair
spring' type as fitted to the Light Tank Mk III. Light Tank Mk II
was fitted on issue with a No I Mk I turret, whilst the Mks IIA and
IIB were fitted with No I Mk 2. Both turrets were rectangular
in shape with sloping front, rear and side plates, they were similar
except that the Mk I had no air louvres (or vents) at the top of
each side plate. These turrets were later slightly modified. Experimental models of this series were designated A4EI6, A4EI8 (Light
Tank Mk IIA) and A4EI7 (Light Tank Mk IIB). Data as for Light
Tank Mk II.

113. Light Tank Mk IIB

114. Light Tank Mk IIB (India Pattern): Specially designed for service in India, these modified vehicles were engined with the
Meadows EPT. The main distinguishing feature of these tanks
was the square bevel sided non-rotating cupola mounted on the
main turret.

115. Light Tank Mk III: Entered service during the early part of
1933 and was similar in layout to the Mk II series except that the
superstructure was extended further to the rear. Fitted with the
modified Horstmann suspension which consisted of twin spring
units (known as the '4 pair spring' type), these later replacing
the single spring units on the Mks II, IIA, and IIB vehicles. The
turret fitted was either the Mk I or Mk II No 2. Both marks of
turret were rectangular in shape with sloping front and sides. The
only difference was in the turret roof plate. 4.5tons; crew 2; I
Vickers .303 or .5 MG; armour 4–12mm; engine 66hp Rolls Royce
6-cylinder; 30mph; 12ft x 6ft 3½in x 6ft 11in.

**116. LIGHT TANK VICKERS EXPERIMENTAL MODEL 1933
India Pattern No I (A4EI9) (L2EI):** Designed in 1933 as a lighter
and faster light tank than those then in service. The hull was
some 2ft shorter and 8in wider than those of the light tanks, Mk II
and Mk III. The number of bulletproof plates was reduced and
their shape simplified with the object of facilitating production.
Improvements were also introduced to increase the rigidity of
the hull, affording better support to the roof which carried a Vickers type turret. Horstmann light double spring suspension was

fitted. This was comprised of two conventional double bogies for each side and no separate rear idler or return roller was fitted. This vehicle received the War Office designation of A4E19 and was also designated L2E1. 3.4 tons; crew 2; 1 Vickers .303 MG; armour 7mm; engine 90hp Meadows EST 6-cylinder water-cooled; 38mph.

117. LIGHT TANK VICKERS EXPERIMENTAL MODEL 1933
India Pattern No 2 (A4E20) (L2E2): Produced also by Vickers-Armstrong Ltd during 1933, this machine was basically similar to the No 1 vehicle, but was modified during manufacture to incorporate several desirable features that included the standard War Department light tank turret. Though produced with armour on the 9mm basis (vertical), this was increased in weight to correspond with the 11mm basis, by additional steel plates secured to the hull; War Office designations were A4E20 and L2E2. The A4E19 and A4E20 became the prototype machines of the Light Tank Mk IV series. 3.9 tons; crew 2; 1 Vickers .303 MG; armour 9–11mm; engine 90hp Meadows EST 6-cylinder water-cooled; 38mph.

118. LIGHT TANK MK IV
This series of light tanks built during 1934 was based on the Vickers Experimental Light Tanks Indian Pattern No 1 and No 2 which had been tested during the previous year as the A4E19 and A4E20. The General Staff decided not to proceed further with the existing Light Tank Mk III but to order a batch of light tanks generally on the lines of the A4E19 and A4E20 and to embody all the improvements, modifications etc that these vehicles had demonstrated as being desirable on their running trials. The first light tank to use the hull as a chassis and to mount automotive components directly onto it. Superstructure of this vehicle was higher than the earlier models of light tanks. The turret was similar to the Mk I pattern fitted to the Light Tank Mk III, but had certain modifications, and was set further back on the vehicle. The suspension was the twin spring Horstmann type fitted with a return roller on the front bogie unit. 4.6 tons; crew 2; 1 Vickers .303 or .5 MG; armour 5–12mm; engine 88hp Meadows ESTE 6-cylinder; 36mph; 11ft 2in x 6ft 8½in x 6ft 11½in.

119. LIGHT TANKS L3E1 (above) AND L3E2 (VICKERS THREE-MAN TANK)
Two light tanks built by Vickers-Armstrong Ltd during 1933 to develop a three-man light tank. They were fitted with a two-man turret armed with two machine-guns. Mounted on the turret top was a large commander's cupola similar to the 'Bishop's Mitre' type fitted to some of the Vickers Medium Tanks. The suspension was similar to that of the Light Tank Mk IV. These two vehicles were built in mild steel and tested under the designations L3E1 and L3E2. They became the prototypes of the Light Tank Mk V. 4.4 tons; crew 3; 1 Vickers .303 and one .5 MG; engine 90hp EST 6-cylinder water-cocled.

120. LIGHT TANK MK V
Built by Vickers-Armstrong Ltd during 1935, this was the first light tank with a two-man turret to enter service. The turret was mounted on a ball race. A .303 and .5 Vickers MG was fitted in the redesigned turret, on top of which was mounted a circular commander's cupola. Hull of the Mk V had a fighting chamber of much larger dimensions than the earlier light tanks, being designed to carry in addition to the machine-gunner, an observer or tank commander. The hull was rectangular in cross-section with flat top plates, a triangular extension at the rear accommodating the fuel tank. Suspension was similar to that of the Mk IV. Only 22 production vehicles were built. 4.15 tons; crew 3; 1 .303 and 1 .5 Vickers MG; armour 12mm; engine 88hp Meadows ESTL 6-cylinder; 32mph; 12ft 1in x 6ft 9in x 7ft 3in.

121. LIGHT TANK MK VI
This three-man tank entered service in 1936 and was the final

development of the lightly armoured Vickers-Carden-Loyd light tank series. Generally similar to the Light Tank Mk V but with a redesigned turret, extended at the rear to accommodate a No 7 wireless set. The suspension was of the type fitted to the Mk V. 4.8tons; crew 3; 1 .303 and 1 .5 Vickers MG; armour 4–15mm; engine 88hp Meadows ESTL 6-cylinder 35mph; 13ft 2in x 6ft 10in x 7ft 5in.

122. Light Tank Mk VIA: Similar in design to the Mk VI, but with a modified Horstmann suspension with the track return roller attached to the hull instead of the top of the front bogie unit. This type of suspension had been tested on a pilot model of the Light Tank Mk V. The circular type of cupola as fitted to the Mk VI was replaced by one that was octagonal in shape and this was fitted with two lookouts in the front half, both of which were provided with glass blocks. A more powerful Meadows engine was installed.

123. Light Tank Mk VIB: This version was the most widely used of the British Light Tanks of World War II. In service with the BEF in France during 1939–40 where it formed a high proportion of the total tank strength. It was very similar to Light Tank Mk VIA, but had a circular commander's cupola similar to that of the Mk VI but fitted with glass block lookouts and a single armoured cooling louvre over the radiator cover plates, instead of the two as on the earlier models. Six Light Tanks Mk VIB were experimentally modified to include rear idler wheels to improve their cross country performance. Some of these were sent on trials in France with the 1st Armoured Division. This form of suspension was similar to that fitted to the Light Tanks Mks II and III. 5.2tons; crew 3; 1 .303 and 1 .5 Vickers MG; armour 4–15mm; engine 88hp Meadows ESTB/A or ESTB/B; 13ft 2in x 6ft 10in x 7ft 5in.

124. Light Tank Mk VIB (India Pattern): Built for the Government of India, before the outbreak of war, these vehicles did not have a commander's cupola, but were provided with a single periscope for the commander which was located in one half of the hinged conical-shaped turret hatch.

125. Light Tank Mk VIC: Last version to be developed in the Mk VI series; fitted with wider suspension wheels and a broader track. The turret was slightly modified and in place of the cupola, the commander was provided with hinged flaps in the turret roof, in the centre of which was mounted a Vickers periscope. On the left side plate was fitted a fan for extracting the fumes of the machine-guns. The .303 and .5 Vickers machine-guns were replaced on this version by the 7.92mm and 15mm Besa air-cooled MGs. 5.2tons; crew 3; 1 7.92mm and 1 15mm Besa MG; armour 4–15mm; 13ft 2in x 6ft 10in x 7ft 5in.

126. LIGHT TANK MK VII TETRARCH
Radical new design by Vickers, initially as a private venture, it was offered to and accepted by the War Office in 1938. It was in production by 1940, though orders were cut back when light tanks were dropped from British armoured divisions. The Tetrarch was first used in action in the Madagascar campaign in 1942. It was subsequently adopted as a glider-borne air-landing tank,

the Hamilcar glider being designed specifically to carry it. The Tetrarch was used in this role in limited numbers at the Normandy landing in 1944 and in the air assault on the Rhine crossing in 1945. One Squadron of these tanks remained in service until 1949–50 by which time gliders had been dropped from military use. The design featured large road wheels with a steering wheel flexing the tracks in similar fashion to the system used on British tracked carriers. 7.5tons; crew 3; I 2pdr (or 3in howitzer in Tetrarch ICS), I Besa MG; armour 16–4mm; 13ft 6in x 7ft 7in x 6ft 11in.

127. A17E1 Prototype

128. Tetrarch ICS: Close support version with 3in howitzer replacing 2pdr gun. Used in small numbers.

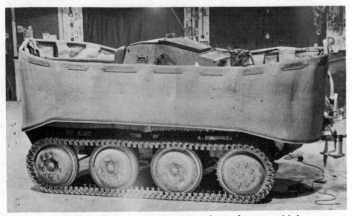

129. Tetrarch DD: Experimental conversion of one vehicle to test Straussler flotation equipment in 1941. Was forerunner of subsequent DD (Duplex-Drive) swimming tanks based on Valentine and Sherman vehicles.

130. Tetrarch I with Littlejohn Adaptor: Reduced bore attachment (Littlejohn Adaptor) was fitted to some vehicles to improve the effectiveness of the 2pdr gun. Other users: .USSR (Lend-Lease, 1942).

131. LIGHT TANK MK VIII HARRY HOPKINS
Designed by Vickers in 1941 as a successor to the Light Tank Mk VII, Tetrarch. Similar characteristics to the Tetrarch were evident in the design but the hull and turret were of improved shape and the armour was thicker. Total of 100 vehicles were built by 1944 but they were never issued for service, light tanks then being obsolete in British military thinking. Some vehicles had the Littlejohn adaptor as for the Tetrarch. 8.5tons; crew 3; armour 6–38mm; engine Meadows 149hp; 30mph; 14ft 3in. x 8ft 10½in x 6ft 11in.

132. LIGHT TANK L4E1
The designation L4E1 was given to an experimental light tank designed by the Superintendent of Design for a modified light tank within the 5ton limit imposed by the General Staff. Work on this vehicle was commenced during the latter part of 1935. Compared

with the Light Tank Mk VI its dimensions were to be 6–7in lower and slightly narrower. The armour thickness was to remain the same as the Mk VI, and estimated weight of the vehicle was to be 4ton 18¾cwt. On completion and after various modifications it was found that the weight of the L4EI had risen to 5ton 3cwt. Trials of this vehicle were completed on 20 June 1938, and no production order was placed. 5.3tons; crew 3; I .303 and .5 Vickers MG, or 15mm and 7.92mm ZB MG; armour 15mm; engine 88hp Meadows EST 6-cylinder; 28–30mph.

133. LIGHT AMPHIBIOUS TANK No 3 (LIE3)

Designed and produced by Vickers-Armstrong Ltd, this amphibious light tank was submitted for trials during June 1939, under the code name LIE3. Attached to the hull were two buoyancy tanks. The road wheels of the modified Horstmann suspension were of a special drum design to increase buoyancy. When afloat the vehicle was propelled by twin screws driven off the sprocket drive shafts. The cowls over the propellers were linked to the steering levers and served to steer the vehicle. LIE3 was fitted with two Vickers tank periscopes, one sited on the top front of the turret, and the other on the front of the drivers armoured hatch. A small sea anchor was carried on the rear deck. The front twin drum road wheels were later replaced by the normal spoked type with a reduction of the return rollers to one per side. Did not go into production. 4.4tons; crew 2; I Vickers .303 MG; engine 88hp Meadows ESTB water-cooled; 4mph in water; 15ft ¾in x 7ft 8in x 7ft 7in.

134. LIE3, rear view.

135. LIGHT TANK ALVIS-STRAUSSLER

This was a private venture built by the firm of Messrs Alvis-Straussler Ltd during 1937 and offered to the War Office. The vehicle was of a novel design, the principle features of which were the provision of two engines, each one to drive the track independently, and a new type of suspension. Each track assembly was attached as a unit at one point at the centre of the vehicle, one assembly on each side. Each separate assembly consisted of two large outside wheels (both of which were rubber tyred, positively driven) and two small inside wheels or track rollers which were idlers. One large driven sprocket and one small track roller formed a bogie. These bogies were hinged to the front and rear of a central swinging beam. Tested without a turret by the War Office, this vehicle was not adopted. 8–9tons; crew 3; engine Two-Alvis SA; 42mph; 15ft 2in x 8ft 3½in x 6ft 9¾in.

136. Rear view of the Alvis-Straussler.

137. LIGHT TANK LOYD EXPERIMENTAL

This two-man light tank was designed by Vivian Loyd in 1942 as a compact lightweight vehicle specifically for airborne operations but did not progress beyond the experimental stage.

138. CRUISER TANK MK I (A9)

Replacement for Medium Tanks Mk I and II (and derivatives), the A9 was to incorporate the best features of the cancelled A6 series at a much reduced cost. Design work carried out by Vickers in 1936. Features included distinctive three-wheel bogies, power traverse for the turret, two auxiliary MG turrets, and a boat-shaped lower hull. Prototype had domed auxiliary turrets, but production vehicles had flat-topped turrets. In service 1938–41. 12tons; crew 6; 1 2pdr, 3 Vickers MG; armour 14–6mm; engine AEC 150hp; 25mph; 19ft 3in x 8ft 4in x 8ft 4in.

141. CRUISER TANK MK II (above) AND MK IIA (A10)

Designed by Vickers as an improved version of the A9, able to act as an infantry tank when required. Subsequently it was considered too lightly armoured for this role and was re-classified as a 'Heavy Cruiser'. In service in 1939 and used in France in 1940 and in the Western Desert in 1941. Features were similar to the A9 but there were no auxiliary MG turrets. Heavier armour obtained by adding extra thickness to the basic hull. Hull MG was omitted originally but was fitted from 1940. The Mk IIA was the main production model, featuring detail improvements. Some vehicles were later reworked with additional armour. 13.75tons; crew 4–5; 1 2pdr, 1 Vickers MG or 2 Besa MG; armour 30mm; engine AEC, 150hp; 16 mph: 18ft 1in x 8ft 3½in x 8ft 6in.

139. A9E1 Prototype.

142. A10E1 Prototype.

140. Cruiser Tank Mk I C.S: As for the basic Mk I but fitted with a 3.7 howitzer instead of the 2pdr. Other users: Germany (few captured vehicles in Western Desert, 1941–2).

143. Cruiser Tank Mk IIA.

144. **Cruiser Tank Mk IIA C.S:** Close-support model with 3.7 howitzer replacing the 2pdr gun.

145. Reworked Cruiser Tank Mk IIA with extra armour over mantlet.

146. **CRUISER TANK MK III (AI3)**
Originated in late 1936 after British War Office observers had witnessed the high speed of the Christie-type BT tanks in service with the Red Army. The Nuffield company were asked to design a tank based on the Christie design as a high-speed replacement for the A9 and A10. The AI3 was based on a Christie vehicle imported from America. Vehicle had Christie suspension, high power-to-weight ratio, and a very high top speed of over 30mph. Simple flat-sided turret was a distinctive feature. Vehicle was developed in under 2 years and was in service in 1939. It was used in France in 1940 and the Western Desert in 1941. 14tons; crew 4; I 2pdr, I MG; armour 6–14mm; engine Liberty 340hp; 30mph; 19ft 9in x 8ft 4in x 8ft 6in.

147. AI3E2 prototype, developed from the Christie machine.

148. AI3E3 production prototype.

149. **CRUISER TANK MK IV (above) AND MK IVA (AI3 MK II)**
Uparmoured version of AI3. Extra plates gave added protection and 20–30mm armour thickness. Hollow 'V' sides added to original AI3 type turret. Some AI3s were reworked to similar standards. In production 1938, and used in France in 1940 and the Western Desert in 1941. Features included Christie suspension and varied patterns of mantlet. Details as AI3 except armour 6–30mm, weight 14.75tons.

150. Cruiser Tank IVA with axle-shaped mantlet.

151. Cruiser Tank Mk IVA with rectangular-shaped mantlet and Besa machine-gun.

152. Cruiser Mk III reworked to Mk IV standards.

153. CRUISER TANK A14E1

Designed to a General Staff requirement for a 'medium' or 'heavy' cruiser tank and partly inspired by the Russian T-28, the A14 was ordered in 1937 but abandoned in 1939 before final completion due to changing requirements. Prototype was built by the LMSR. It had Horstmann suspension with very small road wheels. There were twin auxiliary MG turrets at the front and the planned armament was to be a 2pdr gun. The vehicle weighed 29.5tons and had a 500hp Thornycroft marine engine.

154. CRUISER TANK A16E1

This vehicle was built to the same requirements as the A14E1 and was very similar in size and appearance. It had a Liberty engine and Christie suspension, as in the A13, and was built by the same firm, Nuffield. The prototype was cancelled in 1939 together with the A14.

155. CRUISER TANK MK V COVENANTER (A13 MK III) (above, pilot model)

Trials of the A14E1 showed it to be too slow and generally unsatisfactory. The LMSR were therefore asked to build a new vehicle based on the A13 Mk II and using as many A13 parts as possible. This new design became the A13 Mk III, Cruiser Tank Mk V, later named the Covenanter. This was a low-built vehicle with Christie suspension, and a powerful purpose-built Meadows Flat–12 engine. There were cooling louvres at the front alongside the driver, but the vehicle was plagued with mechanical troubles mainly due to cooling difficulties. These problems restricted the vehicle to training roles only and it was not used operationally. In service late 1940–3. 18tons; crew 4; 1 2pdr, 1 MG; armour 7–40mm; engine Meadows Flat–12, 300hp; 31mph; 19ft x 8ft 7in x 7ft-4in.

156. Covenanter I production model.

157. Covenanter II (Cruiser Mk V*): As Mk I but with modifications to improve the cooling system.

158. Covenanter III (Cruiser Mk V**): Vehicle with built-in cooling modifications, including extra louvres at the rear.

159. Covenanter IV: Vehicle with further cooling modifications.

160. Covenanter C.S: Close-support version with 3in howitzer replacing the 2pdr gun; various marks were converted, the Mk III being shown here.

161. Covenanter with AMRA Mk Ic: The Anti-Mine Roller Attachment was originally conceived about 1937, and consisted of a projecting framework and suspension carried on four spring-mounted and castoring rollers positioned in front of each track of the carrying vehicle, with the object of protecting the track by detonating the mine before the tank ran over it. This device was attached to the tank by two brackets, bolted each side of the vehicle and could be jettisoned when not required. Various versions of this device were made for use with other tanks and they were given the following designations. AMRA Mk Ia for Matilda, AMRA Mk Ib for Valentine, AMRA Mk Id for Crusader and AMRA Mk IIe for Churchill. The Matilda with AMRA Mk Ib was used operationally in the Middle East.

CRUISER TANK MK VI CRUSADER (AI5)

Enlarged version of the AI3 Mk III (Covenanter) design utilising as many common components as possible but with Liberty engine from the original AI3. Ordered 'off the drawing board' in July 1939 and became a major type produced by several factories until 1943. First in service in 1941 and used widely in the Western Desert as the main British type. Total of 5,300 were built. Design featured Christie suspension, multi-faceted turret. Light armour and mechanical unreliability were the main drawbacks to the design. Auxiliary MG turret in Mk I, later removed.

162. Crusader prototype (AI5EI)

163. Crusader I (Cruiser Mk VI): Original production type with auxiliary MG turret and 2pdr gun.

164. **Crusader I C.S (Cruiser Mk VI.C.S):** Close-support model with 3in howitzer replacing 2pdr gun.

165. **Crusader II (Cruiser Mk VIA):** As Crusader I but with added front armour. The MG turret is removed on this vehicle.

166. **Crusader IIC.S (Cruiser Mk VIA.C.S):** Close-support model with 3in howitzer replacing 2pdr gun.

167. **Crusader III:** Final production model fitted with 6pdr gun in place of 2pdr.

168. CRUISER TANK MK VII CAVALIER (A24)

Heavy cruiser tank based upon Crusader design but with thicker armour and 6pdr gun. This was an interim model with a Liberty engine for production while a Meteor-engined model (the Cromwell) was developed. The Cavalier was used only for training. Christie suspension and regular rectangular hull and turret were standard features and the Cavalier was externally almost identical to the Centaur and Cromwell. In service 1942–5. 26.5tons; crew 5; 1 6pdr, 1–2 MG; armour 20-76mm; engine Liberty 410hp; 24mph; 20ft 10in x 9ft 5½in x 8ft.

CRUISER TANK MK VIII CENTAUR (A27L)

This was designed by Leyland as an improvement on the Crusader and Cavalier. The Centaur was an interim type with the Liberty engine pending the availability of the Meteor engine. It was designed for later conversion to Cromwell by the fitting of a Meteor engine when these became available. Centaurs were mainly used for training or special purpose roles. In service 1942–5. 27.5tons; crew 5; varied armament armour 20–76mm engine Liberty 395hp; 27mph; 20ft 10in x 9ft 6in x 8ft 2in.

169. **Centaur I:** Original model with 6pdr gun.

170. Centaur III: Later model with 75mm gun — many were converted to Cromwells by installing Meteor engine retrospectively.

173. Cromwell I: Original early 1943 production model with 6pdr and 2 Besa MG.

Cromwell II: Mk I with wider tracks and hull MG removed to increase internal stowage.

171. Centaur IV: Close-support model with 95mm howitzer. Used by Royal Marines at Normandy landings, June 1944.

174. Cromwell III: Centaur I re-engined with Meteor engine, retaining 6pdr gun.

172. Centaur OP: Vehicle with dummy gun and extra radio equipment for command use.

CRUISER TANK MK VIII CROMWELL (A27M)

Definitive A27 vehicle with Rolls-Royce Meteor engine fitted from start. In 1944 the Cromwell was the most important British built tank by the time of the invasion of France. It was fast and well armed though the 75mm gun was initially delayed. The Cromwell was similar in appearance to the Cavalier and Centaur. Later vehicles (suffix 'w') were of all-welded construction. The Cromwell remained in wide service for some years postwar. 27–28tons; crew 5; varied armament; armour 8–76mm; engine Meteor 600hp; 32–40mph (depending on model); 20ft 10in x 9ft 6½in x 8ft 2in.

175. Cromwell IV: Centaur III re-engined with Meteor engine and with 75mm gun.

Cromwell Vw: Welded hull with 75mm gun.

176. Cromwell VI: Close-support version with 95mm howitzer.

177. Cromwell VII: Cromwell IV reworked with added armour, wider tracks, and reduced ratio final drive.

178. Cromwell VIIw: Cromwell Vw modified as above.

Cromwell VIII: Cromwell VI modified as above, retaining 95mm howitzer.

179. Cromwell CIRD: Vehicle with Canadian Indestructible Roller Device fitted for mine-clearing role. Issued but not used in service.

180. Cromwell II with Vauxhall cast turret: Vehicle fitted experimentally with turret similar to that installed in Churchill VII. Contemplated for production by Vauxhall but not proceeded with.

181. Cromwell II with side skirts: Vehicle with fittings for desert service; not proceeded with.

182. Cromwell 'D' with appliqué armour: Experimental uparmoured model, not proceeded with.

Cromwell OP/Command: Vehicle with dummy gun and extra radio equipment for gunnery or command roles.

183. CRUISER TANK CHALLENGER (A30)
Design instigated in May 1942 to provide a vehicle with a powerful enough gun (17pdr) to take on any known German tank. Original plan was to utilise the A27 (Centaur/Comet) chassis but weight and size of gun and turret necessitated virtual redesign to both longer and wider dimensions. High turret, very long gun, widened centre hull, and Christie suspension were all featured. Vehicle saw only limited service in 1944–5. The Sherman Firefly ultimately undertook the function envisaged for the Challenger. 32tons; crew 5; 1 17pdr, 1 MG; armour 20–102mm; engine Meteor 600hp; 32mph; 26ft 4in x 9ft 6½in x 8ft 9in.

184. Challenger prototype.

185. CRUISER TANK COMET (A34)

This vehicle resulted from an attempt to fit the all-important 17pdr gun to the A27 (Cromwell/Centaur) chassis. A new shortened version of the 17pdr, known as the 77mm gun, was evolved but even so there was a 60% redesign necessary. The A34 was all-welded and introduced return rollers into the suspension (though not on the prototype). Compared with the Cromwell the vehicle had a reshaped turret. Builders were Leyland and the first vehicles were in service in early 1945. They remained in British Army service until the mid 1960s and later in a few cases. 32.5tons; crew 5; 1 77mm, 2 7.92mm MG; armour 14–101mm; engine Meteor 600hp; 29mph; 25ft 1½in x 10ft x 8ft 9½in. Other users: Irish Republic 1950–1970.

186. Comet prototype, with no return rollers.

187. CRUISER TANK CENTURION I (A41)

Originated as an attempt to produce a 'Universal' chassis for combining the old 'cruiser' and 'infantry' tank roles. Completed as a vehicle in the 'heavy cruiser' class to compete as a match for the heaviest German tanks. The war had ended however by the time the first six pilot models were ready for troop trials in May 1945. Features of the design were prominent armoured side skirts (not always fitted) and Horstmann suspension replacing the Christie suspension used on the previous cruiser tank designs. A partly cast turret and sloping glacis plate were other new features. Varied transmission systems and combinations of secondary armament were tried on early development models. From 1945 onwards the Centurion was developed through more than 13 basic marks with many sub-variants and special purpose derivatives. Crew 4; 1 17pdr, 1 20mm Polsten gun or 1–2 Besa MG; armour 17–152mm; engine Meteor 620hp; 21.4mph; 25ft 2in x 11ft x 9ft 8in.

188. INFANTRY TANK MK I MATILDA I (A11)

Stemmed from an original 1934 General Staff requirement for an 'infantry tank' to support infantry in the attack. Machine-gun armament and speed adequate enough to keep up with advancing infantry (ie, walking pace) were basic tactical requirements. Vickers' offer of a light and inexpensive design was accepted and the pilot model was delivered in 1936. It was completely outmoded by later developments by 1939, but nonetheless the Matilda I remained in service for the first year of World War II and was afterwards used for training. Vehicle had a very small plain hull with exposed tracks; it was well armoured for its size. Named 'Matilda' for its duck-like gait and appearance. 11tons; crew 2; 1 MG; armour 10–60mm; engine Ford V-8 70hp; 8mph; 15ft 11in x 7ft 6in x 6ft 1½in.

189. A11E1 prototype.

190. Infantry Tank Mk I with Fowler Coulter Plough: This was an early attempt to develop a plough that could be carried on the front of a tank and be able to uproot the mines in the path of the vehicle as it advanced. This equipment was first evolved in 1937 and fitted experimentally to a Medium Dragon (Gun tractor). After various trials with this device a modified version was tested during 1939 on an Infantry Tank, Mk I. This consisted of a frame projecting in front of the vehicle and resting on two rollers, one in front of each track. Fixed to the frame in front of each roller were placed five coulter or cutting blades in arrow head formation. The whole assembly could be raised or lowered via chains from a power take-off on the rear drive shaft.

INFANTRY TANK MK II MATILDA II (AI2)

Designed as an immediate replacement for the Infantry Tank Mk I, Matilda I, when it was realised that the latter was inadequate for its intended role. Ordered 'off the drawing board' in 1937, a total of 2,987 vehicles was completed between 1940 and 1943 when production ceased. Though relatively small, the Matilda II had a massive appearance with armoured skirts and heavy cast hull armour. The layout closely followed the A7 of some years previously. The Matilda II was the most important tank in the Western Desert fighting in 1940, and the most powerful prior to the arrival of the Germans in that area. There were several special purpose derivatives. 26.5tons; crew 4; I 2pdr or 3in howitzer (CS models) plus I MG; armour 20–78mm; engine 2 AEC diesel 174hp (Mks I/II) or 2 Leyland diesel 190hp (Mks III/V); 15mph; 18ft 5in x 8ft 6in x 8ft. Other users: Australia (1942–53); USSR (1942–4).

191. AI2EI prototype.

192. Matilda I (Infantry Tank Mk II): Original production model with Vickers MG.

Matilda II (Infantry Tank Mk IIA): As Mk I but with Besa MG.

193. Matilda III (Infantry Tank Mk IIA*): As Mk II but with Leyland engines.

194. Matilda IIIC.S or IVC.S: Close-support vehicle with 3in howitzer replacing 2pdr.

Matilda IV and V: Improved production models with minor mechanical refinements. Otherwise externally similar to earlier marks.

195. MATILDA SCORPION

Designed and used in the Middle East during 1942–3, this was the first use of a tank flail device to clear a path through minefields by beating the ground as the tank advanced. Based on the Matilda II, the rotor and flails were carried on a frame that extended some 7ft in front of the vehicle, at a height of 4ft above the ground. The drive for the flail rotor was supplied by an auxiliary Ford engine mounted in a compartment attached to the right-hand side of the tank. In the compartment, behind the auxiliary engine, was placed the flail operator. A modified version, known as the Matilda Scorpion Mk II was also produced; this had improved side arms, and the flail operator was carried inside the tank.

196. Matilda with AMRA Mk Ia: Anti-Mine Roller Attachment used with the Matilda as pusher vehicle.

197. Matilda with Carrot explosive device: Developed in 1942, this consisted of a demolition charge of 600lbs of high explosive carried on the front of an Anti-Mine Reconnaissance Castor Roller device, this in turn was attached to the front of a Matilda tank. The AMRCR and explosive charge was pushed to the obstacle to be destroyed, released from the tank which backed away leaving the AMRCR and explosive charge in position; the charge was then detonated by remote control.

198. INFANTRY TANK MK III VALENTINE (above, Mk I)
This was a design by Vickers based on the chassis and layout of the A10, to meet an urgent 1938 requirement for an infantry tank to supplement the Matilda programme. An 'off the drawing board' order was placed in 1939 and the prototype was completed within a year, on 14 February 1940, leading to the name 'Valentine'. A total of 8,275 were built by 1944 when production ceased. The Valentine was a stable and reliable vehicle though its development was restricted largely by its small size. The vehicle was well armoured. It had a distinctive 'slow motion' three-wheel bogie suspension. Models were progressively upgunned and riveted construction gave way to welding. 16–17tons; crew 3–4; 1 2pdr (Mk I–VII), 1 6pdr (Mk VIII,X), 175mm (Mk XI), 1 MG; armour 8–65mm; engine AEC or GM diesel (except Mk I, gasoline) 131–165hp; 15mph; 17ft 9in x 8ft 7½in x 7ft 5½in.

199. Valentine II (Infantry Tank Mk III*): Improved model with sand shields and AEC diesel engine.

200. Valentine III: Modified turret to take one extra crew member; otherwise as Mk II.

201. Valentine IV: As Mk II but with GMC diesel engine.

Valentine V: As Mk III but with GMC diesel engine.

Valentine VI: Canadian production model built from 1941. GMC diesel engine, cast nose plates (instead of riveted) and Browning MG instead of Besa.

205. Valentine XI: Late 1943–4 production model with 75mm gun and all-welded construction.

202. Valentine VII and VIIA: Improved Canadian production models, the latter with jettisonable external fuel tanks added, and studded tracks. Built 1942–3.

Valentine VIII: Mk III upgunned with 6pdr.

206. Valentine DD: Various marks converted as 'swimming' tanks using the Straussler Duplex-Drive system. Folding canvas screen erected by inflating air tubes. Used for training and perfecting DD techniques, though a few were used operationally in Italy.

203. Valentine IX: Mk V upgunned with 6pdr.

207. Valentine AMRA Mk Ib: Mine-clearing equipment carried on front of tank consisting of rollers on frame supports.

204. Valentine X: 1943 production model with 6pdr gun as built and GMC diesel engine.

208. Valentine Flamethrower (cordite operated): Trials vehicle 1941–2 with flame fuel carried in a trailer and actuated by a cordite charge for ignition of fuel in bursts.

209. Valentine Flamethrower (gas operated): Alternative design to cordite operated equipment, operated by gas pressure. In tests this proved superior and the design was used as the prototype for the Churchill Crocodile flamethrower. These were trials vehicles only.

INFANTRY TANK MK IV CHURCHILL (A22)

Designed initially as a 'shelled area' tank, this vehicle was intended for service on the Western Front which (in 1939) was expected to be similar to 1918 as far as tank operations were concerned. Pilot models were built of the original A20 design to the initial specification and were similar in shape and armament disposition to the tanks of World War I. The A20 was unsuccessful and Vauxhall took over the design from Harland and Wolff and revised the design to meet a new (A22) specification. First production vehicles were delivered in mid 1941 but the early tanks were plagued by mechanical faults and much reworking was necessary. The Churchill was eventually refined into one of the most successful tanks used by the British. It saw service in many special roles, especially with armoured engineer units. Vehicle had a squared-off regular shape with overall tracks and roomy side panniers. Small road wheels, very heavy armour, and relatively low speed made it a stable platform for the attachment of special purpose equipment. 38.5tons (up to Mk VI), 40tons (remainder); crew 5; 1 2pdr (Mks I, II), 1 6 pdr (Mk III, IV), 1 75mm (Mk VI, VII), 1 95mm (Mk V, VIII), 1 3in additionally in Mk I and Mk I CS), 1–2 MG; armour 16–102mm (all except Mk VII, VIII — 25–152mm); engine Bedford 350hp; 15.5mph (12.5mph Mk VII); 24ft 5in x 10ft 8in (11ft 4in Mk VII) x 8ft 2in (9ft Mk VII). Other users: Eire (post 1945); India; Jordan (post 1945); USSR (1942–5).

210. A20 prototype vehicle: with mock-up turret.

211. Churchill I: First production model, 1941, with 2pdr gun in turret and 3in howitzer in nose. First used in action at Dieppe, August 1942.

212. Churchill II C.S: As Churchill I but with positions of guns reversed.

213. Churchill II: As for Churchill I but with Besa MG replacing 3in howitzer in hull.

214. Churchill III: Major redesign with new welded turret and 6pdr gun. Full mudguards fitted as standard (retrospective on earlier marks).

215. Churchill IV: As for Churchill III but with cast instead of welded turret.

216. Churchill V: Close-support tank with 95mm howitzer replacing 6pdr; otherwise as Churchill IV.

217. Churchill VI: As Churchill IV but with 75mm gun replacing 6pdr. In production in 1943 pending production of new largely re-designed model, the Mk VII.

218. Churchill VII: Major redesign (designated A22F) with new hull and turret and 75mm gun; 1944 production. Main type in service in early postwar years.

219. Churchill IV NA75: Conversion by ordnance depots in North Africa (NA) of Mk IV to take 75mm guns salvaged from wrecked M4 Shermans. Complete Sherman mantlet fitted in place of original 6pdr gun. First Churchill type in service (early 1943) with 75mm gun. Used exclusively on Italian Front.

220. Churchill VIII: Close-support model based on Mk VII but with 95mm howitzer replacing 75mm gun. Limited service.

221. Churchill IXLT

Churchill IX, IXLT, X, XLT, XI, XILT: Reworked vehicles with either the original turret (light turret; LT) or the later cast/welded heavy turret of the Mk VII. All armed with 75mm guns and fitted with appliqué armour to bring them roughly to Mk VII standards. Mk III, IV, or VI respectively formed the basis of these rebuilds.

222. Churchill XLT

223. Churchill AVRE: Put into production in early 1944, this was a special conversion of the basic Churchill III and IV for assault engineer units. The 6pdr gun, elevating gear and recoil system were removed and replaced with a 29mm mortar known as the Petard. The Churchills were stripped inside of normal equipment and refitted with special stowage bins to adapt the vehicles for engineers' purposes. Special fittings were provided on the front sides of the AVREs for device attachments.

224. Mk II SBG AVRE: Evolved by the Canadian Army in 1943, as a method for wall or ditch crossing in assault. This consisted of a standard box girder bridge fitted to the front of the AVRE and adapted for quick release. The bridge weighed 4tons, was 34ft long and was controlled by a winch mounted on the rear of the vehicle.

Churchill with carpet laying devices: Evolved for laying rapidly and if necessary under fire, a carpet in a lane over poor ground and over barbed-wire obstacles for the passage of trucks and infantry. These devices consisted of reels or bobbins of various sizes wound with reinforced Hessian matting of different length. The bobbins were carried well above the ground across the front of the vehicle by side arms attached to the sides of the vehicle. When required the weighted free end of the carpet was dropped to the ground whilst the tank ran on to the free end, the bobbin automatically unwinding itself as the vehicle ran forward. On completion of the operation the bobbin was jettisoned. The first use of the carpet device was at Dieppe, this consisted of a small bobbin attached to the front of a Churchill III by brackets.

225. Carpet Device used at Dieppe.

226. Carpet Device TLC.

227. Carpet Device Type A.

228. Carpet Device Type B Mk I.

229. Carpet Device Type C Mk II.

230. Churchill Oke: This was the first flame-throwing equipment to be fitted to the Churchill tank, but was an unofficial one, and had no part in the development of the Crocodile equipment. The Oke device consisted of the infantry flamethrowing equipment 'Ronson' adapted to the Churchill tank. This was achieved by attaching the projector, in a fixed elevation, to the inside of the front track guard. The weapon was aimed by manoeuvring the tank. A disposable fuel tank for the flame projector was carried at the rear of the vehicle. Three Churchill IIs were equipped with Oke equipment and used in the Dieppe raid in August 1942.

231. Front view of a Churchill Oke

232. Churchill Crocodile: Produced in 1943, the Crocodile was a

Churchill Mk VII tank armed with a 75mm gun and co-axial Besa machine-gun in the turret and the flame projector in the hull. A range of about 120 yards was obtainable under favourable conditions, but the generally accepted range was 80 yards. The Crocodile towed an armoured two wheel trailer containing 400 gallons of flame fuel, controls and five pressure bottles containing nitrogen. Connection from trailer to flame projector was through the 'Link' a device through which the pressurised fuel could pass. The fuel trailer, if set on fire, could be jettisoned by a quick release gear.

233. Close-up of Flame projector.

Churchill with AMRA Mk IIe: The Mk IIe Anti-Mine Roller Attachment varied in basic design to the Mk I series, in that it had double roller forecarriage assemblies in place of single roller assemblies, this being due to the wider nature of the Churchill track.

234. Churchill with AMRCR No 1 Mk I: The Anti-Mine Reconnaissance Castor Roller device (AMRCR) was a heavier and modified version of the AMRA and was tested in mid 1943. Like the AMRA, this was a perambulator device attached to, and pushed in front of, the tank for the detection of anti-tank and anti-personnel mines.

235. Churchill with CIRD: Initiated by the Canadian Army during

GREAT BRITAIN   107

1943, the CIRD (Canadian Indestructible Roller Device) followed the same principle as the AMRA and AMRCR being a perambulator device, attached to and pushed in front of the tank. This equipment consisted of two heavy rollers positioned in front of either track, and designed to rotate about a bar after exploding a mine, thus reducing the blast effect on the roller. Various roller sizes, 15.5in, 16in, 18in and 21in in diameter were experimented with.

Churchill with mine ploughs: Development of a tank-propelled mine plough had first begun during 1937 with the Fowler Coulter plough that had been adapted to the Infantry Tank Mk I, but trials of this device were discontinued in 1939. During 1943–4 various types of mine ploughs were again designed and experimented with. Though slightly different in construction, they all worked on the same principle of lifting the mines and deflecting them outwards to the left and right of the ploughing vehicle. One such equipment, the Bullshorn Mk III was used operationally in the North West Europe campaign.

239. Farmer Track Plough.

240. Farmer Deck Plough (early version).

236. OAC Mk I Plough.

241. Bullshorn Mk III Plough.

237. OAC Mk II Plough.

Churchill with mechanical charge placers: To enable obstacles to be breached or demolished, and at the same time give maximum protection to the demolition personnel, a series of mechanical charge placers were developed and experimented with. These methods suspended explosive charges on frames mounted in front of the tank for placing in front or across the obstacles to be demolished. When the frame of explosive had been placed, the tank then reversed and the explosive charge was fired electrically or by pull igniter.

238. Jeffries Plough.

242. The Light Carrot: Developed in July 1942, this was the code name given to an elongated rectangular explosive charge carried on an extension bracket fitted to the nose of the tank, so that it could be positioned against the object to be breached and fired without exposure of the tank crew. The weight of the charge varied from 12lb to a maximum of 25lb. Project abandoned in November 1943.

243. Onion (Jones Onion): Developed in August 1942, this device consisted of a framework attached to the front of a tank so that various charges could be carried by it. The framework measured 9ft wide by 4ft 6in high. It was carried vertically by two side arms attached one each side of the vehicle, these could be jettisoned after the demolition had been completed. When the tank with the exposive device arrived at the obstacle to be attacked a mechanical release cable was pulled allowing the frame of charges to fall. A pair of cranked legs pivoted to the frame met the ground first, so that the frame fell forward and was retained against the obstacle. The tank was then reversed away and the charges fired electrically by a trailing cable. A smaller similar device was known as the Single Onion.

244. Goat Mk III: A further development of the Carrot and Onion devices, this consisted of 1800lb of explosive charges carried on a platform 10ft 6in wide by 6ft 6in long retained in a horizontal position above the nose of the AVRE by side arms, and so designed that contact with the wall or obstacle automatically released the explosive frame in a vertical position. The tank then pushed the frame up against the obstacle and backed off; when the tank was clear of the obstacle, the charges were fired either electrically or by pull igniter.

245. Elevatable Goat: This device was for use against high walls or obstacles, and consisted of a long braced frame carried on the nose of a AVRE in a similar manner to the Assault SBG; fitted under the two main spars were a series of linked charges. On approaching the obstacle the complete assembly was placed against the wall and jettisoned from the vehicle. The linked charges were next released and these fell away from the spars to straddle the wall, the tank retiring to blow the charges.

246. Churchill with Bangalore Torpedoes: This was a simple device of two lengths of Snake piping fitted to a Onion frame assembly. The method of release was similar to the Onion device. Developed for use against light obstacles and barbed wire.

247. Ardeer Aggie: This was an experimental prototype designed with a view to improving on the power of the Petard mortar fitted in the AVRE. The Ardeer projector was a recoilless gun in which the recoil was neutralised by firing a dummy projectile rearwards simultaneous with the discharge of the main projectile. Based on a Churchill III hull, design work on this weapon was begun in September 1943. Tested but found impractical.

248. Infantry Tank Black Prince (A43): Designed in 1943–5 by Vauxhall, this was an enlarged version of the Churchill mounting the 17pdr gun. It was unofficially known as the 'Super Churchill'. Six pilot models were completed in 1945, too late for war service and no production was undertaken. The Black Prince was similar to the Churchill but wider and with heavier suspension. 50tons; crew 5; 1 17pdr, 2 MG; armour 25–152mm; engine Bedford 350hp; 11mph; 28ft 11in x 11ft 3½in x 9ft..

249. INFANTRY TANK VALIANT (A38)
Vickers design based on the Valentine and utilising many Valentine components. Development was taken over by Ruston and Hornsby and a pilot model was ready in mid 1944. The vehicle had suspension based on the Vickers 'slow motion' type, and made extensive use of castings in the hull and turret. Either a 6pdr or 75mm gun could be mounted. The concept was outmoded by 1945 and the project was dropped. 27tons; crew 4; 1 6pdr or 75mm, 1 MG; armour 10–114mm; engine GM diesel 210hp; 12mph; 17ft 7in x 9ft 3in x 7ft.

250. HEAVY ASSAULT TANK (A33)
Essentially an 'infantry tank' version of the A27 Centaur/Cromwell cruiser tank, this vehicle was built by English Electric in 1943. It used the A27 hull as a basis with added armour, wide tracks, and new suspension. First pilot model had American T1 tracks and suspension while second pilot had British 'R/L heavy' suspension. No production order was placed. 45tons; crew 5; 1 75mm, 1 MG; armour 114mm; engine Meteor 600hp; 24mph; 22ft 8in x 7ft 11in x 11ft 1½in.

251. A33 second pilot model.

HEAVY TANK TOG
Designed in 1930–40 under the aegis of a committee composed of the men responsible for British tank development in World War I ('The Old Gang':TOG), this vehicle followed the layout and style of 1918 tanks. Electric transmission was first employed, later replaced by hydraulics. Sponsons with guns were envisaged for the hull sides but were never fitted. By early 1941 after the prototypes had appeared, progress with the Churchill design rendered the TOG tank unnecessary. It was used for some experimental work subsequently. 80tons; crew 6; 1 2pdr, 1 75mm howitzer or 1 17pdr depending on model; armour 12–62mm; engine Ricardo diesel 600hp; 8.5mph; 33ft 3in x 10ft 3in x 10ft.

252. TOG I: Original model with A12 Matilda turret and electric transmission; 75mm howitzer in nose.

TOG IA: TOG I rebuilt with hydraulic transmission.

253. TOG II: Improved model with lower tracks to reduce overall height. Fitted with mock-up turret and 6pdr gun (as illustrated).

254. TOG II*: TOG II modified and used to test turret installation and 17pdr gun as fitted in the A30 Challenger. TOG was in service for trials only from 1940–3 in its various forms.

255. HEAVY ASSAULT TANK TORTOISE (A39)
Super-heavy tank design with limited traverse 32pdr gun intended to outgun and outlast the heavy German tanks and SP guns like the Königstiger and Jagdtiger. The armour was proof against all known German anti-tank guns. With an immense cast hull and no turret, the vehicle was in reality a self-propelled armoured gun rather than a tank. Suspension featured extra-wide tracks and 16 pairs of bogie wheels each side. There was a separate AA cupola for air defence. This was the heaviest British AFV ever completed. Design work started in 1944 but the first of six pilot models was not delivered until 1947. The vehicles were used for trials only and were not put into production. 78tons; crew 7; 1 32pdr, 2 MG; armour 35–225mm; engine Meteor 600hp; 12mph; 33ft x 12ft 10in x 10ft.

256. GRANT MEDIUM TANK
Whereas the Medium Tank M3 had been supplied to Britain under

the Lend-Lease scheme, the British version of this vehicle was purchased directly. The British Tank Commission requested a modification to suit British requirements. This consisted of a new design of turret, that was longer than the original M3 version, having a prominent rear overhang to allow for the installation of wireless equipment in the turret rear. The cupola was eliminated to reduce the vehicle's silhouette and the turret itself was lower, reducing the overall height by about a foot. This version was known as the Grant after General U. S. Grant.

257. Grant Command Tank: British Grant fitted with extra radio equipment for use of senior officers, 37mm gun removed or replaced with dummy barrel.

258. Grant CDL: The CDL (Canal Defence Light) was an armoured housing with a powerful searchlight fitted in place of the original tank turret to illuminate the battlefield in night actions. This was originally a British development.

259. Grant Scorpion Mk IV: British Middle East designed flailing equipment adapted to the Grant Two Dodge engines mounted at the rear drove the flail rotor. Similar equipment was used on the Sherman Scorpion.

260. SHERMAN l7pdr GUN (FIREFLY) (above, IIc)

During the course of the war, most of the basic types of the M4 series were used by the British as combat tanks, these being fitted with 75mm and 76mm guns and 105mm howitzers. Known as the General Sherman, but more often called the Sherman, this tank first entered service with the British when approximately 300 vehicles, mainly M4Als, arrived in Egypt in time to take part in the famous battle of El Alamein during October 1942. From then on, for most of the war, the Sherman became the principal tank of the British armoured force. But undoubtedly the most superior and successful of the British Shermans was the version mounting the l7pdr gun known as the Firefly. In the late part of 1943, it was decided to mount the British high velocity l7pdr gun on to the Sherman. To achieve this, the turret had to be slightly modified and the gun was mounted on its side and adapted for left-hand loading. The original trunnions were used with a new mounting, recoil and elevating gear. Since the l7pdr breech filled almost the whole turret, displacing radio equipment from the rear wall, an aperture was cut in the rear of the turret and an armoured box which also acted as a counterweight was welded on to accommodate the radio sets in a rear extension. An additional hatch for the loader was cut in the turret roof, since the gun breech obstructed his exit through the commander's rotating roof hatch. To provide maximum stowage space inside the hull for the l7pdr ammunition, the hull gunner's position was eliminated, the bow machine-gun was removed, the aperture plated over and an ammunition bin replaced the seat. Thus modified, stowage for 78 l7pdr rounds was provided in the vehicle. Most Fireflies were converted from the Sherman V (US designation M4A4) mainly because the British had large Lend-Lease deliveries of this model, and the next most numerous was basically the Sherman I (M4). Of these a proportion were the late-production M4 type with combination cast and rolled upper hulls. A small number of M4AI (British Sherman II), M4A2 (British Sherman III), and M4A3 (British Sherman IV) were also converted. Apart from giving the M4 series their own designation (ie, Sherman I, II, III, IV and V) the British also applied a suffix letter to the mark number to indicate the armament. 'A' indicated US 76mm gun on any model, 'B' indicated US 105mm howitzer and 'C' indicated British l7pdr. No suffix was used for the US 75mm gun. The suffix 'Y' indicated that the vehicle was fitted with the horizontal volute spring suspension. Thus Sherman IBY showed this vehicle to be a M4 with a 105mm howitzer and fitted with the HVSS, or Sherman IIC, a M4AI equipped with the l7pdr gun.

262. Sherman Firefly VC

263. Another view of the Firefly VC

261. Sherman Firefly IVC

264. Sherman IV

265. Sherman IIA

266. Sherman IIIAY

267. Sherman IBY

268. Sherman DD, screens folded

269. Sherman DD, screens erected

Sherman DD (Duplex Drive): This equipment was devised by the British as a method of converting a normal combat tank into a temporary amphibious tank for sea or river crossing. Developed during April 1943, Sherman DD tanks were used in the Normandy landings. For conversion the tank was waterproofed and fitted with a collapsible screen and 36 rubber air-tubes or pillars. This assembly was attached to a deck that had been welded round the hull of the tank. The rubber pillars were filled by compressed air, carried in two cylinders on the hull of the vehicle, on being inflated the tubes raised the canvas screen which was then locked into position by struts. On entering the water the screen acted as a flotation device. Two small screw propellers, driven from the bevel drive of the vehicle, propelled the tank at approximately 4 knots. On reaching the shore the air was released from the air tubes causing the screen to collapse and the vehicle reverted to its normal combat role. Various marks of Sherman DD equipment existed, later marks having metal framework for the screen.

270. Sherman V Adder: Developed by the British during 1944, the Adder originally known as the Cobra, mounted the flame-projector on a turntable base, fitted over the co-driver's hatch. An armoured container at the rear housed the flame-fuel and other equipment. Other British developments of the Sherman to the flamethrowing role were known as the Salamander of which there were eight variants.

271. Sherman Crocodile: Developed by the British at the request of the US Army, this was an adaptation of the Churchill Crocodile equipment to the Sherman Tank. To retain the bow machine-gun, the flame projector was mounted on a base to the right of the hull gunner's hatch. Four delivered to the US Army, and used in NW Europe, 1944–45.

272. Sherman Rocket Projectors: Improvised in the field by a unit of the British Guards Armoured Division this device consisted of Typhoon Aircraft rocket launchers attached to the turret sides.

273. Sherman with AMRCR No IA Mk I: This was the Anti-Mine Reconnaissance Castor Rollers, adapted for use with the Sherman tank.

274. Sherman with CIRD: The Canadian Indestructible Roller Device, adapted for use with the Sherman tank. Various sizes tested.

Sherman with mine-ploughs: Various types of mine-ploughs were tested on the Sherman tank. These were similar to the Churchill ploughs, but were modified to fit the Sherman hull.

275. Sherman with Jeffries Plough

276. Sherman with Bullshorn Mk III Plough

277. Sherman Pram Scorpion: This experimental model was ready for trials by May 1943. The flail rotor was carried by a pair of side arms that were supported ahead of the tank by two pairs of castor rollers. Motive power for the flails was derived from the tank engine, the rotor being linked to the tank's front driving sprockets. Prototype only.

280. Sherman Crab II: This was similar to Crab I, but was equipped with a contouring device and other modifications. It was more effective than the Crab I on ridges and furrows.

281. Sherman Lobster: Developed early in 1944, this vehicle incorporated the Matilda Baron type of rotor and flail equipment with the Crab type of flail drive. Prototype only.

Sherman Lulu: This was an experimental electrically operated mine detector developed by the British during 1943. The device consisted of three 4ft wooden rollers containing a mine detector coil which in turn, was connected to an indicator unit inside the tank.

278. Sherman Scorpion: This device was similar to the equipment of the Grant Scorpion, drive for the flails being derived from two Dodge engines mounted at the rear of the vehicle.

282. Lulu in travelling position

279. Sherman Crab I: A flail developed by the British in 1943 and placed in production, the Crab based on the Sherman V retained its normal armament. The drive for the rotor was taken by roller chain from the tank propeller shaft, through an aperture in the hull off-side armour, to a carden shaft. The drive from this shaft was taken by a further carden shaft to a spiral bevel double reduction gear on the off-side end of the rotor.

283. Lulu in operating position.

Crusader MK III in Tunisia, January 1943.

Crusader in action in the Western Desert 1941.

Sherman Crabs and Churchill AVREs support assault troops for the attack on Le Havre, September 1944.

Above: Sherman Firefly in Normandy.
Below: Churchill IV tanks advance through Cleve, February 1945.

A Sherman Crab leaves an LCT; Normandy, 6 June 1944.

HUNGARY

INTRODUCTION

Prior to 1940, the only tanks in service with the Hungarian Army were a number of two-man tankettes of Italian origin and a light tank of Swedish design built in Hungary. The tankettes were of the CV.33 type, a 3.4ton two-man vehicle built by the Ansaldo concern of Genoa. Some of the Hungarian CV.33 tankettes were modified by the addition of a small square commander's cupola. The 7-ton three-man light tank was the Swedish Landsverk L-60 design, manufactured under licence by the Manfred Weiss company of Budapest; it was introduced into Hungarian service as the 38M' Toldi (1938). During 1937-8 an experimental light tank, known as the V-4, had been designed by the Hungarian engineer Nicholas Straussler, who later went to Britain, where he designed several armoured cars and light tanks in connection with the firms of Alvis and Vickers-Armstrongs.

With the outbreak of World War II attempts were made in 1940 by the Hungarian Ministry of Defence to obtain tanks from Czechoslovakia; but as the Czech firms of Skoda and CKD/Praga were already committed to building tanks for the German Army, this was unsuccessful. The Hungarians did, however succeed in obtaining the manufacturing rights for one of the latest Skoda products, the S-IIr (T-21), a medium tank development of their former S-IIa (T-11) light tank. This design was adapted to suit Hungarian requirements, the original two-man turret being replaced by a larger three-man type fitted with radio and inter-communication equipments. The motive power was delivered by a Hungarian-made 8-cylinder power plant developing 260hp at 2,200rpm. The suspension, which was similar to that of the CKD/Praga V-8-H medium tank, acted on the road wheels through leaf springs.

The Hungarian prototype, based on the Skoda S-IIr (T-21) design, was completed in August 1941, and soon after it was placed into production as the 40M' Turan I. This vehicle was a 16ton, five-man medium tank armed with a Skoda 40mm gun and two 8mm machine-guns. A later upgunning of the Turan I vehicle led to the Turan II, armed with a 75mm gun housed in a turret with a modified cupola. On the basis of the Turan design, a 105mm self-propelled gun, known as the 40/43 M' Zrinyl was developed from 1942 onwards. The Turan tanks were replaced in 1943 by German PzKpfw III and IV medium tanks.

The PzKpfw 38 (t) was manufactured in its basic form up to 1942; then its chassis was adapted into self-propelled gun carriages, anti-aircraft tanks and tank destroyers. The most famous of these adaptations was the Jägdpanzer 38 (t) Hetzer, whose production was resumed after the war both for the Czech Army (SD38) and for export to Switzerland (G13).

During the thirties, both Skoda and CKD/Praga had also developed some interesting prototypes. Praga had produced a prototype for an amphibious tank, the F-IV-HE, which was extensively tested by the Germans. A pilot model for an 18ton medium tank, the Skoda S-IIr (T-21) was seized by the Germans and given to the Hungarians, who put it into production as the 40'M Turan. Both models are indicative of the high standard of indigenous design attained by Czech tank manufacturers at the time of the German invasion. By 1942-3, the German Heereswaffenamt (WaPrüf 6) requested Skoda to undertake design and development of two armoured vehicles — a 10ton reconnaissance tank designated T-15 and a 22ton medium tank known as the T-25, both to be powered by a Tatra 220hp air-cooled diesel engine; however, neither projects materialised.

I. CV.33 tankettes in service with the Hungarian Army.

4. Toldi.

2. CV.33, Commanders' model.

5. Light Tank, V.4.

3. Toldi, Hungarian version of the Swedish Strv m/33.

6. S-IIr (T-2I) prototype for Turan

7. Turan.I.

8. Turan.I showing suspension.

9. Turan.II.

ITALY

INTRODUCTION

Italy was an early user of armoured vehicles, the first armoured car appearing in 1907. Italy was also the first to use armoured cars in action during the Tripolitania campaign of 1912. However, development of tanks in Italy trailed behind the other major powers, mainly because the Italian front in World War I did not lend itself to AFV operations. The first actual tank design was the Fiat 2000 which originated in 1916–17, and from which two prototypes and possibly four production machines were built in 1918. In the interim, arrangements were made for 100 Renault FT Light Tanks and 20 Schneider Heavy Tanks to be purchased from France. The original plan was for parts to be assembled in Italy but, in the event, complete vehicles were taken over in about August 1918 after some delays in delivery. When this became apparent it was decided by the War Ministry to build an Italian version of the Renault FT, so Fiat undertook design and built it in a consortium which included Ansaldo and Breda.

Initial orders were for 1,400 vehicles but with the Armistice this was reduced to 100, and these tanks, rather larger and better geared than the Renault FT, were delivered in 1923 after numerous delays; model designation was Fiat 3000. During the late 1920s an improved version, the Fiat 3000B, was produced with a 37mm gun replacing the twin MGs of the original design. Various other modifications appeared (as detailed in the reference section) and remained in service well into the Second World War. The next major tank type built was the CV.29, designed in 1929, which was based on the Carden-Loyd Mk VI tankette, four of which were purchased from Britain; the CV.29 was in all respects similar to the British original, and 25 were built.

Fiat and Ansaldo improved on this version to produce the slightly more sophisticated CV.33 series.

Two heavier tanks were produced in 1933–6, as prototypes for possible production; they had diesel engines and differed in details though had similar suspension. Largest was the turretless Carro Armato 12ton Tank of 1933. The lighter of the two tanks, the Carro Armato 8ton Tank appeared in 1936 and featured a 37mm gun in the hull front and an MG in the turret. From this prototype was developed the M.11 of which 100 were ordered in 1938. About this time the designation system for tanks was changed and the old CV type (Carro Veloce 33) became 'L' (for Light, L.33).

Meanwhile a greatly improved version of the L.33 appeared, the L3/35 which had better armour and a superior engine. There were several variants of this vehicle including a flamethrower. A further improved model was the L3/38 of 1938 which featured new suspension and other detail changes. In 1936 Fiat-Ansaldo built prototypes of 5ton vehicles which were light tanks considerably bigger than the L3/35 and fitted with turrets and 8mm MGs; this type was known as the L.6.

Of all the new designs the M.11 was the most acceptable but its limitations were realised, especially its thin armour. This led to a heavier development, the M.13, which had thicker armour, an AA machine-gun and a 47mm gun in the turret. M.13s entered service early in 1940 and by late 1940 there were 250. Eventual orders up to 1942 totalled 1,900 and the M.13 very much undergunned and under-armoured by British or German standards, became the main Italian battle tank. While a neat design, however, it was no match for opposing British vehicles in the Western Desert.

There were several variants of the M.13 (or M13/39); a very late model, produced in 1942, was completely re-engined and changed in detail, this was designated the M14/41. Finally came a major improvement in the M15/42 which appeared in 1942. It had a petrol engine (replacing diesel) and a longer high-velocity gun. Only a few of these were built as M-series tank production was ended in March 1943 in favour of the Semovente self-propelled gun, a variant of the M.14 with turret replaced by a low barbette in the manner of the German Stu G III assault gun.

The last Italian medium tank design was the 'Sahariano' which appeared in early 1943 as a close copy of the British Crusader tank which the Italians had greatly admired. This was a fast vehicle with Christie suspension quite different to all preceding designs. However, Italy's withdrawal from the war late in 1943 terminated her attempts at tank development. Other medium tanks used by Italy were French vehicles captured by the Germans in 1940, including the SOMUA and Renault R.35.

In the light tank field the L.6 was ordered in 1939 with the idea of replacing the numerous L3/33 and L3/35 vehicles which were by that time very outmoded. Nearly 600 were ordered for delivery in 1940–41 but this was reduced to about half so that the remaining chassis could be used for Semovente production. Variants of the L6/40 included command tanks and munition carriers. Some L6/40 vehicles were used by the Germans. The only Italian heavy tank was the P26/40 which was partly inspired by the Russian T–34 in having a well sloped hull plate. Design was started in late 1940 and a 75mm gun and 20mm cannon were the main weapons. Due to a more pressing need for existing tanks, the prototype was not ready until March 1942 and after successful trials 500 vehicles were ordered. The first few were ready in late 1943 but the Italian Armistice prematurely terminated production and the Germans seized (and used) the few P.40 vehicles available.

A developed vehicle, the P.43 was planned for 1943, having a better turret and lower overall height, but this prototype was never completed. Italian designs, though well thought-out, fell short of the standards of British, French, German and American tanks, mainly because they were too small and thinly armoured: like the British the Italian-built tanks were more suitable for colonial operations in the 1930's but in contrast to Britain, Italy had insufficient industrial resources to re-arm quickly after the outbreak of war. While Britain had a good supply of tanks to make good her tank deficiencies, Italy never enjoyed such good fortune from her hard pressed ally, Germany, so that even the heaviest and most advanced Italian tank, the P.30 of 1943, barely matched the size and hitting-power of contemporary designs.

Fiat 3000B tanks on transport trailers.

CV.33 tankettes on manoeuvres, 1940.

M.11—39 medium tank, production model, undergoing trials in 1938.

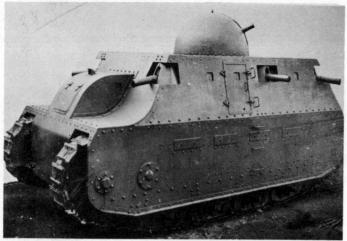

I. FIAT 2000 MODEL I7 (TIPO 2000) HEAVY TANK

The first tank built in Italy; largely a private venture by Fiat who donated two vehicles to the Italian Army in February 1918. Consideration of the design started in August 1916 and building started in October 1916. First vehicle ready in June 1917, hence 'Model 17'. Four more vehicles built in 1919 and these vehicles remained serviceable until the early 1930s. Prototype vehicle had cylindrical turret and lacked gun mounts initially. Box-like superstructure with seven MGs giving all-round field of fire. Prominent canopy at front for driver and front drive. Sprung bogies. Spherical turret with additional 14mm MG, in all later vehicles: Imaginative and effective design for its period. Last vehicle in service (1934) had its two front hull MGs replaced by 37mm semi-automatic cannon. 40tons; crew 10; 65mm gun plus 6 MG; armour 15–20mm; engine (gasoline) 240hp; 4.5mph; 24.27ft x 10.17ft x 12.46ft.

4. FIAT 3000 MODEL 1921 (above)/MODEL 1930 (CARRO-ARMATO) LIGHT TANK

Italian-built version of the Renault FT (see France, plate 6) originally intended to be a direct copy but greatly changed by Fiat, the builders. Owing to extra development time it was too late to see war service. Prototype model built by June 1920, tested 1921, and production models in service 1923. Modified version was built as a result of early experience with the Model 1921. The Fiat 3000 was similar externally to the Renault FT but was fitted with a transverse rear engine, mounted lower in the hull. Model 1921 had MG armament and Model 1930 had a 37mm gun and a prominent cupola. Trench crossing tail on both models as built but removed in 1933. 5.5tons (6tons); 2 MG (1 37mm gun); armour 6–16mm; engine (gasoline) 50hp (63hp); 13mph; 13.63ft (14.07ft) x 5.37ft (5.47ft) x 7.2ft. (Details in parentheses for Fiat 3000B). Other users: Albania (c. 1932–9); Ethiopia (1927–33); Latvia (c. 1933–9); also tested by Denmark, Greece and Spain, but not taken into service.

2. Fiat 2000 prototype

5. Fiat 3000 prototype (unarmed)

3. Fiat 2000 rear view

6. Fiat 3000 Model 1930 (Fiat 3000B): Prototype (above with tail) tested in 1929. More powerful engine, 37mm gun in turret, towing eyes added and prominent exhaust silencers. Gun offset from centre.

7. Fiat 3000B production model

Fiat 3000B Wireless Tank: Commander's model with added aerial frame prominent on turret.

8. Fiat 3000B Modified (L5–21): 1936 modification with twin 37mm guns in turret; trench-crossing tail deleted.

9. CARRO VELOCE 29 TANKETTE

Fast tank to accompany infantry (virtually a machine-gun carrier) and for reconnaissance. Based on the Vickers Carden-Loyd Mk VI (see Britain, plate 55), four of which were purchased from Britain in 1929. Built by Fiat-Ansaldo, a total of 21 being completed in 1929–30. Similar to Carden-Loyd original design but with wider tracks and Italian MG armament. Powered by Ford Model T engine. Armoured head covers for driver and gunner. Usually towed small tracked ammunition trailer, also derived from a British design. Armed with single shielded 6.5mm gun. 1.7tons; crew 2; 1 MG; armour 4–9mm; engine (gasoline) 20hp; 25mph; 8.1ft x 5.6ft x 4ft.

10. FIAT ANSALDO L3, CARRO VELOCE 3 (above, first prototype) / CARRO VELOCE 33 TANKETTE

Designed by Ansaldo and closely derived from the basic Carro Veloce 29 (see above) in 1931–2. Officially tested and design finalised in 1933. Total of 1,300 ordered initially, later increased. Built by Fiat-Ansaldo. Numerous variants and improved models (see below). Widely used and widely exported. The vehicle was airportable beneath an aircraft and could tow a tracked ammunition trailer. It was distinguished by being very low and small, and lacking a turret, the gun(s) being set in the superstructure. Riveted and bolted construction was used throughout and the vehicle was of very simple shape. Rear engine and front drive. MG armament except in special variants (see below). 3.15tons; crew 2; 1 MG or 2 MG (see below); armour 5–15mm; engine (gasoline) 43hp; 26mph; 10.4ft x 4.67ft x 4.25ft. Other users: Afghanistan (1936–?); Albania (1938–40); Austria (1935–9); Bolivia (1937–?); Brazil (special export model with Madsen MG, 1938–c. 1946); Bulgaria (1936–9); China (1936–9); Greece (captured vehicles, 1941), Hungary (1934–8); Iraq (1936–41); Spain, Nationalist (1936–9).

11. CV 3 Second Prototype: With water-cooled MG and beam suspension.

12. CV 3 Third Prototype: With air-cooled MG and scissors suspension.

13. **Carro Veloce 33** (above, an early production type): The original production model, 1933–5. Prototypes had various types of suspension and armament. Armed with Fiat 6.5mm Type 14 MG, or twin 8mm MGs from 1935.

14. **Carro Veloce 33/II** (CV35, unofficial designation; above, early production type): Bolted construction. Twin 8mm MGs. Improved vision ports on later vehicles.

15. CV33/II from front showing twin MG armament.

16. **CV 33/II late production models**

17. A CV 33/II fitted experimentally with torsion bar suspension.

18. **CV Fiat-Ansoldo L38:** Improved 1937–8 model with stronger suspension, new tracks, episcope for driver, and Breda MG. Many older vehicles were retrospectively modified to this standard. From 1940 some vehicles were rearmed with a 20mm Solothurn anti-tank gun, as in the illustration above.

19. **L35/Lf** (later L3–35Lf in 1940): Flamethrower conversion of any of the three production types. Featured a 500kg armoured fuel trailer towed behind the vehicle. Flame-gun was mounted in the hull, replacing MGs. On some later vehicles the fuel tank was mounted on the rear superstructure. Range up to 100 metres. 'Lf' stood for 'lanciafiamme' (flamethrower); known as 'Carro d'assalto lanciafiamme'.

20. L35/Lf flamethrower tanks in action.

21. Late model L35/Lf flamethrower tank with fuel tank on vehicle rear.

22. **CV 33 L35/r Command/Radio Tank:** Any of the production models with radio installed and prominent bowed aerial. Vehicles used in the command role usually had armament removed to allow the fitting of a map table internally.

23. CV 33 L35/r Command Tank (no armament).

24. **CV 33/II Carro Veloce Passerella:** Bridgelayer ('passerella') conversion with winch and A-frame produced by Engineer Corps in 1936. Few only produced, not used in combat.

25. CV 33/II special export model for Brazil with torsion bar suspension and 13.2mm Madsen MG.

Other variants: Recovery Vehicle (unarmed and with towing equipment); Tank Destroyer (1939 prototype, not adapted); Radio Controlled Demolition Tank (conversion by a tank unit); AA Tank (L3 with 8mm MG on AA mount in limited service).

26. CARRO ARMATO MODEL 32, 12TON MEDIUM TANK
An experimental turretless vehicle built in 1933 by Ansaldo to meet a requirement for a 'breakthrough' tank to replace the Fiat 3000 models (see above). Powered by Fiat 643N truck engine; armed with 45mm howitzer and four ball-mounted MG. Side doors. Three-man crew. Not adopted for production and used only for trials. 12tons; crew 3; 45mm howitzer plus 4 MG; engine (gasoline) 75hp; 14mph; 16.36ft x 5.97ft x 6.44ft.

27. CARRO ARMATO 8TON LIGHT TANK
Experimental model derived from the Carro Armato Model 32, but lighter and equipped with a purpose-built V-8 diesel engine. The armament consist of a 37/40 gun in the right-front hull super-structure and two 8mm Breda machine guns in a small revolving turret. After various modifications this machine became the pro-totype vehicle for the M.II series. 8–10tons; crew 3; 40mm gun, 2 MG; engine (diesel); 19mph.

work began in 1939; testing 1940; production in 1941. Production models carried a 20mm Breda gun and a coaxial 8mm MG. Order was completed by late 1942, many of the original total being converted to Semovente SP guns (used by the Germans, 1942–4) The L 6–40 was similar to the 5ton series in appearance but with improved and strengthened suspension and with longer ground contact. These vehicles in their various forms saw service from 1940–4. After the war some were used by the militia until 1952 6.8tons; crew 2; 20mm gun plus 1 MG; armour 6–40mm; engine (gasoline) 68hp; 26mph; 12.6ft x 6.1ft x 6.15ft.

28. FIAT-ANSALDO 5TON SERIES (CARRO CANNONE) LIGHT TANK

Á series of experimental prototypes designed as possible replacements for the CV 33 series, being larger, heavier, and better armed. The first prototype (early 1936) had no turret and a 37mm anti-tank gun in the superstructure. The second prototype (above) was the same vehicle (late 1936) now fitted with a turret containing a twin 8mm MG mount. The third prototype was similar but the 37 mm gun was now moved into the turret. This became the forerunner of the L 6–40 light tank series. There was thus a turret in all but the first prototype, rounded in the second and faceted in the third. The prominent superstructure carried the turret offset to the left. Bogie suspension was by torsion arms. These vehicles were used only for trials and training. 4.75tons to 5tons; crew 2; 37mm gun plus 2 MG; armour 12mm; engine (gasoline) 42hp; 20–25mph; 11.48ft x 5.57ft x 6.49ft.

31. Pilot model with two 8mm Breda MG

29. Fiat-Ansaldo 5ton, third prototype main gun in turret.

30. FIAT-ANSALDO MODEL L 6–40 LIGHT TANK

Derived directly from the 5ton light tank series and designed and built by Fiat-Ansaldo mainly for export sales. After testing by the Italian Army, a production order for 283 (later reduced) was given with the object of replacing the CV 33 series light tanks. Design

32. Pilot model with 37/26 gun and coaxial 8mm MG

33. M.6, Production Pilot model with 20mm Breda automatic gun

34. L6 If: Prototype flamethrower conversion. Not adopted.

L6–40 Centro Radia: Command tank with two radios and prominent aerials. Turret sometimes removed, or superstructure built up with dummy gun.

37. MII/39 front view

35. FIAT-ANSALDO L3 PROTOTYPE LIGHT TANK
This experimental model was built by Fiat-Ansaldo in 1937 on the chassis of a CV 33/II light tank (see above). It retained the original MG armament but had enlarged superstructure and mounted a turret with 20mm automatic cannon. Not ordered for production.

36. CARRO ARMATO M II/39 MEDIUM TANK
Directly evolved from the Carro Armato 8ton of 1935 vintage (see above) and of similar dimensions, with the same diesel engine and 37mm gun. It differed in having superior sprung bogie suspension, the 37mm gun remaining in the superstructure. Impetus for its adoption came after early operations by Italian-equipped Nationalist forces in the Spanish Civil War in 1936 had shown up the inadequacy of the little CV 35 light tanks. A redesign of the Carro Armato 8ton prototype was ordered, Ansaldo and Fiat being asked to build 100 of the new vehicles under the designation Carro Armato MII(8T). First deliveries were made in early 1939 and were completed by 1940. The M II/39 was of riveted construction with rear engine, front drive, side access doors, and the manually operated turret was offset to the left. There was a stowage box formed within the hull at the rear. Owing to its very light armour and small size the M II/39 was obsolescent by the time it went into action in Libya in 1940. Many vehicles were swiftly knocked out and the type was withdrawn from service early in 1941. IItons; crew 3; 37mm gun plus 2 MG; armour 6–30 mm; engine (diesel V8) 105hp; 2Imph; 15.5ft x 7.08ft x 7.33ft. Other users: Few captured and used temporarily by Australian forces in the Western Desert, early 1941.

38. CARRO ARMATO M 13/40 MEDIUM TANK
To form the spearhead of the Italian tank force in the rearmament period of 1940 a completely new tank was designed under the direction of General di Feroleto who was appointed Inspector-General of mechanised forces with the specific task of modernising the range of available AFVs. The M 13/40 design was based broadly on the MII/39 but was bigger, carrying the main gun — a new high velocity 47mm weapon — in the turret, with the secondary MG turret moved to the hull (reverse arrangement to the M II/39. Thicker armour and other refinements were also incorporated. First deliveries of production vehicles, built by Fiat and Ansaldo, started in mid 1940, 250 vehicles out of the 1,900 initial order being delivered by the end of 1940. First experience with these vehicles in the desert showed the need for added filters and other 'tropical' parts. These were duly fitted and the opportunity was taken, with later machines, to substitute an uprated engine. Vehicles so fitted — and all late production vehicles — were known semi-officially as M 14/41 but there were few external differences. However, early vehicles had dustguards only at the front end forward of the turret line while later vehicles had full-length dustguards. The M 13/40 was first in action in December 1940 in Libya and proved to be a very practical design with a good high velocity gun, though it was no match for the heavy British infantry tanks like the Matilda. Subsequent production included a Semovente SP gun on this same chassis which eclipsed the value of the original tank design. The armour of the M 13/40 was inadequate for 1940. A total of 1,960 vehicles were built. 14tons; 47mm gun and 2 MG; armour 9–30mm; engine (diesel) 105hp; 2Imph; 16.18ft x 7.33ft x 7.8ft.

39. MI3/40 Armoured Observation Post: This OP vehicle had a modified turret with a rangefinder and cupola. Early production type is shown — note jerricans on engine cover. Gun was a dummy. Details as for standard vehicle.

40. M 13/40 late production

4I. CARRO ARMATO M I5/42 MEDIUM TANK

Much revised design based on the late production version of the M 13/40, the M 14/41. Evolved late in 1942, the vehicle featured a petrol engine in place of the diesel engine, increased power, more speed, and a heavier high-velocity 47mm gun (Model 47/40). The hull shape was altered to take the new engine and vents were added on the engine cover plates. The exhaust pipes were given armoured shrouds and the side access door was moved from the left to the right side. Finally electric and hydro-dynamic traverse was provided for the turret. Extra stowage points were welded on the hull sides in various positions to take jerricans, though these were not always fitted. Details otherwise were as for the M 13/40. The M I5/42 was short-lived, however, only 82 being made before production of this class of tank was halted in March

1943 in favour of 100 per cent Semovente SP gun production. (The Semovente stayed in production until Italy surrendered in September 1943 and was on the same medium type chassis as the tank.)

42. CARRO ARMATO P 26/40 HEAVY TANK

Conceived on Mussolini's orders in 1940 to provide the Italian Army with a heavy tank which it then lacked. The Inspector General of Mechanisation invited both the mechanisation department and the Ansaldo company to submit two alternative designs each for consideration. One of the Ansaldo designs was chosen and given the temporary designation P.75. A wooden mock-up was ready for approval by December 1940. The vehicle was in the 20 ton class and was to have a 75mm gun-howitzer and 20mm cannon in the turret. A 330hp V-12 diesel engine was to provide power and frontal armour was to be 40mm. There was considerable delay in sorting out design details, however, and engine testing alone took most of 1941 when the prototype vehicle finally appeared in October of that year. By this time weight had gone up to 23tons and the maximum armour thickness to 50mm. The first prototype had the short 75/I8 gun which was later replaced by the more powerful and longer 75/32 piece. By this time a new and more powerful 75mm gun had appeared, the 75/34; this was now put in the P 26/40, production of which was finally authorised by May 1942 when 500 were ordered. This order was later doubled when production work started on these vehicles early in 1943 after further delays. However, by the time Italy surrendered in September 1943 only 2I had been built. Production types had extended dustguards and a modified rear end to provide stowage for tools and equipment. A few were taken over by the Germans after the Italian surrender but the type saw little or no combat. 26tons; crew 4; 75mm plus MG; armour 14–50mm; engine (diesel V-12) 275hp; 22mph; 19.09ft x 9.18ft x 8.26ft.

43. Carro Armato P26/40 first prototype with short 75/I8 howitzer as originally designed.

44. Carro Armato P 26/40 second prototype with long 75/32 gun.

Carro Armato P 43: Project for an improved version of the P 26/40 featuring a new enlarged, but lower, turret with sloping sides and cupola. Provisional order was placed for 150 vehicles but the surrender of Italy took place in September 1943 before the prototype could be completed.

Carro Armato P 43 bis: Variant on the P 43 with wider but less sloped turret and lacking the cupola. Not built. Both the P 43 and P 43 bis were in the 30ton class and were generally similar in size to the P 26/40.
30tons; crew 4; 75mm gun; armour 50–100mm; engine (gasoline) 480hp; 25mph (estimated); 20.2ft x 9.97ft x 7.34ft.

45. CARRO ARMATO CELERE SAHARIANO MEDIUM TANK
A close copy of the British Crusader tank, which latter much impressed the Italians when they encountered it in the Western Desert. Shape and size were based closely on the Crusader and Christie suspension was used. The design was specifically intended for desert fighting as implied by the name. However, by the time the prototype was ready in early 1943 the North African campaign had ceased and the project was cancelled. The prototype had a 47mm gun but a 75mm gun was earmarked for production models.
18tons; crew 4; 47mm gun and MG; engine (gasoline) 250hp; 44mph.

FOREIGN TYPES IN ITALIAN SERVICE
The following types were purchased from abroad or obtained from other sources to equip Italian units in the 1915–45 period.

Renault FT: 100 vehicles supplied by France in 1918 for training and familiarisation while the Fiat 3000 Light Tank was developed.

Schneider CA: 20 vehicles supplied by France in 1918. Little used.

Carden-Loyd Mk VI Tankette: 25 purchased from Vickers in 1929 and used to gain tank experience on exercises and as a basis for an Italian-derived design, the CV 33, which was a close copy.

Somua: Captured French tanks supplied by Germany in 1941 and used for training and to equip a reserve unit in Italy.

46. Renault R–35: Captured French tanks supplied by Germany in 1941 and used to equip two reserve tank battalions in Italy. These French types were of limited value due to lack of spare parts.

PzKpfw VI, Tiger Ausf E: Germany supplied 36 Tiger I tanks in the early summer of 1941 to equip a new crack armoured division, the 'Mussolini' (1st) Armoured Division. These vehicles saw only limited employment due to the Italian surrender in September 1943. The remaining vehicles at this time were returned to German hands.
A few captured T–34s are known to have been manned by Italian crews on the Russian front in 1943.

Fiat 3000B tanks showing both variations — twin 8mm machine-guns and 37mm cannon.

Above: C.V.33 and CV.35 tankettes pass on review, 1938.
Below: M.11—39 medium tanks.

JAPAN

INTRODUCTION

Japan's first step toward mechanisation occurred in 1918 when some Mk V tanks were received from England. Further wartime pattern tanks, such as the French Renault FT (called 'Ko', or 'A' in Japan) and the British Medium Mk A, were delivered some time later. Not much more was accomplished until 1925, when two tank companies were established, one of them being an experimental unit attached to the Chiba Infantry School which conducted the study of tank tactics. Until then, Japan had not produced any tanks of her own, but during 1925 a domestic design programme was launched which was later to become original in several ways.

Japanese tank design started with a rather ambitious design which was both sophisticated and clumsy. Completed at the Osaka Arsenal in March 1927, this prototype was known as the 'Experimental Heavy Tank, I'; it weighed 22tons and featured a main turret, armed with a 57mm gun, and two subsidiary turrets, each housing a machine-gun. It was apparently influenced by the contemporary trend to multi-turrets affording a wide field of fire and many guns — such a policy was exemplified abroad by the French Char 2C (1920), the British Independent (1926), the German NbFz (1933) and the Russian T-35 (1933), the latter being the only one to reach quantity production status. The second Japanese heavy tank model was simply a rebuild of the former one which was carried out in 1930 under the designation of 'Experimental Heavy Tank', with only a few modifications. The multi-turret formula was the subject of continuous development up to 1935, a newly constructed pilot model appearing in 1932 under the designation of Type 91 heavy tank which, owing to its year of completion, was sometimes designated Type 92, itself followed by an ultimate prototype, the Type 95. The interest evinced by the military authorities did not result in a quantity production order, however, and the whole concept was abandoned in favour of smaller and lighter single-turreted machines.

In order to keep themselves technically abreast of the most advanced foreign designs, the Japanese had purchased from abroad some contemporary tanks including samples of the Vickers Mark C and Vickers-Armstrongs Six-Ton tanks as well as a few Vickers Carden-Loyd Mark VIB tankettes. The French Renault concern was awarded a production contract for a few dozen of an offspring of their wartime FT light tank — the 8ton NC tank which became designated as the 'OTSU' or 'B', in the Japanese Army.

From the Vickers C tank the Osaka Arsenal derived an 8ton, four-man light tank pilot model armed with a 57mm gun. The promise evinced by this machine resulted, in 1929, in the Mitsubishi Heavy Industries company receiving an order for the development of a projected design, the 'I-GO' the prototype of which was completed in 1931. The 'I-GO' was adopted as the Type 89 medium tank, a 12ton vehicle armed with a 57mm gun and capable of a speed of 25kph. The Type 89 was placed in production during 1931 just in time to be involved, together with some OTSU (Renault NC.I) tanks, in the 'incident' which

occured at Shanghai in 1932 as a result of Japan's aggressive policy towards China. The petrol-engined Type 8▢ was retained in production until 1936.

The year 1933 was an important date in the histor▢ of Japanese tank devlopment. During this year Majo▢ (later Lieutenant-General) Tomio Hara designed his bel▢ crank 'scissor' type suspension (resisted by horizonta▢ or sloped coil springs) which was to become widely use▢ on subsequent Japanese tanks, from the Type 94 tankett▢ up to the Type 5 CHI-RI medium tank, the last Japanes▢ prototype of World War II. In 1932, Mitsubishi Heav▢ Industries had produced an air-cooled diesel engin▢ suitable for installation in tanks, and in 1933 this engin▢ was experimentally fitted in a Type 89 medium tank▢ This initiated a large scale tank 'dieselisation' policy i▢ Japan. After trials under extreme climatic conditions▢ this diesel power plant was standardised for driving th▢ subsequent Type 89 medium tank production model▢ which became designated as the Type 89-OTSU (Typ▢ 89-B). The earlier gasoline version was then redesignate▢ Type 89-KO (Type 89-A).

In the early thirties, the Japanese considered a limite▢ mechanisation policy. At first, studies were concentrate▢ on wheeled armoured cars, but terrain conditions i▢ the Far East favoured tracked machines and such ▢ vehicle was finally preferred. The design was undertake▢ by Ishikawajima and resulted in the machine-gun arme▢ Type 92 combat car, for which a welded constructio▢ was employed.

The development of a line of small vehicles classifie▢ as tankettes ('MAME SENSHA' in the Japanese nomen▢ clature) had also started around 1932, when the Imperia▢ Army began to evince interest in an armed and armoure▢ tractor able to tow a tracked trailer carrying supplie▢ and ammunition up to forward positions of the front line▢ The first Japanese tankette, known as the Type 94▢ (1934), constituted an entirely original type of construc▢ tion although certain details of design may be trace▢ to foreign types. Further development of the basic desig▢ led, from 1936 onwards, to a modification of the origina▢ trackwork which was now fitted with a trailing idler▢ This increased the ground contact length and the vehicl▢ gained in cross-country mobility. Further adaptation o▢ the Type 94 tankette gave rise to a dieselised prototyp▢ version which in turn formed the basis for the improve▢ Type 97 TE-KE tankette, a diesel engined 4.5ton midge▢ tank armed with a 37mm gun. After the TE-KE furthe▢ development of the tankette was abandoned, th▢ Japanese Imperial Staff having begun to appreciate tha▢ the entire concept was outdated.

While heavy tank and tankette designs lapsed, th▢ medium and light tank programmes progressed to im▢ proved models. Advancing to a more modern mediu▢ tank resulted in competition for production orders be▢ tween two models, the 10ton CHI-NI and the 15to▢ CHI-HA, both carrying a 57mm gun. At this time th▢ Japanese military authorities were sensitive to cost con▢ sideration, and so the less expensive CHI-NI wa▢ favoured at first; however, in 1937 when Japan becam▢

involved in full-scale war with China, the more powerful CHI-HA was finally chosen, being standardised as the Type 97 CHI-HA (1937) medium tank and placed in production by Mitsubishi Heavy Industries. On the basis of the CHI-HA design several specialised vehicles were developed, namely the SHI-KI command tank, the SE-RI recovery tank and a mine-clearing vehicle.

In the meantime the line of development previously initiated with the Type 92 combat car had also been discontinued. Instead it was followed with the design of a light tank which was to be coupled with the Type 89 medium tank within the newly formed mechanized brigade in Manchuria. Prototype construction was undertaken by Mitsubishi in the form of a 7ton, 37mm gun light tank, known as HA-GO, which was powered by the same diesel engine as the Type 89-B medium tank. The HA-GO was standardised as the Type 95 (Kyugo) light tank in 1935 and its production started at the end of the same year. It had a speed of 40kph and a cruising range of 242km and despite numerous shortcomings, was highly praised by its crew — in fact, it gained a popularity out of proportion to its actual fighting value. This rather undeserved reputation resulted in its being maintained in full-scale production for far longer than was necessary, since more potent successors, such as the Type 98 KE-NI and the Type 5 KE-HO, had been designed in the meantime.

Developed in the late thirties as a successor to the HA-GO, the Type 98 KE-NI featured a refined layout and a suspension system located within the hull. In this form it was designated Type 98-A, but an alternative design, the Type 98-B was produced as a prototype with four large road wheels suspended on individual bell crank bogies interconnected by coil springs. The Type 98-A KE-NI entered limited production from 1942 onwards.

Beginning in 1933, the Japanese had also devoted much time to research on amphibious tanks. It is probable that British and Russian experiments in this line had influenced the Japanese in their decision to produce such a vehicle, and the resulting design probably drew its inspiration from the Vickers Carden-Loyd Light Amphibious Tank of 1931. Interest evinced by the Japanese Imperial Army crystallised in the form of two prototypes of the SR-I, or I-GO, a light tank armed with a single machine-gun. With the I-GO, Japan pioneered water-jet propulsion for amphibious tanks. Further development let to the SR-II, or 'RO-GO' which like its predecessors, did not go beyond the prototype stage and an attempt to build an amphibious version of the Type 92 combat car ceased after trials with a pilot model. Another design, the SR-III, was developed from the SR-I/III in 1939; a production programme was set up for it but did not reach fruition and after this Army interest in amphibious tanks lapsed.

Over the years Japan had set up a tank industry, partly composed of government owned establishments (Zoheisho) in Japan and Manchuria, and partly of civilian subsidiaries belonging to larger automotive firms and naval shipyard concerns. Some of the latter merged into new groups specialising in the design and construction of armoured vehicle prototypes as well as in their mass-

production. Foremost among these was Mitsubishi Heavy Industries which became the largest Japanese producer of armoured fighting vehicles and military diesel engines. Branches of the Ishikawajima Dockyard and Engineering Co and the Tokyo Gas and Electric Co were merged together in 1937 with the DAT Motor Co to form the Tokyo Jidosha KK concern. From this a branch of the former TGE developed separately as Hino Motors in May 1942. This firm alone produced several light tanks. Other companies involved in the tank production ring were Hitachi, Ikegai, Niigata and Kobe Steel Works, while Mitsubishi, Nihon, Kobe and Daido also acted as armour plate suppliers.

As priority was given to aircraft and naval vessels (which were the prestige weapons of the time) Japanese tank production always suffered in consequence. Only 6,450 Japanese tanks were produced from 1931 to 1945; of this total, Mitsubishi alone contributed about 3,300 light and medium tanks. During the war years, Japan's tank industry remained short of steel and skilled labour and the situation was further complicated by the increasingly destructive American air raids which started in 1943. The difficulties were such that by 1943 Japanese tank production had already fallen to 750 units — in figure which contrasts significantly with the 29,497 units produced in the United States during the same year. In 1945 it was decided to concentrate on the defence of the home islands and high priority was theoretically given to tank production for the first time: but this decision remained without real practical effect. From 1941 to 1945 the Japanese Ordnance Department had, however, displayed a considerable effort in terms of design and development.

The development potentialities of the CHI-HA led the Mitsubishi concern to evolve an improved model which was designated Type I CHI-HE (1941). Powered by the new Type 100 V-12 high-speed diesel engine, the CHI-HE weighed 17tons and was armed with a 47mm high-velocity gun which had a greater penetration capability than the 57mm tank weapon. The Type I CHI-HE medium tank began to leave the assembly line in 1941–2 and became the most successful Japanese tank to see wartime service. Its inadequate production rate, however, necessitated the conversion of the former CHI-HA model by replacing the original turrets with those of the Type I CHI-HE. This more advanced version was redesignated Type 97 SHINHOTO CHI-HA (or 'modified turret CHI-HA') to distinguish it from the obsolescent basic model. As had been done with the CHI-HA, the Shinhoto CHI-HA was also developed into some specialised variants, such as the KA-SO observation tank and a bulldozer tank, while the CHI-HE design led to the Type 2 HO-I Gun Tank.

Following the appearance of the CHI-HE, the development of the medium tank proceeded on a progressive basis. The next step forward, the 1943 Type 3 CHI-NU (there having been no Type 2) offered an increase in fire-power over its predecessor, having a larger turret with a 75mm anti-tank gun patterned after a French Schneider field gun. This resulted in an increase in the combat weight to 18.5tons.

The Navy's first amphibious tank was the Type 2 KA-MI, a 12.5ton vehicle armed with a 37mm gun and based upon the Army's HA-GO design. It was followed by the heavier Type 3 KA-CHI which featured the same Type 100 diesel engine as the Army's Type I CHI-HE medium tank. In 1944 a tracked landing craft, the Type 4 KA-TSU appeared and in 1945 the chain of development which had started with the Type 2 KA-MI ended with the Type 5 TO-KU pilot model. Although the Japanese Navy's amphibious tanks did not resemble any other of the Japanese tank types, there were certain features and technological trends which they shared with some Army tanks — the most obvious being the use of the bell crank 'scissor' suspension system and the installation of a Type 100 diesel power plant for some of the later models.

The most remarkable achievement of the Japanese tank industry had been the wide scale 'dieselisation' policy initiated in 1933 with the Type 89 medium tank. They developed several families of air-cooled diesel engines including 6-, 8- and 12-cylinder variants based on the same size of cylinder. This policy embodied the advantage of reducing the fire hazard, lowering the fuel consumption and eliminating difficulties inherent in procuring high-grade petroleum. In 1945 Japan could be claimed to be the most advanced nation in this particular field of development — way ahead of the United States, Germany, Britain and even Russia.

A larger model, the 30ton Type 4 CHI-TO, emerged in 1944 as a prototype. It carried a more powerful 75mm gun adapted from an anti-aircraft weapon and was powered by a V-12, 400hp diesel power plant of a newly developed series.

The last of the long line of medium tanks developed by Mitsubishi Heavy Industries from the former CHI-HA was the Type 5 CHI-RI (1945), a 37ton vehicle which represented the ultimate advance of Japanese tank design during World War II. The CHI-RI was in essence a lengthened CHI-TO and no major changes were made to the earlier designs, apart from the addition of a hull-mounted 37mm gun of very questionable utility. The CHI-RI prototype was powered by a derated version of a water-cooled aircraft engine of German origins. This was not due to a reversal of policy in favour of petrol engines, but rather to the lack of diesel motor developing a sufficient output.

From 1941 onwards, a progressive development programme, based upon both the Type 95 HA-GO and the Type 98 KE-NI light tanks, had also been undertaken. Unfortunately it remained mainly experimental and of a restricted nature. Light tanks Type 3 KE-RI and Type 4 KE-NU were obtained by upgunning the former Type 95 HA-GO, firstly with the 57mm low-velocity gun then with the 47mm high-velocity gun of the medium tank range. Another new light tank, the Type 2 KE-TO, was no more than a similar development of the former Type 98 KE-NI.

However, a new layout was adopted for the last vehicle in the light tank category — the promising 10ton, 47mm gun armed KE-HO, designed by Hino Motors. The KE-HO

resulted from the need for a better and more heavily armed light tank than the HA-GO and even the KE-NI; unfortunately it never reached production status, although the prototype was ready and had been evaluated as early as 1942. Preparation for its quantity production as the Type 5 KE-HO light tank had been undertaken by 1945 but the Japanese surrender precluded these plans. Such a long delay was largely due to the users' reluctance to modify the earlier models, and perhaps also to the overloading of the Japanese war industry during the critical years 1943–4.

Perhaps the most significant advance in Japanese tank development was represented by the unique family of amphibious tanks for which the Japanese Imperial Navy had laid down a requirement in the early 1940s. The basic design was to be original in two ways at least — an extremely interesting flotation system was achieved by the attachment of empty bow and stern pontoons which could be released at will from inside the tank when it was ashore; and it could be also transported aboard a submarine and launched from it.

The Japanese tank designation system
Japanese tanks were designated by a type number indicating the last two digits of the year in the Japanese calendar in which production was initiated. The year was taken from the legendary foundation of the Japanese Empire — 660BC western terms — which was their year 0. The European equivalent of a Japanese year is thus found by subtracting 660. Thus a tank labelled Type 95 (the last two digits of 2595) was a model of the year 1935 in western chronology. From 2601 onwards, the last digit of the Japanese year was used, i.e. Type I (1941), Type 2 (1942) and so on. In some cases the type number was followed by a word descriptive of its function classification and a code letter given by the manufacturer; thus:
Type 97 CHI-HA was Model 1937, Medium 'C'.
Type 94 TK was Model 1934, Tankette.
Type 98 KE-NI was Model 1938, Light 'D'.

Type 92 Combat Cars, China, 1937.

Type 94 tankettes advance over the plains of Northern China.

Type 95 light tanks in Malaya, 1942.

1. MEDIUM MK A (WHIPPET)

After World War I Japan purchased several foreign types for evaluation including a number of British Whippets which were obtained in 1922 and used for several years, being withdrawn about 1929. For vehicle details see British section. Some Mk V tanks were also purchased from Britain.

2. KO-GATA SENSHA

This was the Japanese designation given to the Renault FT, a number of which were purchased from France from 1922 on. All were the FT 18 model with 37mm guns. Some remained in service until 1940. For vehicle details see French section.

3. OTSU B (OTSU–GATA SENSHA)

In 1927 Japan purchased Renault NCI tanks from France and these stayed in service until about 1940. Many were subsequently modified with Japanese diesel motors replacing the Renault gasoline engines. For vehicle details see French section.

Also purchased in the twenties were the Vickers Medium C tank, Carden-Loyd tankettes, and Carden-Loyd amphibious tanks. Details of these are given in the British section.

4. EXPERIMENTAL TANK No I

First Japanese design, the Experimental Tank No I, completed at the Osaka Arsenal early in 1927. It was a multi-turret vehicle carrying a short 57mm gun in the main turret and machine guns in the front and rear subsidiary turrets. It ran over 19 small bogie wheels per side grouped in pairs and supported by a two-stage leaf spring suspension. Main turret was surmounted by a stroboscopic vision device. 20tons; crew 5; I 57mm gun plus 2 6.5mm MG; engine (I, gasoline) 140hp, liquid cooled; 12.5mph.

5. EXPERIMENTAL HEAVY TANK

Experimental Tank No I of 1927 was modified and rebuilt as the 'Experimental Heavy Tank' by 1930. Weight decreased by 2tons by making the armour thinner; tracks and gearbox were modified and it had 17 bogie wheels per side instead of 19. The tank was up-gunned with a 70mm gun. 18tons; crew 5; I 70mm gun plus 2 6.5mm MG; engine (I, gasoline) 140hp, liquid cooled; 12.5mph.

6. HEAVY TANK TYPE 91

A new prototype construction built at the Osaka Arsenal in 1931. Like its predecessor, it ran over 17 bogie wheels per side, suspended by a two-stage leaf springs system. Neither a strobo-scope nor cupola was fitted in the main turret. New gearbox and slightly wider tracks were introduced. Officially, it was referred to as Type 91 Heavy Tank, but owing to its year of completion, it was sometimes known as Type 92. 18tons; crew 5; I 70mm gun plus 3 6.5mm MG; engine (I, gasoline aircraft type) liquid cooled; 16mph.

7. HEAVY TANK TYPE 95

Culmination of the Japanese multi-turret tank concept which stemmed from the original Experimental Tank No I, via the Experimental Heavy Tank and the Heavy Tank Type 9I. It featured a front sub-turret armed with a 37mm gun, a main turret housing a 70mm gun forward and a machine gun in the rear, and a rear sub-turret fitted with a machine-gun. It ran on 9 road wheels each side, suspended by leaf springs. Supported by 4 return rollers, the tracks were rear driven from a petrol motor. Riveted construction. Only one pilot model was built in 1934. 24tons; crew 5; I 70mm gun plus I 37mm gun plus 2 6.5mm MG; armour I2–30mm; engine (I, gasoline aircraft type, 6-cylinders) 290hp, liquid cooled; I3.7mph; 21.25ft x 8.8ft x 9.5ft.

8. TANKETTE TYPE 94, TK

Early in the thirties, the Japanese Army asked for an armoured tractor able to pull a tracked trailer for supplying ammunition in the forward battle area. A defensive weapon was also specified and the design turned out as a 3ton turreted vehicle, very similar in appearance to the Vickers-Carden-Loyd commercial light tank of this time. This vehicle was standardised as 'Tankette, Type 94' (not 'Type 92' as wrongly stated by American Intelligence during World War II). Both welded and riveted constructions are used throughout the hull. Running gear included 4 rubber tyred bogie wheels per side, mounted on bell cranks resisted by compression springs. Mounted offset to the right, the turret had neither powered nor manual traversing gear being traversed by shoulder pressure against the machine-gun. When open, the driver's hatch interfered with the machine-gun traverse, so the turret was often carried facing to the left. Powered by a petrol motor. 3.5tons; crew 2; I 7.7mm MG; armour 4–12mm; engine I Type 94 (gasoline, 4-cylinders), 32hp, air-cooled; 25mph; I0.08ft x 5.33ft x 5.33ft.

9. TANKETTE TYPE 94, TK MODIFIED

From 1936 onwards, a modified version of the basic Type 94 tankette was produced, embodying a trailing idler, a lowered drive sprocket and an increased ground contact length for the tracks. Interior of the driving and fighting compartments as well as the turret were lined with asbestos panels to afford protection against heat radiation. 3.5tons; crew 2; I 7.7mm MG; armour 4–12mm; engine I Type 94 (gasoline, 4-cylinders), 32hp, air-cooled; 25mph; II.08ft x 5.33ft x 5.8ft.

TANKETTE TYPE 94 (DIESEL PROTOTYPE)

Diesel version of the earlier tankette built as a prototype. The driver was located to the left instead of to the right as in the former variants. Experience gained with this vehicle played a part in the design of the Type 97 tankette.

I0. TANKETTE TYPE 97, TE-KE

The final development of the Japanese tankette concept and somewhat larger than previous designs, weight and dimensions having been substantially increased over the Type 94. More room in the turret allowed for a 37mm gun, though a 7.7mm machine-gun was still sometimes used as an alternative. Rear three-quarters of the turret roof was hinged to form an entrance hatch. The hull had been fully redesigned, the glacis plate was simplified and had better deflection angles, and the diesel engine had been transferred to the rear. Versions of this vehicle were also used as front line observation post vehicles or as forward area armoured ammunition carriers. They were all externally similar. 4.7tons; crew 2; I 37mm gun or I 7.7mm MG; armour 4–16mm; engine I (diesel, 4-cylinders) 65hp, air-cooled; 25mph; I2.I7ft x 6.25ft x 5.83ft.

II. COMBAT CAR, AMPHIBIOUS, TYPE 92 A-I-GO

The Japanese tried to develop their Type 92 combat car into an amphibious vehicle. The all-welded hull was made waterproof and redesigned to give more room and buoyancy. Floats were added and a single screw propelled the machine in water. Did not progress beyond the prototype stage but experience gained with it was beneficial for further research.

14. COMBAT CAR TYPE 92 (EARLY PRODUCTION)
The first production model of the Type 92 combat car was slightly heavier than the prototype. It featured a new running gear which consisted of 6 small rubber tyred bogie wheels mounted in pairs on three semi-elliptic springs on each side. The centre-guide tracks were front sprocket driven and had an increased ground contact length. This was not found fully satisfactory and was modified once again. 3.5tons; crew 3; 1 13mm and one 6.5mm MG; armour 6mm; engine (1 Ishikawajima, gasoline, 6-cylinders) 45hp, air-cooled; 21.6mph; 12.85ft x 5.33ft x 6.04ft.

12. AMPHIBIOUS TANK SR-II, RO-GO
A further design for the Army, it was similar in size to the SR-I, but much improved. Features included Horstmann style suspension, eight sided turret, retractable buoyancy vane on the front (operated by screw and pinion). Two propellers in enclosed channels provided propulsion. 4tons; crew 3; 2 7.7mm MG; armour 6mm; engine 1 gasoline, air-cooled; 25mph on land, 4.9mph in water; 16.66ft x 6.16ft x 7.83ft.

AMPHIBIOUS TANK SR-III
The final design of an amphibious tank contemplated for the Japanese Imperial Army in 1939. It was adopted and a production programme was set out but as no further need was developed, this was cancelled. 3.8tons; crew 2; 1 7.7mm MG; armour 4-10mm; engine (1, 4-cylinders) 72hp; 30mph on land, 5.7mph in water; 13.77ft x 5.75ft x 6.25ft .

15. COMBAT CAR TYPE 92 (LATE PRODUCTION)
An improved version of the original production model. Major change lay in the trackwork in which the 6 small bogie wheels were replaced by 4 larger and spoked rubber tyred wheels grouped in two bogies resisted by helical coil springs acting on bell cranks. Large numbers of both early or late production models were produced. Details as above.

AMPHIBIOUS TANK SR-I, I-GO
Designed in 1933 as an amphibious tank for the Japanese Imperial Army, the SR-I or I-GO did not go beyond the prototype stage. Featured two buoyancy chambers overhanging the tracks, one on each side. The trackwork included 4 twin-wheeled bogies grouped in two sets which were suspended by leaf springs. Supported by 3 return rollers, the track tops slightly sloped down to rear idler wheel. Only two pilot models were built, one of them being water-jet propelled. 1 6.5mm MG; engine (1 Mitsubishi, diesel), air-cooled.

13. COMBAT CAR TYPE 92 (PROTOTYPE)
A heavy tankette specially designed for cavalry support purposes in 1931. Longer, wider and higher than that of tankettes, the box type hull extended forward to form a bulge which accommodated a ball-mounted machine-gun. A further machine-gun was carried in an all-round traverse turret. Armament was either two 6.5mm light machine-guns or one 13mm and one 6.5mm machine-gun. The prototype tank ran on 4 rubber tyred bogie wheels on each side, paired in two bogies and supported by semi-elliptic leaf springs. Supported by 4 return rollers, the tracks driven by front sprockets. One of the very first armoured vehicles of welded construction. 3.2tons; crew 3; 2 6.5mm MG or 1 13mm and 1 6.5 mm MG; armour 6mm; engine (1 Ishikawajima, gasoline, 6-cylinders) 45hp, air-cooled; 25mph.

16. LIGHT TANK TYPE 95, HA-GO

The most oustanding Japanese tank of World War II. Developed from 1933 to give speed and mobility in the newly created mechanised brigades. The Type 95 featured a turret offset to the left, a prominent built-out front machine-gun compartment and two rounded bulges in the centre of the superstructure, overhanging the tracks. Hull and turret were of riveted and bolted rolled plates, with some welding in places. It ran on two twin-wheel bogies per side, operating through bell cranks and resisted by horizontally mounted helical compression springs. Air-cooled diesel engine was of very advanced design and furnished a high output in relation to its weight. Power drive was transmitted to the front sprockets through a sliding gear gearbox giving four forward speeds and one reverse, steering was by clutch and brake method. Produced up to 1942, mainly by Mitsubishi. 7.4tons; crew 3; 1 37mm gun plus 2 7.7mm MG; armour 6–12mm; engine (1 diesel, 6-cylinders) 110hp, air-cooled; 25mph; 4.08ft x 6.75ft x 7.50ft.

17. LIGHT TANK TYPE 95, HA-GO (MODIFIED)

To improve its cross country performance, the Type 95 HA-GO was tested with a modified trackwork. Wheels were coupled in pairs by low attached bogie bolsters of inverted triangular shape. This modification was mainly intended for use in Manchuria but did not proceed further.

18. LIGHT TANK TYPE 98-A, KE-NI

Refined development of the HA-GO, planned with two different running gears and suspensions. The Type 98-A ran on 6 wheels grouped in three bogies each side, with their springing system located inside. The driver, who controlled the tank through a steering wheel, was positioned in the centre front. Tracks remained front driven. KE-NI also disclosed more extensive use of welding in its construction: armour protection was heavier and more suitably shaped. There was neither hull nor turret rear machine-gun and no cupola above the turret. As Type HA-GO was highly praised by its users, KE-NI was not placed in production until 1942 and it seems that no more than two hundred were built. Powered by a supercharged diesel engine. 7.2tons; crew 3; 1 37mm gun, 2 7.7mm MG; armour 6–12mm; engine (1 diesel, 6-cylinders) 150hp; air-cooled; 31.1mph; 13.46ft x 6.96ft x 5.96ft.

19. LIGHT TANK TYPE 98-B, KE-NI

Developed as an alternative for the sub-type 98-A. Featured a 4 large wheel Christie type running gear with rear drive and no return rollers. Suspension was by individual bell cranks connected by coil springs. Did not go beyond the experimental stage.

20. LIGHT TANK TYPE 2, KE-TO

Developed on the basis of the Type 98-A KE-NI from which it differed only in being armed with a 37mm Type 1 (1941) tank gun instead of the Type 100 (1940) tank gun of the same calibre. Although successful trials were achieved, production of this tank was delayed until 1944, as the users were fully satisfied with the Type 95 HA-GO. Only a few were built. 7.2tons; crew 3; 1 37mm gun, 1 7.7mm MG; armour 6–16mm; engine (1 diesel) 150hp; air-cooled; 31.1mph; 13.46ft x 6.96ft x 5.96ft.

LIGHT TANK TYPE 3, KE-RI

The Type 3 KE-RI light tank was a standard Type 95 HA-GO upgunned with a 57mm gun. This development did not go beyond the prototype stage owing to the inconveniently restricted turret space. Details as KE-TO except 7.4tons; 57mm gun; engine 110hp; 14.13ft x 6.79ft x 7.42ft.

LIGHT TANK TYPE 4, KE-NU

A further attempt to increase the firepower of the standard Type 95 HA-GO; it resulted from combination of the Type 95 hull with turret and 57mm gun of the Type 97 CHI-HA medium tank. This development involved a larger turret ring and other minor modifications. Several prototypes were built but only a few were so converted. 8.4tons; crew 3; 1 57mm gun, 2 7.7mm MG; armour 6–25 mm; engine (1 diesel, 6-cylinders) 110hp, air-cooled; 25mph; 14ft 1½in x 6ft 9½in.

LIGHT TANK TYPE 5, KE-HO

Very last prototype in the light tank series. Designed in 1942, the one prototype disclosed very satisfactory test results. However, its mass production was not considered prior to 1945 by which time it was too late. The chassis was of new design and the tank was armed with the 47mm Type 1 tank gun. Powered by a supercharged engine. 10tons; crew 4; 1 47mm gun and 1 7.7mm MG; armour 8–20mm; engine (1 diesel, 6-cylinders) 150hp, air-cooled; 31mph; 14ft 4½in x 7.33ft x 7.33ft.

21. LIGHT TANK TYPE 89 (PROTOTYPE)
Stemmed from the Vickers Mark C, a British commercial tank of which the Japanese bought a sample in 1927. It featured a prominent 'nosed' front offset to the left, a hull machine-gun mounted to the right of the driver's plate and a rounded turret with no cupola above its flat top. Suspension consisted of 9 small bogie wheels suspended by leaf springs and 5 return rollers mounted along a girder. The transmission provided four forward and two reverse speeds. Very few tanks of this type were made before the design progressed to a heavier model reclassified as Medium Tank Type 89. 9.8tons; crew 4; 1 57mm gun, 2 6.5mm MG; engine (1 Mitsubishi, .gasoline, 6-cylinders) 105hp, liquid-cooled; 15.5mph.

22, 23. MEDIUM TANK TYPE 89-KO
From the British Vickers Mark C and a 9.8ton tank produced as a prototype, the Japanese developed a battle tank standardised as Medium Tank Type 89 (1929). They produced this tank in two sub-types: Type 89-KO (89-A) and Type 89-OTSU (89-B). Type 89-KO (89-A) had a petrol engine adapted from an aircraft power

unit and featured a box type hull, slightly sloped glacis plate with a door to the right, vertical front plate above this with a hull machine-gun mounted to the right and a small hat-like cupola hinged to the top of the turret. It ran on 9 small bogie wheels per side, the leading one being independently mounted, and the upper track portion was supported by 5 small return rollers mounted along a girder. Protective skirting covered the leaf spring suspension. 12.7tons; crew 4; 1 57mm gun and 2 6.5mm MG; armour 10–17mm; engine (1 Mitsubishi, gasoline, 6-cylinders) 105hp, liquid-cooled; 15.5mph; 18.8ft x 7.17ft x 8.48ft.

24. MEDIUM TANK TYPE 89-OTSU
From 1936, after trials under cold weather conditions in Manchuria, Type 89-OTSU (89-B), a diesel variant of Type 89-KO, entered production with a straight 6 cylinder diesel motor. Production was mainly in hands of Mitsubishi but other concerns in Japan and Manchuria were also involved owing to requests of users and to various plants involved in manufacture, some changes and improvements slightly affected the exterior appearance throughout the production stage. One (above) featured a one-piece front plate with the driver's position to the left; a new cupola and a redesigned aperture for mounting the 57mm gun.

25. Another one featured a one-piece front plate with the driver's position to the right, a two-piece split cupola hatch, redesigned skirting plates, 4 return rollers and manganese steel parallel toe-type track shoes.
Later some tanks of these types were fitted with ditching tail-pieces. Steering was by clutch and brake and the transmission included a four-speed gearbox with high and low ranges. 13tons; crew 4; 1 57mm gun, 2 6.5mm MG; armour 10–17mm; engine (1 Mitsubishi, diesel, 6-cylinders) 115hp, air-cooled; 15.5mph; 18.8ft x 7.1ft x 8.4lft.

26. Type 89-OTSU, showing the undltching tail

27. EXPERIMENTAL MEDIUM TANK CHI-NI

An experimental tank designed in 1936 as a competitor to the CHI-HA. By this time the Japanese General Staff favoured lighter and cheaper-to-produce tanks and the CHI-NI was preferred to the heavier CHI-HA. One pilot model was built in 1937 and successfully tested, but when the war with China broke out, the more powerful CHI-HA was selected and standardised. CHI-NI running gear included 8 small road wheels suspended by horizontal compression springs acting through bell cranks and it had 3 return rollers each side. Turret had no co-axial machine-gun. 9.8tons; crew 3; I 57mm gun plus I 7.7mm MG; armour 25mm; engine 135hp; 18.5 mph.

28. MEDIUM TANK TYPE 97, CHI-HA

The Type 97 CHI-HA was the competitor to the less costly CHI-NI. When the war between Japan and China broke out, the CHI-HA was selected for mass production as the Type 97 (1937) medium tank. Mitsubishi being the leading contractor. Its design followed generally the lines of the light tank Type 95 HA-GO but it had a two-man turret, a more powerful armament and a thicker armour. The CHI-HA ran on 6 double rubber tyred wheels per side; it had a bell-crank suspension with helical springs but no shock absorber. Mounted in pairs, the 4 centre wheels operated against horizontally mounted compression springs while the front and rear wheels acted on slopingly mounted compression springs. Drive was carried through a four-speed sliding-gear box combined with a high and low transfer case giving in all eight forward and two reverse gears. Steering was by clutch and brake method. Internal communication was by 12 push buttons in the turret connected to 12 light panels and a buzzer in the driver's compartment. This was the most successful Japanese tank design and the best in service in the war years, though it was no match for Allied tanks. 15tons; crew 4; I 57mm gun plus 2 7.7mm MG; armour 8–25mm; engine (I Type 97, diesel, V-12) 170hp, air-cooled; 23.5mph; 18.01ft x 7.66ft x 7.33ft.

29. COMMAND TANK SHI-KI

This tank was adopted from the CHI-HA medium tank as a command vehicle for Japanese armoured regiments. It differed in having the 37mm gun located in the hull front in place of the machine-gun. Another variant carried a 57mm gun duplicated in the hull front. The SHI-KI model featured several improvements in matter of vision and communication and incorporated a directing device. The distinctive feature was the frame type radio aerial around the turret.

30. RECOVERY TANK SE-RI

The SE-RI was designed and equipped for rapid recovery of disabled vehicles and had been developed by Mitsubishi from the CHI-HA medium tank. Recovery equipment was rather simple including a rear light jib for lifting and steel wire ropes for towing, and the turret was of conical shape. 15.4tons; crew 4; 2 7.7mm MG; armour 8–25mm; engine (I Type 97, diesel, V-12) 240hp, air-cooled; 25mph; 18.17ft x 7.66ft x 7.32ft.

31. MINE CLEARING TANK G

The Japanese converted a few of their CHI-HA medium tanks as flail tanks for mine destroying. The device consisted of two revolving drums carrying rows of chains which exploded mines on contact, largely copied from the Allied flail device. Main armament (57mm gun) was retained in the turret.

32. MEDIUM TANK TYPE 97, SHINHOTO CHI-HA

A development of the original CHI-HA tank. As the demand for a new medium tank, the Type I CHI-HE, exceeded production abilities, the Type 97 CHI-HA was modified: its original turret housing a 57mm short gun was replaced by one from the Type I which mounted a high velocity 47mm long barrelled gun. This interim vehicle was known as Type 97 SHINHOTO CHI-HA ('New turret CHI-HA') and was first placed in operation in 1942. 15.8tons; crew 4; 1 47mm gun plus 2 7.7mm MG; armour 8–25mm; engine (1 Type 97, diesel, V-12) 170hp, air-cooled; 23.5mph. 18.01ft x 7.66ft x 7.76ft.

Observation Tank KA-SO: This tank was adapted as a command vehicle from the SHINHOTO CHI-HA medium tank. It carried a dummy 47mm gun in the turret but retained the real rear turret and front hull machine-guns. It had several specialised equipments which made it suitable for a leading role. Externally it was visually identical to the SHINHOTO CHI-HA.

33. Bulldozer Tank: The Japanese converted a few of their SHINHOTO CHI-HA medium tanks to take a bulldozer attachment. This was attached low to the ground level, between the first and second road wheels and was operated by cable.

34. MEDIUM TANK TYPE I, CHI-HE

This was a refined Type 97 CHI-HA armed with a long barrelled 47mm Type I anti-tank gun. Improvements included a redesigned straight superstructure front plate, a new turret, welded armour with its thickness raised up to 50mm and a more powerful engine. Production began during 1941. It was slightly longer and higher than the Type 97 CHI-HA. 17tons; crew 5; 1 47mm gun plus 2 7.7 mm MG; armour 8–50mm; engine (1 Type 100, diesel, V-12) 240hp, air-cooled; 27.3mph; 18.76ft x 7.66ft x 7.83ft.

35. GUN TANK TYPE 2, HO-I

Based upon the Type I CHI-HE medium tank, the HO-I was designed as a complemental self-propelled gun. It was armed with a 75mm Type 99 short barrelled gun housed in an all-round traverse turret. The HO-I was standardised in 1942 but no large quantity was produced. 16.7tons; crew 5; 1 75mm gun plus 1 7.7mm MG; armour 12–50mm; engine (1 Type 100, diesel, V-12) 240hp, air-cooled; 27.3mph. 18.76ft x 7.66ft x 8.4ft.

36. MEDIUM TANK TYPE 3, CHI-NU

Generally similar to the Type I CHI-HE but carried a larger turret housing the 75mm Type 3 tank gun, adapted for anti-tank purposes from the Type 90 field gun, itself a licensed French Schneider weapon. The turret was provided with side and rear doors. Only a few production CHI-NU were built in 1944. 18.5tons; crew 5; 1 75mm gun plus 1 7.7mm MG; armour 8–50mm; engine (1 Type 100, diesel V-12) 240hp, air-cooled; 24mph; 18.5ft x 7.66ft x 8.6ft.

37. MEDIUM TANK TYPE 4, CHI-TO

Similar to the earlier models but longer, with 7 bogie wheels on each side. Carried the 75mm Type 4 long barrelled tank gun which was developed from anti-aircraft weapons; armour thickness was increased to 75mm. It did not go beyond the experimental stage and only six machines of this type were produced. 30tons; crew 5; 1 75mm gun plus 2 7.7mm MG; armour 12–75mm; engine (1, diesel V-12) 400hp, air-cooled; 28mph; 20.75ft x 9.41ft x 9.41ft.

38. MEDIUM TANK TYPE 5, CHI-RI
Still larger and heavier, although generally similar to the previous designs, the CHI-RI had 8 bogie wheels per side. It carried the same 75mm gun as the CHI-TO but it had an additional 37mm Type I tank gun in the front hull. Since the Type 100 series of diesel motors with power output over 500hp was still under development, the CHI-RI was temporarily engined with one BMW V-12 petrol engine of 500hp. The end of the war precluded development beyond prototype stage. 37tons; crew 5; 1 75mm gun, 1 37mm gun, 2 7.7mm MG; armour 12–75mm; engine (1 BMW, gasoline, V-12) 550hp, liquid-cooled; 28mph; 23.98ft x 10ft x 10ft.

39. AMPHIBIOUS TANK TYPE 2, KA-MI
The KA-MI appeared in 1942 and became the most successful and best known Japanese amphibious tank. Basically a development of the Type 95 HA-GO light tank, it was intended to be used by the Imperial Navy landing forces. Two (bow and stern) detachable floats assured buoyancy and stability in water and could be discarded when the tank came ashore. Two screws propelled the KA-MI in water and steering was effected by two rudders connected through steel cables to a handwheel located in the turret. All-welded construction, and openings to the turret race could be sealed by rubber seals. Suspension was similar to that of the HA-GO but the compression springs were mounted within the hull. 12.5tons with pontoons; crew 6; 1 37mm gun, 2 7.7mm MG; armour 12mm; engine 1 diesel, 6-cylinders, 115hp, air-cooled; 23mph on land, 6mph in water; 24.58ft (with pontoons) x 9.16ft x 7.5Ift.

40. AMPHIBIOUS TANK TYPE 3, KA-CHI
Large and heavy amphibious tank based upon the CHI-HE design.

It was powered by the Type 97, V-12 diesel motor. Like the KA-MI, it carried fore and aft pontoons which could be removed for land operation. Running gear featured 8 road wheels and 4 return rollers per side, the road wheels being grouped in two sets of 4 resisted by externally mounted compression springs acting on bell cranks. The turret was surmounted by a circular chimney provided with an escape hatch. This could be discarded once on land. 28.8tons (with pontoons); crew 7; 1 47mm gun plus 2 7.7mm MG; armour 50mm; engine 1 Type 100, diesel, V-12, 240hp, air-cooled; 20mph on land, 6.5mph in water; 33.75ft x 9.8ft x 12.5ft.

41. AMPHIBIOUS TANK TYPE 5, TO-KU
Slightly larger and heavier than the KA-CHI, the Type 5 TO-KU amphibious tank featured an increased firepower: it carried a 47mm gun and a machine-gun in the front hull while the turret mounted a naval 25mm cannon and a machine-gun. Designed too late in the war, the TO-KU was not put into production. 29.1tons (with pontoons); crew 7; 1 47mm gun plus 1 25mm gun plus 2 7.7mm MG; engine 1 Type 100, diesel, V-12, 240hp, air-cooled; 20mph on land, 6.5mph in water; 35.45ft x 9.83ft x 11.08ft.

42. AMPHIBIOUS WHEEL/TRACK TANK, TRIAL TYPES 1 AND 2 (above)
Experimental vehicle produced in 1928 to test feasibility of wheel or track locomotion and amphibious capability. Could be driven at equal speed in either direction. Based in essence on the Citroën-Kégresse half-track idea, a vehicle of this type having been purchased from France. Type 1 had a boat-shaped hull with domed turret and stroboscopic vision cupola.

43. Type 2 was the same vehicle rebuilt with larger domed turret and no cupola, single propeller at rear operated via a power take-off from the main drive.

44. RADIO-CONTROLLED TANK NAGAYAMA
Converted Fordson agricultural tractor which retained its rear spudded wheels to act as sprockets for the tracks which were added. It was given a boiler plate enveloping body with raised cupola over the driving position. Used for radio control experiments and was not armed. (Between 1934 and 1945 Japan produced several very small remote control tanks as demolition vehicles, and in 1936 one Type 94 tankette was also converted to radio control for trials).

NEW ZEALAND

I. 'BOB SEMPLE' TANK
This was an International Harvester agricultural tractor fitted with a box-like superstructure which had loopholes for rifle fire from within. It was named after the New Zealand Defence Minister whose idea it was. Four vehicles were built in 1940–I. The design was unstable and the tactical value was limited. 20–25tons; 8mph.

2. SCHOFIELD WHEEL-AND-TRACK TANK
Named after its designer, this vehicle was conceived for local production utilising chassis parts from the standard GMC 6cwt commercial truck, an engine from the same source, and suspension units from a Universal Carrier. Open-topped turret had a 2pdr gun. The wheels were on pivoted arms and were utilised for road running. Tracks were used cross-country. Only prototypes were built. II,680lb; crew 3; I 2pdr, I MG; armour 6–I0mm; engine Chevrolet 6-cylinder, 29.5hp; 25.7mph on tracks, 45.6mph on wheels; I3ft Iin x 8ft 6½in x 6ft 7½in (on tracks).

British and American types used by New Zealand tank units, 1939–45: (see relevant sections for further details).
M4 Medium Tank (Sherman) (various models).
M3 Light Tank (various models).
Infantry Tank Mk III, Valentine III (some converted to CS role with 3in howitzer replacing 2pdr gun).
Infantry Tank Mk II, Matilda (various marks)

POLAND

INTRODUCTION

After the First World War, Poland was revived as an independent state by grouping together the territories previously occupied by Germany, Russia and Austria. The new Polish national army came into being soon afterwards from a nucleus formed by a Polish corps which had been organised in France. Interest in armoured vehicles soon appeared, when units of the Polish Army were sent for training periods with the French Army. One regiment of tanks, equipped with Renault FT machines, arrived in Poland in June 1919 and one of its battalions took part in the Russo-Polish conflict of 1919–20, which soon took a quite different form from the former entrenched type of warfare which had prevailed on the Western front. In Poland, small mechanised forces, combining armoured cars with motorised infantry and truck-drawn artillery, were often engaged in deep raiding parties.

The Russo-Polish War was ended by a peace treaty in 1921, and the Polish armoured forces were reorganised along French lines. While the armoured cars were given to the Cavalry, the tanks became part of the Infantry and were established into a tank regiment with three battalions.

Between 1923 and 1930, most of the activities of the Poles in the tank development field were concentrated on continuous attempts to improve the Renault FT tank. One of the first stages in this direction was by substituting new laterally flexible tracks — designed by S. Kardaszewicz — which were composed of twelve steel cables fitted with steel grousers. Although the speed was increased to 12kmh (7.5mph), the Kardaszewicz tracks were not accepted as standard and a similar fate occured to another pattern with steel plates introduced by an officer of the 1st Tank Regiment. Later, it was decided to up-date the Renault FT, at least as far as armament was concerned, by fitting it with a newly designed turret carrying both a 37mm gun and a coaxial 7.92mm Browning machine-gun. Some other redesigns were to increase the performance to 13kmh. A number of Renault FT tanks were also rebuilt into specialised variants including smoke producer tanks and radio/command tanks.

From late 1924 onwards, numerous conferences were held by the Polish military authorities on the subject of constructing a domestic heavy tank capable of a breakthrough role as well as infantry support missions. A light tank was also considered as a replacement for the Renault FT. Despite opposition from the Chief of the Infantry branch, the KSUS department drew up a specification for a new tank. Dated 1925, this specification requested a weight of 12tons, an armament composed of a gun with a maximum calibre of 47mm, complemented by one heavy and one light machine-gun, all-round vision equipment and an electrically started engine which could drive the tank at a speed of 25kmh, with a range of action of 200–250km. The go-ahead was given for a competition between the Polish S.A.B.E.M.S. and 'Parowoz' companies and a Czech firm, for the design of a so-called WB-10 tank. Sophisticated designs and even prototypes were submitted by the competitors, but trials conducted with them revealed that they were not acceptable. The WB-10 project was therefore terminated without further development.

In 1928, there appeared in Great Britain the two-man Vickers Carden-Loyd Mark VI tankette, a truly outstanding design which attracted a great deal of attention. This tiny tracked armoured vehicle could be either used as a machine-gun carrier or as a light tractor, and it was sold to numerous foreign states in one form or another. Poland purchased one sample from Vickers-Armstrong Ltd and soon went on to produce a domestic development based upon a similar formula. Designated TK.I, the Polish tankette was a 1.75ton, 2-man vehicle powered by a Ford motor. Through an intermediate model, the TK.2, further development led to the somewhat heavier TK.3 which was accepted as the production model. The TK.3 became the first armoured tracklaying vehicle manufactured in quantity in Poland. It was produced under the parentage of the state-run PZI institute, and orders for 300 machines were fulfilled from 1931–32 onwards. A TK.3 was demonstrated in Yugoslavia as a competitor for the Czech Skoda S-I (MU 4/T-1) tankette but no order was placed for it.

By the late twenties, little progress had been made in procuring new equipment. Several foreign tanks, such as the Czech wheel-and-track KH.50, the French Renault FT M.26/27 (with Citroën-Kégresse trackwork) and the Renault NC. I (NC.27) had been demonstrated in Poland but no procurement programme had been planned. The year 1930 was however marked by a significant event: the infantry tank regiment, the cavalry armoured car squadrons, and the artillery armoured trains, were all combined into an independent branch of the service. With a new internal organisation including two tank regiments, one armoured car group, and two armoured train groups, this was called the Bron Pancerna.

The need for a more powerful armoured vehicle — the tankettes being incapable of an actual combat role — forced Poland to turn her attention to a further Vickers product, namely the Vickers-Armstrong Six-ton tank, (Vickers Mark 'E'), which was soon to gain a worldwide reputation for a whole decade. In fact, between 1930 and 1939, Vickers-Armstrong Ltd sold over 190 machines of that type (tanks and tractors) to foreign countries — Bolivia, Bulgaria, China, Finland, Greece, Japan, Portugal, Russia and Thailand (Siam) — but the largest order came from Poland with a total of 50 (other sources give 38) tanks with either the single and twin turret arrangement.

The fact that the Vickers-Armstrong Six-ton tank was well within the capacity of the Polish technology, and as it offered some potential for further development, the PZI design bureau was entrusted with the study of a homemade copy. Subsequently PZI produced the 7 TP, a 9ton twin turreted tank which was to be a considerable step forward in design over the Vickers original. At first, the Armstrong-Siddeley engine of the Six-ton was replaced by a licence-built Saurer 6-cylinder diesel engine which developed 110hp, so making the Polish 7 TP the first diesel-powered tank to reach production status. The 7 TP armour was also 4mm thicker than the Six-ton armour. The first 7 TP to be built by PZI left the works in 1934 and production continued at a slow tempo up to 1939.

Around the mid thirties, the question of designing tanks in Poland had become a very controversial matter. Two schools of thought were in opposition: the first one defended the launching of domestic design and production programmes while the second one, represented by the Chief of the Armoured Force himself, considered this as a waste of time and money which could be better spent in purchasing well-proven foreign tanks.

One of the favourite fads of certain tank designers between the mid twenties and the mid thirties were the multi-turret tanks, relying on several guns and machine-guns to be able to fire simultaneously on different targets. While Germany and Japan more or less investigated the three-turret formula, only Britain and Russia translated it into fact with their A.9 and T–28. As late as 1936, Poland also dallied with the formula and drew up her 20/25 TP project of which three alternatives were proposed. The first one came from the government-owned BBT design bureau and was to have a weight of 23tons, a crew of seven and an armament composed of one 40mm (or 75mm) gun with three machine-guns, two of them being located into front sub-turrets. Maximum armour thickness was specified at 50mm. The second one, issued by the KSUS Committee, explored a diesel-engined 22ton tank, with a crew of six, a 35mm thick armour and the same armament as for the BBT variant. The third and last edition of the 20/25 TP project was a proposal from the PZI concern which put forward a design for a 7man, 25ton diesel-powered tank with an armour up to 80mm; being already outmoded since its design stage, the whole project was cancelled. It would have been a waste of money, and of limited Polish industrial resources.

Surprisingly enough, the development of the tankette concept had been continued in Poland over the years, through progressive steps. In 1933, the TK.3 had given rise to the TKS, slightly heavier than its parent. Powered by a Polski-Fiat motor, the TKS had armour protection capable of withstanding small calibre AP bullets, embryonic forms of optical equipment consisting of a periscope and a sighting telescope and a strengthened suspension. This newly patterned tankette had been put into production in 1934, with an order for 390 vehicles. Following the lines already taken by Vickers-Armstrongs Ltd with their Carden-Loyd Patrol Tank (1932), the next stage in the Polish tankette development emerged during 1934. It was a turreted midget tank designated TKW, of which only a few prototypes were constructed. An ultra-light self-propelled gun, fitted with a 37mm Bofors anti-tank gun mounted in the front plate, was designed on the basis of the TKS and became known as the TKS-D. A small number of such vehicles were constructed in 1936 but the design was rejected after trials. The TK series was finalised as the TKF; this variant was powered by a Polski-Fiat engine and carried two machine-guns, one of which was capable of anti-aircraft fire. In 1936 also, it was decided to investigate the possible adaptation of either the Danish Madsen or the Swiss Solothurn 20mm cannon for this type of vehicle but the trials conducted with these foreign weapons proved to be very deceptive and a homemade weapon of this calibre was eventually conceived. The Polish 20mm FK cannon was ready in 1938 and its mounting on TK.3 and TKS tankettes started in 1939 after suitable modifications of the vehicles. Only a few were so modified when the war broke out and brought to an end further Polish armoured fighting vehicle development.

When trying to find further successful foreign designs, Poland had turned her interest to the United States where, by 1928, J. Walter Christie introduced his fast tank chassis which utilised a new coil spring suspension acting on pivoted arms. Considerable interest in this Christie fast tank had been shown by the United States, Russia, Poland and later — via the Russian BT — by Great Britain. Orders for nine machines — five for the United States, two for Russia and two for Poland — of the newly developed Model 1931 had been accepted by the firm run by J. Walter Christie, the US Wheel Track Layer Corporation, of Linden, New Jersey, USA. However, Poland defaulted to take delivery of her two samples which were later purchased by the US Army to supplement the five machines originally ordered.

Polish interest in Christie tanks was to resume in 1936 when BBT drew up plans for a wheel-cum-track fast tank of its own but based upon the American design as far as the suspension system and the twin purposes running gear were concerned. The Polish version of the Christie tank was to mount the same Bofors turret and 37mm gun as the last Polish version of the Vickers Six-ton tank and be powered by an American La France V-12 cylinder motor developing 210hp. A prototype, designated the 10 TP, was actually built in 1938 and undertook trials. It was contemplated as the main equipment for the four mechanised cavalry brigades foreseen in the modernisation programme of the Polish Army, which had been laid down in 1936–7.

Some time later, a start was made on another project along the same lines but intended to run on tracks only. This 14 TP, as it was known, was to have increased armour to that of the 10 TP and therefore a greater weight. As far as the maximum speed was concerned, this would have been greatly reduced in comparison with its parent, the 10 TP which could run on wheels at a speed of 75kmh. Neither the 10 TP nor the 14 TP, of which the uncompleted prototype was destroyed in September 1939, reached production status. Such an unfortunate fate for these tanks which showed so much promise would probably not happened if the development of a Polish-made Christie tank had begun as early as 1932–3, on the basis of the 1931 machine which had been ordered then rejected.

While the production of the modified twin turret model 7 TP was proceeding slowly, it was decided to introduce a single version carrying a Bofors gun (the turret being manufactured by this same concern). This variant appeared in 1937, but the production was restricted by the difficulties of making armour plates and of procuring the turrets from Sweden. Afterwards, in 1939, some quibbles about its unsuitable armour thickness brought PZI to evolve a heavier variant with an improved engine, welded armour thickened up to 40mm in front, a strengthened suspension, wider tracks and a turret with a rear overhang which could accommodate both transmitter and receiver radio sets. The up-armoured 7 TP, which now weighed 11tons, did not have time to go beyond the prototype or, at best, pre-production stage.

Meanwhile other tanks were under development at the PZI design bureau in the form of two ultra-light tanks which came into being on a common basis, namely the PzInz. 130 and the PzInz. 140. The former was a variant developed specifically as an amphibious tank and consequently was fitted with a rudder and a three-blade propeller for steering and propulsion in water. Prototypes of both models were constructed in 1936–37, using the same PzInz. 425 6-cylinder engine as a power plant. Contemplated for standardisation as the 4 TP, the PzInz. 140 was fitted with a turret which could accommodate a 20mm FK light automatic cannon and a coaxial 7.92mm machine-gun, while the amphibious PzInz. 130 was intended to be fitted with the same turret but carrying only either one or two machine-guns. At one time, it was hoped that the 4 TP (PzInz. 140) would be amenable to a 37mm gun armament but this project was abandoned. Both models were tested during the autumn of 1937 and showed some promise but also revealed defects such as overloading of the suspension and, for the PrInz. 130, a lateral instability when swimming. From the purely military point of view, it was evident that such ultra-light tanks would be below an acceptable level of fighting capability because they were too thinly armoured and too lightly armed. In consequence no preparations for quantity production of these models were undertaken and the final fate of both prototypes is unknown. Two self-propelled gun projects, designed along the same lines, were also dropped.

With the political crisis which arose between Poland and Germany over the question of Danzig, it became vital to complete the mechanisation programme of the mid-thirties. In 1937, two horse cavalry regiments had already been converted — on paper — into motorised units, and the 10th (Motorised) Cavalry Brigade had been raised. This was later followed by a second large unit of this type. The formation of eight independent tank battalions was also considered, but if the weak point of the motorised brigades was the lack of suitable tanks, there were no tanks at all for the independent battalions. As a stop-gap measure until a range of new tanks could be produced, the Polish Armament Ministry decided to spend a French military loan granted in 1936 for the purchase, amongst other military equipments, of the complement for two tank battalions. Purchase of the S-35 was negotiated, but since this tank was not available for export orders, 100 light tanks of the R-35 type were ordered in April 1939. By August 1939 however, only one battalion, deducted from the French orders in production, had been received.

With the advent of the Second World War, Poland had 169 7 TP tanks, 50 Vickers Six-ton tanks, 53 Renault R-35 tanks, 67 Renault FT tanks, 693 TK and TKS tankettes and 100 armoured cars. Of course the Bron Pancerna was greatly outnumbered by the German Schnelle Truppen which were able to line up no less than 3,195 tanks (1,445 PzKpfw. I, 1,226 PzKpfw. II, 98 PzKpfw. III, 211 PzKpfw. IV and 215 PzBfw), supplemented by a number of formerly Czech PzKpfw. 35 (t) and PzKpfw. 38 (t), organised into 6 regular panzer divisions, 1 provisional improvised division and 4 light divisions. The famous Blitzkrieg tactics — combining an armoured sword-thrust at a vital point and deep sweeping actions with air dive bombing attacks — propounded by General H. Guderian, was employed for the first time and completely decimated the Polish armies in three weeks. Strangely enough, the R-35 battalion was not engaged in action, and on 17 September 1939, was evacuated to Rumania.

The unfortunate German-Polish War did not put an end to the Polish armoured forces. Many Polish soldiers having escaped to France, one 'brigade polonaise', with two battalions of R-35 tanks, was raised with them from April 1940 onwards. They fought gallantly during the French disaster and a number of them were, once again, evacuated to England. They formed, via an Army Tank Brigade and a reborn 10th Cavalry Brigade, the nucleus of an armoured division. Created in the spring of 1942, with Covenanter then Crusader III tanks, and later with Cromwell and Sherman tanks, the 1st Free Polish Armoured Division fought in Normandy, Belgium, Holland and Germany. Another Polish armoured brigade, formed in 1943 from personnel saved from Russian camps, had been engaged on the Italian front and later expanded into the 2nd Polish Armoured Division. Both units were demobilised after the war. When Poland was re-established as a state closely allied with Russia, the new Polish armoured forces received Soviet patterned tanks which were later built by Poland herself.

Renault FT: These French light tanks were in service from 1919 to 1930 with first line regiments, and for some time afterwards were used for training. During 1923 attempts were made to improve this vehicle by fitting a track that consisted of twelve flexible steel cables to which were attached steel cross plates. Though this increased the speed by 7.5mph it was not adopted.

Renault FT Modified: During 1932 a new type of turret was designed that was capable of mounting a 37mm gun and a co-axial Browning M.1920 heavy machine-gun. This turret was constructed of armourplate some 16–20mm thick and weighed 36lbs more than the original turret.

TANK PROJECT WB-10

First Polish tank design, the WB-10 originated from a 1925 specification to which three companies submitted designs for both wheeled and tracked amphibious tanks. Trial vehicles were built but later rejected and the project dropped.

1. TANKETTE TK.1

Two-man tankette prototype built in 1929, developed on the basis of the British Vickers-Carden-Loyd Mk. VI machine-gun carrier, one of which was purchased during that year. The TK.2 was a similar prototype vehicle. 1.75tons; crew 2; 1 7.92mm MG; armour 3–7mm; engine Ford 4-cylinder Model A 40hp, air-cooled; 31.1mph; length 7ft 9in., height 3ft 5in.

2. Tankette TK.3: Built in 1930, this was an improved version of the TK.1 and TK.2 models with an enclosed superstructure and slightly heavier armour. Quantity production was begun in 1931 and 300 machines were built. In 1931 a four-wheeled trailer was devised that could be towed behind the tankette and when it was necessary to travel on a road, the tankette was driven onto the wheeled chassis, the tracks removed and a chain drive was taken from the tankette drive sprocket to the rear axle of the trailer. The combined vehicles were steered by the tank driver from within the tank. 2.4tons; crew 2; 1 7.92mm MG; armour 3–8mm; engine Ford 4-cylinder Model A, 40hp air-cooled; 28.6mph; 8ft 5½in x 5ft 10in x 4ft 4in.

3. TK.3 mounting wheeled trailer.

4. TK.3 geared to wheeled trailer.

5. Tankette TK.3 Modified: During 1936 to 1939 experiments were made to modify and up-gun the TK.3, this included a redesigned front superstructure and the fitting of a 20mm automatic cannon in a large ball mount. A few TK.3 vehicles were converted to this standard.

6. Modified TK.3 showing redesigned front superstructure.

7. Tankette TKS: Developed in 1933, this was an up-armoured version of the TK.3 with thicker armour, a Polish-built Fiat engine, wider tracks and a strengthened suspension. The glacis plate was designed to incorporate a single ball-mounted machine-gun, and new vision and sighting devices were included. Quantity production of 390 vehicles commenced in February 1934. Twenty of these vehicles were built with cast armour. 2.6tons; crew 2; 1 7.92mm MG; armour 3–10mm; engine Polish built Fiat 4-cylinder 40hp air-cooled; 24.9mph; 8ft 5in x 5ft 9½in x 4ft 4½in.

10. Tankette TKS-D: This consisted of a 37mm Bofors anti-tank gun mounted on a reinforced front plate in the modified TKS model. The design was dropped after prototype trials during 1936.
Tankette TKF: This was the final attempt to modernise the TK tankette, this variant was equipped with an uprated Fiat engine, and armed with a combination mount that was comprised of a 7.9mm heavy machine-gun Wz 25 and a 9mm machine-gun Wz 28 mounted in a high angle mantlet at the front of the vehicle to enable it to engage low-flying aircraft. 2.6tons; crew 2; 1 9mm and 1 7.92mm MG; engine Polish Fiat 4-cylinder, 46hp, 26.1mph.

8. TKS captured by the Germans during the invasion of Poland.

11. LIGHT TANK 7 TP
Polish development of the Vickers-Armstrong's 6ton (Mark E) tank, twin turret model. It was powered by a Polish-built (Swiss-patterned) Saurer diesel engine and it entered in production in 1934. It had a thicker armour than the Vickers 6ton. 9.4tons; crew 3; 2 7.92mm MG; armour 17mm; engine 1 diesel 6-cylinder, 110hp; 19.9mph; 15ft 1in x 7ft 11in x 7ft 0½in.

9. Tankette TKW: During 1934 it was decided to equip a TK tankette with a fully rotating turret, the vehicle's superstructure was increased in height and a small armoured compartment was provided for the driver. The turret was mounted to the right of the driver and was armed with a heavy machine-gun. Only a few prototype vehicles were built.

12. Light Tank 7 TP: Single turret development of the preceding 7 TP, armed with a 37mm Bofors anti-tank gun and a coaxial 7.92 mm MG. Armour 15mm max. It was placed in production from 1937 onwards.

16. IO TP

13. Vickers 6ton Tank supplied to Poland.

Medium Tank 14 TP: Similar to the IO TP, it had a heavier armour and was designed to run on tracks only. Powered by a German Maybach motor The uncompleted prototype was destroyed in 1939. 14tons; crew 4; I 37mm gun, 2 7.92mm MG; armour 50mm (max); engine I gasoline 12-cylinder, 300hp air-cooled; 3l.lmph.

Heavy Tank 20/25 TP: Multi-turret design proposed in three alternatives by 1936. Not produced. Similar to the British Vickers-Armstrong's 'sixteen-tonner' and the Russian T-28. Contemplated with either a petrol or a diesel powerplant.

14. Light Tank 7 TP improved: Improved version of the single turret 7 TP, with a heavier welded armour, a new turret overhanging to the rear, a new engine, a strengthened suspension and wider tracks. IItons; crew 3; armour 40mm (max); engine I diesel 6-cylinders, 110hp.

17. SMALL TANK 4 TP (PZ.INZ. I40)
4ton, two-man light tank designed in 1936 as a reconnaissance vehicle. Its engine was offset to the right while the one-man turret was located to the left. It featured a torsion bar suspension. It did not go beyond the prototype stage. 4.3tons; crew 2; I 20mm automatic cannon, I 7.92mm MG; armour I7mm (max); engine I gasoline 6-cylinder, 95hp; 34.2mph; 12ft 7¼in x 6ft l0in x 6ft lin.

15. WHEEL-AND-TRACK FAST TANK IO TP
Polish development of the Christie wheel and track design. It was powered by an American La France, V-I2 motor and embodied an improved Christie coil spring suspension. The prototype was still on test when Poland was invaded, and all work on it ceased. I2.8tons; crew 4; I 37mm gun, 2 7.92mm MG; armour 20mm; engine I gasoline 12-cylinders, 210hp; 3l.lmph on tracks, 46.5mph on wheels; 17ft 8½in x 8ft 4½in x 7ft 2½in.

18. SMALL AMPHIBIOUS TANK PZ.INZ. I30
Amphibious tank based on the same chassis as the 4 TP (PzInz. I40). It featured a rudder, a three-blade propeller and the tracks assisted in propulsion in the water. Like the PzInz. I40, the PzInz. I30 was not accepted for production. 3.9tons; crew 2; I–2 7.82mm MG; armour 8mm (max); engine I gasoline 6-cylinders, 95hp; 37.3mph on land, 6.3mph in water; 13ft l0in x 6ft l0in x 6ft 2in.

19. Pz.Inz. I30 on water trials.

SWEDEN

INTRODUCTION

The first tank built in Sweden dates from 1921; patterned after a German wartime prototype, the LK.II, it was designated Strv m/21 ('Strv' for 'Stridsvagn' or 'Tank' in Swedish). J. Vollmer, the German engineer who had designed the LK tanks, also designed the Swedish machine and supervised its building, in order that despite the Versailles Treaty, he could carry on further tank development outside the jurisdiction of the Allied Control Commission charged with overseeing the German armament industry. The Strv m/21 was a 9.5ton machine-gun armed vehicle of which ten were built, and formed into a tank company thereby constituting the first Swedish armoured unit. In 1929 these tanks were brought up to date by receiving a new engine, a new power train and other improvements; they were subsequently redesignated as Strv m/21-29.

By this date the AB Landsverk company, whose factory was located at Landskrona in Southern Sweden, had come into being with German assistance. It was not long before they became involved in the armoured vehicle business to the mutual advantage of both Germany and Sweden. The Swedish concern acquired a high standard of technical knowledge from an exchange of technicians, industrial know-how and design studies whereas Germany, whose domestic tank development was still forbidden by the terms of the Versailles Treaty, could keep alive designs and experiments for her future Panzerwaffen. AB Landsverk initiated their programme of original tank design development in 1929 with the L-5, an experimental chassis combining both wheeled and tracked running gears. The L-5 pilot model was never fully completed but the basic design was developed further into the L-30 and L-80.

During the early thirties, AB Landsverk soon became one of the leading exponents of fast and versatile light and medium tanks. In 1931, they evolved an 11ton medium tank armed with a 37mm gun, the L-10, which was of relatively advanced conception. A small batch of L-10 tanks was produced for the Swedish Army under the designation Strv m/31. The company then put forward one of the most attractive light tank designs of the early thirties — the L-60, a 7ton vehicle armed with a 20mm cannon, for which a manufacturing licence was granted to the Hungarian Weiss company (the licence-built L-60s being used by the Hungarian Army as the 38M' Toldi). Later the L-60 proved to have a certain potential with a more powerful armament, and Landsverk progressed with various designs for the Swedish Army. In 1933–4 the tank department of the company had also turned their attention to ultra-light tanks of less than five tons in weight. They designed two such machines, the L-100 and the L-101. The L-100 prototype, developed in 1934, was a small 4.5ton tank armed with a single machine-gun and with a striking speed of 55kph. It seems that the L-101 design (which actually preceded the tank possessing the earlier designation) was dropped soon after the first drawing-board studies. Along with these types Landsverk had proceeded with the design of two wheel-and-track tanks, the L-30 and the L-80, which

represented the ultimate development in this type of armoured vehicle. The L-30 was tested by the Swedish Army as the Strv fm/31 ('f' indicating 'försöks' or 'test') but was not accepted for production.

Thus, by 1935 the AB Landsverk company had laid out six designs for either fully-tracked or tracked-and-wheeled tanks, weighing from four to eleven tons. All of them could be considered to be amongst the best of their time — they introduced some technical innovations such as independent suspension, magnifying optical instruments and co-axial machine-guns. They possessed clean lines and foreshadowed several of the features found later on German and Russian tanks, an outcome of the fruitful collaboration between Germany and Landsverk.

The first, albeit timid, move of the Swedish Army towards mechanisation dates from 1936, when the Government decided to organise one tank battalion within each of two old and glorious infantry regiments. Surprisingly enough, the Swedish Army's order for tanks was not awarded to AB Landsverk but to the Czech CKD/Praga concern, for a 4.5ton export light tank known as the AH-IV-Sv ('Sv' standing for 'Sverige' or 'Sweden'). This tank was built under licence by the Jungner company and redesignated Strv m/37. However, the next step forward was a Landsverk product, accepted as the Strv m/38 and derived from the earlier L60 which had proved amenable to a 37mm gun armament. Progressive development of the basic design led to the Strv m/39 and the Strv m/40 (Strv 33), two 10ton 37mm gun light-medium tanks, the latter being the first actual Swedish tank to attain a moderate production status, at first into its 'L' and then into its 'K' variants.

On the eve of World War II the shortage of tanks remained so acute that Sweden decided to purchase another CKD/Praga tank, the 11ton 37mm gunned TNH-Sv. Tanks on order for Sweden were seized on the production line when Germany invaded Czechoslovakia in March 1939, but, by an agreement signed between the Germans and the Swedes, the Scania Vabis concern was licenced to build the TNH-Sv which became designated Strv m/41 (Strv 35) in Sweden. The same tank had served extensively as the PzKpfw 38 (t) in the German Army during 1939–40 and its potentialities were further illustrated by the numerous self-propelled gun motor carriages developed later from its chassis.

Abroad the pressure of war had stimulated extensive development work on increasingly heavier tanks, a correspondingly uninterrupted race towards more powerful armament as well as better protection and an increased production tempo. In Sweden design and industrial resources had remained centred around the 10–11ton 37mm gun tanks and the Swedes were not prepared to be drawn into the arms-race; so from 1942 onwards all Swedish tanks in service were outclassed by their foreign contemporaries. As an attempt to bring their tank design up to current European standards, AB Landsverk produced a 22ton battle tank, the Strv m/42 (Strv 71), carrying a short 75mm gun; but by the time quantity deliveries were possible, in 1944, it was already obsolete.

1. STRV m/21
Designed by J. Vollmer, who built the German tanks of World War I, the Strv m/21 was patterned after the LK.II. It was powered by a sleeve valve type engine located in front, the driver and crew being in rear. The sprung suspension was protected by armour skirts. Ten machines of this type were built. M21 Command Tank was equipped with two-way radio; others had receivers only. 9.7tons; crew 4; I 6.5mm MG; armour 14mm; engine I Daimler 4-cylinders, 55hp water-cooled; 18ft 8½in x 6ft 9in x 8ft 3¼in.

2. Strv m/21–29: The Strv m/21–29 was a rebuild (1929) of the older Strv m/21. The modifications included a more powerful Scania Vabis engine (85hp), a new power train, heavier armour and other minor details.

STRV (LANDSVERK) L-5
The first design to be laid out by AB Landsverk appeared in 1929 as an experimental chassis for a wheel-and-track vehicle with a duplicate running gear. Designated L-5 by its manufacturer, the prototype remained uncompleted. The wheels were carried outside the trackwork. 5.2tons; crew 4; engine I 6-cylinder, 80hp water-cooled; 16ft 5in x 8ft 0½in.

3. STRV M/31 (L-10)
The L-10, which appeared in 1931, was one of the best tanks

produced by the AB Landsverk company and was singularly advanced for its time. Both hull and two-man turret were welded construction. Suspension system combined leaf and coil springs and it was powered by an engine of German origin. The L-10 was radio equipped and incorporated excellent optical sighting and vision devices. In 1934, a few were delivered to the Swedish Army as the Strv m/31. 11.5tons; crew 4; I 37mm gun, 2 MG; armour 9mm; engine I Büssing V-6-cylinders, 140hp air-cooled; 17ft 0¾in x 7ft 0¾in x 7ft 3½in.

4, 5. STRV (LANDSVERK) L-30 (STRV fm/31)
Retaining the same turret and similarly powered by a German engine, the L-30 was a wheel-and-track tank developed in parallel with the L-10 of 1931. Changeover from wheels to tracks and vice-versa could be done in 20 seconds even while the tank was running. Its wheeled running gear was fitted with balloon types. The L-30 was tested by the Swedish Army under the designation of Strv fm/31 but was not accepted for production. 11.5tons; crew 3; I 37mm gun, I MG; armour 6–14mm; engine I Maybach V-12 150hp water-cooled; 17ft 0¾in x 8ft 0½in x 7ft 4½in.

STRV (LANDSVERK) L-80
The L-30 was succeeded by the L-80, produced in prototype form in 1933. It was lighter and smaller than the L-30 but faster both on wheels and tracks. The wheel/track changing gear was similar to the one of the L-30. After the L-80 no further development of this type of vehicle was undertaken in Sweden and it was one of the last, if not the last, wheel-and-track designs featuring a duplicate running gear. 6.5tons; crew 2; I 20mm gun, I MG; armour 7–13mm; engine 100hp; 35kph on tracks, 75kph on wheels; 12.14ft x 9.02ft x 6.89ft (on tracks).

6. STRV (LANDSVERK) L-60

In 1934, the L-60 appeared, an AB Landsverk Light Tank, which introduced several design innovations later adopted on German and Russian tanks. A few samples were sold to Eire and its production under licence was undertaken by the Weiss Company of Budapest on the behalf of the Hungarian Army (38'M TOLDI). Through a series of modified variants that consisted of L.60A, L60B, L.60C (37mm gun). L.60D (new turret and 37mm gun and twin MG) the L.60 was progressively upgunned, and from 1938 onwards evolved into the Swedish Army Strv m/38-m/40 series. 6.8tons; crew 3; I 20mm cannon, I MG; armour 6–13mm; engine I Büssing NAG, V-8-cylinders, 160hp water-cooled; 15ft 1in x 6ft 7in.

7. STRV (LANDSVERK) L-100

An ultra light tank, the L-100, was proposed by AB Landsverk in 1934. Armament was to be a single machine-gun with a 20mm cannon as an alternative. The vehicle had a high power to weight ratio (29hp/ton) and a long track base which gave a stable gun platform over rough country. Mechanical layout followed that of the L-60. 4.5tons; crew 2; 2 MG or I 20mm cannon; armour 9mm; engine I 6-cylinders, 30hp water-cooled; 34.1mph; 13.4ft x 5.4lft x 6.07ft x 185cm.

STRV (LANDSVERK) L-101

The L-101 was a 1933 design proposal for an ultra light tank destroyer armed with a 20mm cannon. There is no evidence that the L-101 design ever got beyond the drawing board stage.

8. STRV m/37

Czech CKD/PRAGA design (AH-IV-Sv) built under licence in

Sweden from components delivered in crates by Czechoslovakia 50 vehicles of this type were assembled by the Jungner compan in 1938–9. The Strv m/37 was radio equipped. It featured th Praga four-wheel trackwork supported by half-elliptic leaf spring and it carried two coupled machine-guns in a turret offset to th left 4.5tons; crew 2; engine I Volvo, 85hp water-cooled; 37.2mph

9. STRV m/38

The L-60 series was evolved into the Strv m/38 with a 37mm gun replacing the 20mm cannon. The Strv m/38 was powered by a Swedish power plant of lower output and steering was controlle by means of a steering wheel. Only a small batch was produced by AB Landsverk in 1939. 8.5tons; crew 3; I 37mm gun, I 8mm MG armour 13mm; engine I Scania Vabis 6-cylinders, 142hp water cooled; 27.9mph.

10. Strv m/39: A progressive development of the Landsverk L-60 series via the Strv m/38, the Strv m/39 was produced only in small quantity in 1940. It featured a redesigned gun mantlet with two coaxial machine-guns. Steering levers replaced the steering wheel of the former model. 9tons; crew 3; I 37mm gun, 2 8mm MG engine I Scania Vabis, 6-cylinders 142hp, water-cooled.

11. Strv m/40 L (Strv 33): Another tank to be built to the L-60 basic design was the Strv m/40. It featured a number of technical improvements such as a hydraulic pre-selective gearbox combined with a high/low transfer box. The Strv m/40 was the first Swedish tank to reach the quantity production status. After being phased out the Swedish Army's service, some samples were sold to the Dominican Republic. 9.5tons; crew 3; I 37mm gun, 2 8mm MG; armour 24mm; engine I Scania Vabis 6-cylinders, 142hp water-cooled; 27.9mph; 16ft 1in x 6ft 11in x 6ft 10in.

160   SWEDEN

12. Strv m/40 K: The 'K' version was the late production model of the Strv m/40 whose manufacture was resumed by another manufacturer in 1944. It incorporated, along with some minor differences, a slightly heavier armour, with an up-rated engine to compensate. 10.9tons; crew 3; 1 37mm gun, two 8mm MG; engine 1 Scania Vabis 6-cylinders 160hp water-cooled; 27.9mph.

13. STRV m/41 (STRV 35)
Czech design (TNH-Sv) first ordered from CKD in 1938. Tanks on order were seized by Germany with the occupation of Bohemia

and Moravia (1939) but Sweden acquired a manufacturing licence for this tank which was built by the Scania Vabis company in two sub-models: S/I with a 145hp engine and S/II with a 160hp engine. In all 238 machines were delivered to the Swedish Army. The undercarriage was similar to the one of the Strv m/37 models (AH-IV-Sv) but embodied two return rollers instead of one. From 1962 onwards the Strv m/41 was rebuilt as an armoured personnel carrier designated Pbv.301 (11.5ton, 10men, 20mm cannon, 45km/h). 10.5tons; crew 3; 1 37mm gun, 2 8mm MG; armour 25mm; engine 1 Scania Vabis 6-cylinders, 145/160hp water-cooled; 27.9mph.

14. STRV m/42 (STRV 71/IKV. 73)
First Swedish 75mm gun tank, the Strv m/42 was designed by AB Landsverk in 1941–2. It ran on 6 road wheels each side, individually sprung by torsion bars. The Strv m/42 could be fitted with either one or two power packs. In 1958–60, it was modernised and rebuilt as the Strv. 74 (26ton, 4 men, 75mm gun, 45km/h) wih a long-barrelled gun. 22.5tons; crew 4; 1 75mm gun, 3 8mm MG; armour 40–80mm; engine(s) 1/2 320/410hp, water-cooled; 27.9 mph; 20ft x 8ft x 8ft 6in.

M4A3 medium tanks in action in France, July 1944.

M4A1 medium tanks in action, New Guinea, 1944.

M4(105mm) medium tanks move towards Bitburg, February 1945.

U.S.A.

INTRODUCTION

The first American tank designs appeared in 1916, after British and French tanks had been used in action in Europe, and before the American declaration of war they were essentially of a 'private enterprise' nature. The C. L. Best Tractor Co. demonstrated a mock-up tank which was essentially an armoured body with traversing turret mounted on a CLB 75 agricultural tractor. Another 1916 tank was the miniature HA 36 built by an engineer of the Holt Tractor Co. This was a reduced size one-man vehicle with a motorcycle engine, based in layout and characteristics on the lozenge-shaped British Mk I tank.

Early in 1917 the Holt company built two more prototype tanks at two different tractor plants. One of these vehicles, the G-9, consisted of an armoured body with a small rotating turret, placed on a Holt 10ton tractor — in essence, this was exactly the type of vehicle which Colonel Swinton had suggested to the British War Office. The other Holt vehicle was the Special 18, popularly known as 'Scat the Kaiser'. None of these early designs was taken up.

America declared war on Germany in April 1917, and it was then that official interest in tanks began. An expeditionary force was sent to France and the Army Command decided that it should include tank forces. In July 1917 it was officially decided to form a tank corps with light and heavy tanks. Staff considerations of requirements and procurement took until October 1917, when it was planned to order the British Tank Mk VI for American service, a total of 600 being needed. The Mk VI, an improvement on the Mk V, was still in the project stage at this time.

After analysing the effect of the Cambrai tank battle however, the staff officers on the tank corps project decided that a longer, more powerful vehicle was desirable.

This led to the adoption of the British Mk VIII Tank, then in the design stage, as an 'International' tank for Britain, America and France. A tank production treaty was drawn up in January 1918, with over 1,000 vehicles planned for each nation with a special factory in France to build them. There was a delay in implementing the programme, due to shortage of materials and only 100 vehicles (plus prototypes) were completed since the project was dropped when the war ended. It was 1919-20 before these vehicles were in service and they formed the backbone of the US Army's tank strength until the early 1930s. Mk IV, Mk V and Mk V* Tanks were supplied by Britain to the US Army in France as an interim measure for the heavy tank battalions. For the standard light tank the US Tank Corps adopted the Renault FT which was already in French service.

Arrangements were made to build a copy of the Renault in America, but in practice this necessitated a major redesign due to the variation in engineering standards between France and the USA. The American vehicle, known as the 'Six-Ton Special', later as the M1917 was greatly delayed and not in service until 1919. The American light tank battalions in France were, in the meantime, equipped with Renaults. Five heavy and 20 light tank battalions were planned for the AEF but the

tank corps had still not reached full strength at the cessation of hostilities.

In America there were several other projects under way in 1918. Chief of these were the Skeleton Tank, the Steam Tank, and the Holt Gas-Electric. There was also a Three-Wheel Holt Steam Tank and, in the heavy category, the Studebaker Tank, a troop and supply carrier intended for Anglo-American use, which was cancelled later that year.

Most notable of the new designs however, was the Ford Two-man Tank, designed for mass-production and utilising Ford Model T automotive components. Only a few vehicles were built of the 15,000 ordered. A larger vehicle, the Ford Three-man Tank was designed and ordered in quantity, but once more production was cancelled at the end of the war.

Immediately after the Armistice there was a rapid run-down of forces, a major reduction being the Tank Corps itself which was disbanded in 1920. Responsibility for tanks was passed to the Infantry who took over the few tanks which remained, including the 100 new Mk VIIIs. Funds were severely limited but a few prototypes including the M1921 and its derivatives, were built in the 1920s.

In 1922 a Tank Board was set up to define future AFV policy. This Board confirmed that tanks were mainly an infantry support weapon to facilitate 'the uninterrupted advance of the rifleman in the attack'. Two main types were proposed, a light 5ton tank capable of truck transportation, and a medium tank of up to 15tons. This weight limit was conditioned by the capacity of contemporary army bridging equipment. The new ruling meant that the prototypes then being produced (all in the 25ton class) were outside official requirements, though all were completed and tested. A 37mm gun, .30 machine-gun, and a top speed of 12mph were basic characteristics laid down for the 15ton tank. Design studies over the next few years led to the T1 series of tanks, produced from 1926 to 1931 in varying forms and fulfilling the 15ton requirement. The light tank requirement, meanwhile, had been dropped by 1926 as the Army considered the 15ton tank sufficient.

Other tank development work in America in the 1920s was carried out independently by the engineer, J. Walter Christie, who had novel ideas about the necessary characteristics of armoured vehicles. He was an advocate of fast, light tanks with big powerful engines and an effective suspension for high speed running. Christie had produced a self-propelled gun during World War I and built his first tank, the M1919 at the end of the war. From Christie there then came a succession of designs. His independent suspension system was combined with the ability of all his designs, for running on wheels only, the track being removed. The US Army tested most Christie designs and built a small batch in 1930 for the Infantry (Medium Tank T1) and Cavalry (Combat Car T1).

By this time the Cavalry had seen the need for mechanisation and the Combat Car T1 was the first of a number of designs acquired for cavalry units. In practice the Combat Car was a tank built for the Cavalry scouting rôle, but the different nomenclature was necessary to bypass the law of Congress of 1920 which made tanks the sole province of the Infantry.

In 1932 General MacArthur became Army Chief of Staff and instituted a full mechanisation programme for the Army. The Light Tank T2 developed from the TIE4, and Combat Car T5 (both vehicles with common chassis and mechanical parts) were developed from this time. By 1935 these were standardised as the Light Tank M2AI and Combat Car MI respectively. From the M2AI light tank and Combat Car MI, the whole series of light tanks, through the M3 and M5 of World War II fame, were developed.

In the medium tank field there was no new development until 1927 when a 22ton tank the MI apeared. Superficially this was similar to the British medium tanks of the time, though it had a 57mm gun. A small number of Christie Medium tanks was also built. Betwen 1930 and 1936 came the T2, T3, T3E2 and T4 all improvements on the original Christie TI design. There were 16 of the T4s, the most numerous output of a single design since the Mk VIII tanks of 1919.

In 1938 Rock Island Arsenal, the Ordnance Dept's main weapons design and production centre, produced a new medium tank design, the T5. This abandoned Christies' suspension system and instead utilised the volute system of the M2 series of light tanks. A series of developments from the T5 led to the M2 and M2 AI medium tanks of 1939–40, the US Army's most powerful tanks of their day. The Armament of these remained a 37mm gun however.

America was, of course, neutral at the outbreak of World War II, but the Army Staff lost no time in analysing the success of the early German campaigns, the invasion of Poland, and later of France. The German tanks had, in some cases, 50mm and 75mm guns, and weapons of this calibre were clearly going to arm more and more German tanks. The standard American tank gun was still 37mm and the chance was taken in America's great rearmament programme of 1940 to redress the balance. This led directly to the design and production in 1940–42 of the Medium Tank M3 (Lee) and its improved successor the M4 (Sherman). The M3, based on the M2/M2 AI chassis, had its 75mm gun in a sponson while the M4 had a turret-mounted gun. By 1942 when the Lend-Lease Act had become operative, these two vehicles became the key to Allied tank superiority over the Germans, able to outmatch in firepower all types of German tanks then in service.

Prior to the Lend-Lease Act, Britain purchased M3 medium tanks and these were modified to meet British requirements. They were known as the Grant.

The massive expansion of the American armed forces, in 1941–42, was largely achieved by co-opting industry for war production and development on a grand scale. In the case of tanks, where prewar production facilities were only available at Rock Island Arsenal, the enormous output required was achieved by using the resources of the automobile and engineering industries. Vast new arsenals were built in the main industrial centres of America, such as Detroit, managed and leased by commercial undertakings. Firms like Ford, Chrysler, Fisher, Baldwin, Lima, and Massey-Harris were involved in big operations of this nature. In many cases these firms originated ideas, or modifications which were taken up by the Ordnance Dept, or they produced designs to meet Ordnance requirements.

Over 40,000 vehicles based on or derived from the M4 Medium Tank were built in the 1941–5 period and the M4 was developed into dozens of different production models and special purpose variants. Major effort following standardisation of the M4 was devoted to the improvements of a technical nature which managed to keep the design and firepower abreast of German tanks. The Ordnance Department, in fact, sponsored a whole series of medium tank replacement designs, the T20 to T26 series vehicles, which were intended as M4 replacements. Only the T23 saw limited production but was not put into combat service. Instead of diversifying effort on new tank production, the Army used many features, such as the suspension, guns, turret and so on developed for the T20–T26 series, and incorporated these into the basic M4 design.

By 1944, however, there was a need for a vehicle with much heavier firepower. The German Ardennes offensive of December 1944, where the Königstiger and Panther tanks enjoyed great success against the M4 finally ended delays in getting a heavier tank into service. This was the M26 'Pershing' developed from the original T26 series of Medium Tank and mounting a 90mm gun. By the war's end efforts were concentrated on developing tanks with even heavier guns, though these designs did not see war service. As the war progressed, production and design schemes were rationalised to give a series of standard tank chassis in each class which would also be used as a basis for special-purpose variants. The 'Light-Weight Combat Team' in this scheme was based on the M24 'Chaffee' Light Tank, an excellent design which replaced the M3/M5 series of Light Tanks. The 'Medium-Weight Combat Team' was based on the M4A3 Medium Tank, the Ford-engined variant of the Sherman which was chosen as the standard type for US Army service. The 'Heavy-Weight Combat Team' was based on the M26 Pershing Tank. In practice these three schemes for standardised chassis types were not fully implemented until after 1945 since production of many earlier vehicles could not be phased-out due to demand on the fighting fronts, until early 1945.

I. CLB 75 TANK

Built by the C. L. Best Tractor Company in 1916, this was one of the first American attempts in tank design. Demonstrated at San Francisco early in 1917, it was simply the standard C. L. Best agricultural tractor with a simulated armoured body, armed with two light cannon in a revolving turret.

2. HA 36 TANK

Designed and built at the Holt Tractor factory in 1916, this was a one-man machine powered by a motorcycle engine operating through a special transmission. Tracks were made of link chain on which were bolted wood cleats. Fitted with dummy weapons, the HA 36 resembled in miniature the British heavy tank of that period.

3. CATERPILLAR G-9 TANK

Constructed by the Holt Tractor Company, this was one of several designs devised by the Holt Co. This machine was based on the Holt 10ton 75hp tractor, and consisted of an armoured box type hull surmounted by a small revolving turret in front and a larger one at the rear. Tested by the US Army Ordnance Department in 1917, the G-9 was not adopted.

4. HOLT GAS-ELECTRIC TANK

First American vehicle designed as a tank from the start, it was built in April 1917 jointly by the Holt and General Electric (latter providing drive units). Holt 90hp petrol engine operated a General Electric generator, which provided the current to drive two electric motors, one motor for each track. Varying the current to each track-driven motor steered the tank, a brake on each motor shaft holding the track on the side of the turn. The main armament, a Vickers 2.95in mountain howitzer was mounted low down in front of the machine and two Vickers machine guns were carried in side sponsons. Only one prototype machine built. 25tons; crew 6; 75mm Howitzer, 2 MG; armour $\frac{1}{4}-\frac{5}{8}$in; engine Holt 4-cylinder 90hp water-cooled; 6mph; 16ft 6in x 9ft 1in x 7ft 9$\frac{1}{2}$in.

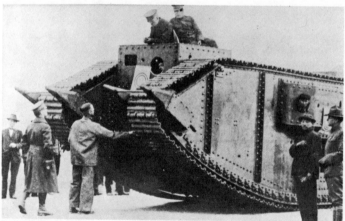

5. STEAM TANK

Produced by the US Engineer Corps during 1918, and based in layout and characteristics on the British Mk IV tank. It was built as a means to carry a flamethrower that had been developed by an officer in the Engineer Corps. The Steam Tank was planned to be steam driven so as to utilise steam from the boilers to provide pressure for the flame projector: this proved impracticable and an auxiliary 35hp petrol engine was installed to provide the pressure for the flame device, by this means the oil was put under a pressure of 1,600lbs per sq in and projected, ignited through the flame nozzle to a range of 90ft. The vehicle's motive power was supplied by two 2-cylinder steam engines, each with its own kerosene burning boiler, and each driving a track. As first fitted, the flame projector was in the front plate, but was later located in a small turret above the front cab. 50tons; crew 8; 1 Flame-thrower, 4 MG; armour $\frac{1}{2}$in; engine 2 2-cylinder Steam Engines 500hp; 4mph; 34ft 9in x 12ft 6in x 10ft 4$\frac{1}{2}$in.

6. THE THREE-WHEELED STEAM TANK

The third tank to be designed in the United States. Built by Holt in 1918, this vehicle consisted of a box-type armoured hull constructed on a tricycle wheel assembly. The hull was carried at the front by two 8ft diameter tractor wheels, and the rear of the vehicle was supported by a triple disc steering roller to which was attached a small steel plate, (a tail for trench crossing). Each front drive wheel had its own power unit, which consisted of a Doble 2-cylinder 75hp engine and kerosene fired boiler. Main armament, a 2.95in mountain howitzer was mounted low in the front of the machine, .50 Browning machine-guns were carried in ball mounts in the hull sides. One Prototype built. 17tons; crew 6; 75mm Howitzer, 2 MG; armour $\frac{1}{2}-\frac{3}{4}$in; engine 2 Doble 2-cylinder Steam Engines 150hp; 5mph; 22ft 3in x 10ft 1in x 9ft 10in.

7. THE SKELETON TANK

Built by the Pioneer Tractor Co of Winona, Minnesota during 1918, this vehicle was designed with the object of developing a light machine capable of crossing wide trenches. A lozenge-shape was achieved in skeleton form using ordinary iron pipes joined by standard plumbing connections. A box-like fighting compartment of $\frac{1}{2}$in armour plate was suspended between the track frames, containing a crew of two and the driving unit, which consisted of two Beaver 4-cylinder engines each of 50hp with forced water-cooling. Drive was via a shaft to the rear sprocket carried in a small container between the rear horns of the tracks. A turret surmounted the fighting compartment, armed with a .30 cal machine-gun. 9tons; crew 2; 1 MG; armour $\frac{1}{2}$in; engine 2 Beaver 4-cylinder 100hp; 5mph; 25ft x 8ft 5in x 9ft 6in.

8. FORD 3TON TANK (above, with original gun mounting)

Though designated 'tank' this vehicle was originally developed

as an MG or ammunition carrier. Designed by the US Ordnance Department in 1918, it was planned to utilise where possible, standard Ford automobile components, since the Ford Motor Company were to mass-produce these vehicles. The two man crew sat in the front of the machine, with the driver to the right, a cupola being provided for him. The gunner sat to the left, manning the .30cal machine-gun which had an arc of fire of 21°. In the early models the machine-gun was enclosed in an armoured tube carried in a ball mounting. This was replaced on later models by a heavier type of gun tube and mounting. Power was by two Ford Model T engines situated at the rear of the vehicle, each with its own electric starter, and a simple transmission system with a gearbox for each track. In October 1918 a prototype machine was sent to France for troop trials and met with the approval of the American Tank Corps, subject to certain reservations. It was planned to put the Ford Tank into mass-production, 15, 015 vehicles being ordered. However only 15 of these were built before all orders were cancelled after the Armistice. Some of these completed vehicles arrived in France in January 1919 to undergo trials as 75mm gun tractors. 3.1tons; crew 2; 1 MG; armour $\frac{1}{4}-\frac{1}{2}$in; engine 2 Ford Model T, 4-cylinder 45hp; 8 mph; 13ft 8in x 5ft 6in x 5ft 3in.

9. Ford 3ton Tank with heavier gun mounting

10. Ford 3ton Tank as tractor in France, towing 75mm gun and limber

11. FORD THREE-MAN TANK MARK I

As a result of the trials of the 3ton tank, the American Service of Supply requested the Ordnance Department to build a larger three-man version. This was to overcome the main failing of the two-man vehicle, its lack of gunpower. The three-man version was to be armed with a 37mm gun, turret mounted, and a machine-gun in the right front of the hull. While similar in layout to the two-man machine, it was longer and heavier. As with the Ford 3ton tank a separate Ford planetary transmission was used for either track, but the two Ford Model T engines were replaced with one 60hp Hudson 6-cylinder unit. Tests showed this vehicle to be unsatisfactory, and orders were cancelled in 1919. 7.5tons; crew 3; 37mm gun, 1 MG; armour 0.37–0.5in; 16ft 6in x 6ft 6in x 7ft 9in.

12. Studebaker Supply Tank: Ordered by the British War Mission in New York during 1918, from the Studebaker Pierce Arrow Corp, Indiana, this vehicle was planned for mass-production as a supply and troop carrier to be used in the battle operations of 1919. Similar in design to the British tanks of that period it lacked gun sponsons and was powered with a 4-cylinder 100hp aero engine. With the advent of the Armistice the contract was cancelled.

13. Tank Mark VIII 'Liberty': British design of 1917 for Inter-Allied use by terms of Anglo-American Tank Treaty. America was to build 1,500 vehicles of this type in the USA during 1918–19 and was to use a proportion of the vehicles that were to be built at a new Allied tank factory being erected in France at Neuvy-Pailloux. Production plans were delayed by material shortages and other factors and only the prototype was running at the time of the Armistice. Plans for full scale production were then cancelled, but it was decided to complete 100 vehicles using available components from the original production programme, and these were built at the Rock Island Arsenal during 1919–20. These vehicles differed from the British version only in the use of Browning machine-guns instead of the Hotchkiss, and in the use of the Liberty instead of the Rolls Royce engine. These machines remained in service until 1932. When withdrawn they were stored until the outbreak of the war in 1939; many of them were then handed over to Canada for training. One vehicle was modified during 1929 with a new cooling system by Heat Controlled Motor Co, with external power ventilator on hull side. Another Mark VIII was modified in 1925 by replacing the commander's box cupola with a stroboscope cupola similar to that of the French 2C.

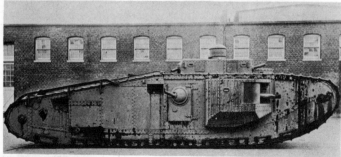

14. Mark VIII with stroboscope cupola

15. Mark VIII used for training in Canada, 1940

16. RENAULT FT LIGHT TANK
Standard tank for the light battalions of the newly formed tank arm. It was planned to build this vehicle in America. However only 10 American-built vehicles arrived in France before the war's end, and US light tank units were wholly equipped with vehicles supplied by France, about 514 in all.

17. BRITISH MARK V HEAVY TANK
The heavy battalions of the American Tank Corps were to be equipped with British tanks pending development and production of the Mk VIII Liberty Tank. Mk V and Mk V* tanks were supplied by Britain to American units in France, and American crews were also trained in England by the British Tank Corps using Mk IV and Mk V tanks.

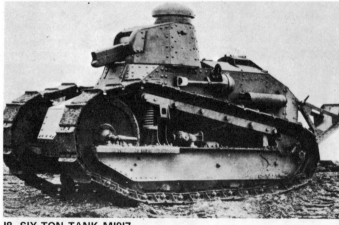

18. SIX-TON TANK M1917
To equip the light battalions of the American Tank Corps then being formed in 1917, it was recommended that the French Renault

FT tank be adopted. Specimen vehicles were obtained, and with manufacturers drawings these were shipped to the United States. Owing to the differences in the French (metric) and American engineering standards, it became necessary to carry out a virtual redesign, which also incorporated a number of improvements and changes. The steel-rimmed wooden idler wheels of French design were replaced with all-steel types, a bulkhead was constructed between the engine and crew's compartment, the Renault engine was replaced with a 4-cylinder Buda with the addition of a self-starter, and a new gun mount was installed that would permit the mounting of either a .30 cal machine-gun or 37mm gun. Under the code name of Six-Ton Special Tractor initial orders were placed for 1,200 vehicles, this was later increased to 4,400. The principal contractors for building the vehicles were the Van Dorn Iron Works, Maxwell Motor Co, and C. L. Best Tractor Co, all working under the supervision of the US Ordnance Department. By II November 1918, a total of 64 vehicles had been completed, ten of which actually arrived in France before the war ended. A total of 950 of the Six-Ton Tank were built before production ceased, and were the standard US light tanks until 1931. (Under the Lend-Lease Act in 1940 329 of these vehicles were sent to Canada where they were employed as training machines. 7.25tons; crew 2; I 37mm gun or I MG; armour 0.25–0.6in; engine Buda 4-cylinder 42hp water-cooled; 5.5mph; 16ft 5in x 5ft 10½in x 7ft 7in.

never been satisfactory, the air-cooled Franklin engine gave promise of permitting a modification likely to prove practical in modernising these outmoded machines. During 1929, arrangements were made to install this engine in a Six-Ton Tank: this was achieved by removing the Buda engine complete with clutch, radiator with fan and other minor parts, enlarging the engine compartment, and installing a modified Franklin air-cooled engine complete with clutch and with fan on a crank shaft. New idler track rims were fitted to reduce the noise which would arise from the increased speed of the machine. With an increased speed of 10mph and the noice reduced by 50% the trials of the machine proved successful. The War Department decided to modify 6 additional vehicles for service with the Mechanised Force newly formed in 1930. A more powerful Franklin engine was used with suitable modifications to the cooling baffles. After delivery of these six modified tanks, the first modified version was reworked accordingly. Modifications of the 6ton 1917 model were later discontinued due to a decision by the Chief of Infantry to cease developments in wartime produced tanks. 7.Itons; crew 2; I 37mm gun or I MG; armour 0.25–0.6in; engine Franklin 6-cylinder 100hp air-cooled; 10mph; 17ft 3½in x 5ft 10½in x 7ft 7in.

21. Pilot model for the M1917AI

19. M1917 in Canadian service as training machines.

20. SIX-TON TANK M1917AI
As the water-cooling system in both light and heavy tanks had

22. CHRISTIE MEDIUM TANK M1919
Designed by J. Walter Christie with experience gained from the construction of the Wheel-and-Track 8in Gun Motor Carriage in World War I. Built by the Front Drive Motor Co in 1919 to become the first postwar tank to be built in America. Originally projected as a dual purpose tank or truck chassis the M1919 had a low box type of hull which was divided into three compartments, driver, gunners and engine. A circular turret 5ft in diameter and 2ft 6in. high, mounting a 57mm gun in a large ball mount, formed the upper part of the fighting compartment, surmounted by a small dome-shaped turret armed with a ball-mounted Browning machine-gun. Both turrets had a 360° traverse. For road running the tracks were removed and stowed on the hull sides, and the centre wheels were raised. 13.5tons; crew 3; 57mm gun, I MG; armour 0.25–1in; engine Christie 6-cylinder 120hp water-cooled; 7mph; 18ft 2in x 8ft 6in x 8ft 9in.

23. Christie Medium Tank MI92I:

This was the 1919 medium tank rebuilt by the Front Drive Motor Co in 1921. The hull was reshaped, with the engine and final drive still at the rear, but with a re-arrangement of the crew's positions. The gunners were now transferred to the front of the vehicle where the main armament with two coaxial machine guns had been mounted on the front plate. The driver and commander were placed behind the fighting compartment, with the commander to the right, beneath an all-round vision cupola. Suspension was modified to two large sprung centre wheels replacing the smaller spring type of the MI9I9. Like its counterpart, this vehicle also had the ability to run on wheels or tracks. I4tons; crew 4; 57mm gun, 2 MG; armour 0.25–0.75in; engine Christie 6-cylinder 120hp water-cooled; 14mph; 18ft 2in. x 8ft 6in x 7ft 1in.

24. MEDIUM TANK MI92I (MEDIUM A)

In 1918 the Caliber or Westervelt Board was appointed to formulate a forward-looking policy and programme for artillery development and design. The report and recommendation of this board had however some influence on AFV development. The recommendation of this board in connection with tanks, was to develop one type, a medium which would replace both the 6ton (Renault type) and the Mk VIII of British design, combining in one basic vehicle the necessary characteristics of both these machines. The development of a medium tank was begun in 1919 under specifications laid down by the Chief of Tank Corps. The proposed vehicle was to carry as principal armament, a cannon of not less than 2.28 in or over 3in to be armoured against .50 armoured-piercing bullets at close range, be able to cross a 9ft trench, to carry a crew of five and to weigh approximately 20tons. The first machine built to conform with these specifications was the vehicle designated Medium Tank MI92I or Medium Tank A; this was produced at the Rock Island Arsenal to an Ordnance design. Powered with a Murray and Tregurtha marine engine, the weight of this vehicle fully loaded was 41,000lb. The armament consisted of a coaxial 57mm gun and a .30 machine-gun in a forward-mounted fully-rotating turret; superimposed on this turret was a smaller turret with a second machine-gun. One pilot model was built. 23tons; crew 4; 57mm gun, 2 MG; armour ⅜–1in; engine Murray-Tregurtha marine, 6-cylinder 250hp water-cooled; 10mph; 21ft 7in x 8ft 0in x 9ft 6in.

25. MEDIUM TANK MI922

Completed at the Rock Island Arsenal in 1923, this vehicle incorporated features of the Medium 1921, and adapted certain features from the British Medium D, including the flexible tracks with cable suspension and the track frame, with the rear of the frame higher than the front. This was intended to give the vehicle greater tractive ability in climbing out of trenches. By this time the development of these vehicles was hampered by new weight restrictions for this class of tank, having now being limited to 15 tons by a new War Department policy. This was imposed by the limited capacity of rail transportation, average highway bridges and field pontoons to carry tanks over 15tons. This amounted practically to scrapping the two experimental medium tanks, since the MI92I weighed 23tons and the MI922, 25tons. It was however decided to continue with the trials of these vehicles to obtain data for use in the development of a 15-ton tank. 25tons; crew 4; 57mm gun 2 MG; armour ⅜–1in; engine Murray-Tregurtha marine, 6 cylinder 250hp water-cooled; 15mph; 25ft 11in x 8ft 10in x 9ft 11½in.

26. MEDIUM TANK TI

Designed by the Ordnance Department, and built at the Rock Island Arsenal in 1925, this vehicle incorporated improvements found necessary in the trials of the Medium Tanks, MI92I and MI922. Similar in design to the Medium MI92I, this vehicle weighed 22tons and with its Packard engine had a speed of 14mph. Standardisation of this vehicle as Medium Tank MI was recommended in 1928 with concurrence of the Chief of Infantry, and was approved by the War Department, but approval was later withdrawn. The Medium Tank TI was modified in 1931 with improved ventilation and by installing a 338hp Liberty engine in place of the special Packard used. With this modification its designation was changed to Medium Tank TIEI. 22tons; crew 4; 57mm gun 2 MG; armour ⅜–1in; engine Packard 8-cylinder 200hp water-cooled; 14mph; 21ft 6in x 8ft x 9ft 4½in.

27. MEDIUM TANK T2

Designed to conform with the War Department's limit of 15tons for tanks, the T2 was built by J. Cunningham Sons and Co in 1930. This vehicle bore a likeness to the British Vickers Medium Tank. It was equipped with a Liberty V-12 liquid-cooled engine, and was armed with a semi-automatic 47mm gun and .50 cal machine-gun in the turret. It had a secondary armament in the right front hull plate that consisted of a 37mm gun and .30 cal machine-gun. This dual hull mounting was later replaced by a single .30 cal machine-gun. While having the same general armour protection as the TI, the T2, weighed only 15tons and in addition had a maximum speed of 25mph. Only one pilot model was built. 15.6tons; crew 4; 1 47mm, 1 37mm gun, 2 MG; armour 0.25–1in; engine Liberty V-12, 12-cylinder 312hp, liquid-cooled; 25mph; 16ft x 8ft x 9ft 1in.

28. CHRISTIE MI928

This was a turretless vehicle designed by Christie and built in 1928 by the US Wheel and Track Layer Corporation. Its main feature was its ability to run at high speed on wheels or tracks. Suspension was the original of what was to be known as the Christie suspension, and consisted of four large weight-carrying wheels on each side, mounted on arms connected to long adjustable springs housed vertically inside the side of the hull. When running on the road wheels the tracks were carried on shelves along the hull sides. The engine and final drive were placed at rear, the fighting compartment in the centre and the drive at the front of the vehicle. Though no turret armament was fitted, a mock-up gun was mounted in the nose of the vehicle and a pedestal mount for a machine-gun was fitted in the crew's compartment. On October 4 1930, Christie demonstrated his convertible model to an Army Board, as a result of which five modified machines were ordered by the US Army. Two of these tanks were also sold to the USSR under licence to become prototypes of the Russian BT tank. The Polish government also contracted for two machines but defaulted and these two machines were later accepted into the US Army. 8.6tons; armour .5in; engine Liberty 12-cylinder V type 338hp water-cooled; Track 42mph, Wheels 70mph; 17ft x 7ft x 6ft.

29. MI928 on wheels

30. CHRISTIE MI931 MEDIUM TANK T3

Produced in 1931 by the US Wheel and Track Layer Corporation and accepted into the US Army under the designation of T3 Medium Tank, these were the five modified versions of the Christie MI928 machine, now fitted with a 37mm gun and coaxial .30 cal MG in a fully traversing turret, the nose gun being eliminated. Four of them (Nos. 1, 3, 4, 5) were in 1932 delivered to the US Cavalry and re-designated Combat Car TI. The 37mm gun being replaced by a .50 cal MG. 11tons; crew 3; 37mm gun, 1 MG; armour $\frac{5}{8}-\frac{1}{2}$in; engine Liberty V-12 338hp water-cooled; Wheels 46mph, Track 27mph; 18ft x 7ft 4in x 7ft 6in.

31. Medium Tank T3 running on wheels

Medium Tank T3EI: This designation was given to the two machines that had been contracted for by the Polish Government, who had defaulted, the vehicle being acquired by the US Army. Similar to the T3, except that they were gear driven when operating as wheeled vehicles instead of chain driven.

32. Medium Tank T3E2: In 1932 the infantry ordered an additional five modified T3 tanks but as Christie failed to fulfil the terms of the contract with the Ordnance Department the order went to the American La France and Foamite Company where they were built, designated T3E2. Major change was a sloped widened nose and enlarged turret. II.5tons; crew 4; 37mm gun, 5 MG; armour $\frac{3}{8}$–$\frac{1}{2}$in; engine Curtiss 12-cylinder 435hp water-cooled; Wheels 15.26mph, Tracks 25mph; 18ft 9in x 8ft x 7ft 8in.

33. T3E2 running on wheels

Medium Tank T3E3: Similar to the T3E2, but with controlled differential steering and other minor modifications. Built by American La France and Foamite Company in 1936.

34. MEDIUM TANK T4

The Medium Tank T4 of which 16 were produced during 1935 and 1936 was also of a convertible design, built by the Rock Island Arsenal. The design was based on the Combat Car T4, the chassis being strengthened to carry the increased weight of armour. I3.5tons; crew 4; 3 MG; armour $\frac{1}{2}$–$\frac{5}{8}$in; engine Continental 7-cylinder 268hp air-cooled; Wheels 35mph, Tracks 15–20mph; 16ft 1in x 8ft 2in x 7ft 3in.

35. Medium Tank T4EI: Built at the Rock Island Arsenal during 1936, this version was fitted with a barbette type superstructure mounting 6 machine-guns, and was later standardised together with Medium Tank T4 as Medium Tank MI Convertible, Limited Standard. I5tons; crew 4; 6 MG armour $\frac{1}{2}$–$\frac{5}{8}$in engine Continental 7-cylinder 268hp air-cooled; Wheels 40mph, Tracks 25mph; 16ft 1in x 8ft 2in x 7ft 4in.

36. MEDIUM TANK T5 (above, phase I)

With the appearance of the Medium Tank T5, built at the Rock Island Arsenal during 1938, began the design of the medium tank that was to develop through World War II. Designed in the interest of economy standardisation to use as many parts of the Light Tank M2 as possible, the convertible Christie type of suspension was replaced by that of the vertical volute spring type. But even at this period the conception for the role of a tank was principally as an infantry weapon, this being emphasised by the armament of six .30 cal machine-guns sited on a barbette type superstructure to give all round fire. A rotating turret with a 37mm gun was mounted on the barbette. Various versions of this vehicle appeared undergoing changes in, armament, track and suspension, and engine. I5tons; crew 5; 37mm gun, 6 MG; armour Iin; engine Continental radial 7-cylinder 250hp air-cooled; 20mph; 17ft 3in x 8ft 2in x 9ft.

37. Medium Tank T5 Phase III (M2 Pilot): Similar to T5, Phase I, but with larger engine (346hp Wright Radial) and wider tracks.

38. Medium Tank T5EI: Phase I fitted with twin 37mm guns and Guiberson radial diesel engine.

42. M2 with E-2 Flame Projector: This was an experimental mounting of the E-2 flamethrower unit upon the M2 Medium Tank. The main armament was replaced by the flame projector, two flame fuel tanks being installed inside the vehicle. The propellant air tanks were carried on the rear deck.

39. Medium Tank T5E2: This was the Phase III model reworked. A 75mm Pack Howitzer was installed in the modified right front of the vehicle; the bow and rear corner machine-guns were retained. A small six-sided cupola with range finder and machine-gun replaced the turret. This was a test vehicle in the development of the Medium Tank M3. Crew 5; 75mm Howitzer, 8 MG; armour I–I¼in; engine Wright Radial 9-cylinder 346hp air-cooled; 18ft x 8ft 7in x 9ft 3in.

40. Another view of T5E2

43. Medium Tank M2AI: The M2AI was practically identical to the M2, except for thicker armour and a larger turret. Bullet deflection plates were attached to the front glacis plate as a protection for the driver's eyes. A supercharger was fitted to the engine to increase its rating to 400hp. Various other modifications were introduced. Standardised in 1940, it was already technically obsolete compared to the German Pz.Kpfw III and IV which were fitted with 5cm or 7.5cm guns. 23tons; crew 6; I 37mm gun, 8 MG; armour I¼in; engine Wright Radial 9-cylinder 400hp air-cooled; 30mph.

41. MEDIUM TANK M2
This was the T5 Phase III design standardised in June 1939 as the Medium Tank, M2. Production of 15 vehicles commencing at Rock Island Arsenal in August 1939. 19tons; crew 6; I 37mm gun, 8 MG; armour Iin; engine Wright Radial 9-cylinder 350hp air-cooled; 26mph; 17ft 8in x 8ft 7in x 9ft 4½in.

44. M2 fitted with British designed turret for trials

47. M3 with E3 Flame Projector: Developed in 1942, the 75mm sponson was blanked off and the 37mm gun replaced by the flame device.

48. M3 with Mine Exploder Device TI: Developed in 1940, this consisted of two roller units pushed before the tank and one roller unit trailed behind. Variations of this device existed from TI to TIE6, for adaptation to M3 and M4 Medium Tanks.

45. MEDIUM TANK M3 (above, early production model)

At a meeting in August 1940, between the Chief of the newly formed Armoured Forces and representatives of the Ordnance Department and specifications of a new medium tank were planned. It was to be a tank with heavier armour mounting a 75mm gun, and it was proposed that the 75mm gun be turret mounted. However, as insufficient development work had been done on the problem of mounting a gun of this calibre in a revolving turret, it was decided to use as a prototype the T5E2 Medium Tank, since experiments had already taken place with this vehicle, when a 75mm pack howitzer had been mounted in a modified sponson. With the T5E2 as a basis, it was therefore agreed that the projected medium tank would mount the 75mm gun in the right sponson, and the turret mounting of the gun would follow later. The resulting vehicle was the Medium Tank M3 of which the pilot model was ready by January 1941, with production vehicles coming into service by the middle of 1941. This was the first American medium tank to be produced in quantity under the defence programme, prior to the entry of the USA into the war. The Medium Tank M3 was dimensionally similar to the M2A1 and had the same Wright radial air-cooled gasoline engine and vertical volute suspension. The M2 75mm gun (M3 in later models) was in a limited traverse mount in the right sponson and a 37mm gun offset to the right was carried in a fully traversing turret. Turret and sponson were cast and the rest of the hull riveted, though changes were made in subsequent models. As originally designed the M3 had side doors; these were eliminated in late production models. Most important innovation of all however, was the installation of gyro-stabilisers for both the 75mm and 37mm gun allowing the vehicle to fire with accuracy while on the move. Six basic production models of the M3 were produced, and they were subsequently supplied under the Lend-Lease Act to the British forces where they were known as the Lee, after Robert E. Lee. Some were also supplied to Russia. Initial production type from April/August 1941 onwards. Riveted hull, side doors. 60,000lbs; crew 6; 75mm gun, 37mm gun, 3 MG; armour 1½–2in; engine Wright Continental R-975 9-cylinders 340hp; 26mph; 18ft 6in x 8ft 11in x 10ft 3in.

49. Medium Tank, M3A1: This was identical mechanically to the M3, but had a cast upper hull. Side doors were later eliminated to strengthen the structure, and provision made for an escape hatch in the hull floor. 60,000lbs; crew 6; 75mm gun, 37mm gun, 3 MG; armour 1½–2in; engine Wright Continental R–975 9-cylinder 340hp; 26mph; 18ft 6in x 8ft 11in x 10ft 3in.

46. M3, late production model

50. M3A1E1: This was an M3A1 used as a test vehicle with triple 6-cylinder Lycoming engines.

51. M3A5E1: This was a test vehicle to try Twin Hydramatic transmission.

52. Medium Tank, M3A2: This was mechanically identical to the M3, but had an all-welded hull mainly to reduce weight but also because it was superior to riveting in armoured vehicles. Some M3, M3AI and M3A2 models were fitted with Guiberson diesel motors owing to the shortage of Wright Continental motors and these vehicles were designated with the suffix '(Diesel)'. 60,000lbs; crew 6; 75mm gun, 37mm gun, 3 MG; armour 1½–2in; engine Continental R–975 9-cylinder 340hp; 26mph; 18ft 6in x 8ft 11in x 10ft 3in.

53. Medium Tank, M3A3: All welded hull as M3A2, but fitted with twin General Motors 6–71 diesel engines of 375hp. These were standard bus and track diesel engines that were in production and were authorised as an alternative power plant. Side doors were welded up or eliminated on later vehicles of this mark. 63,000lbs, crew 6; 75mm gun, 37mm gun, 3 MG; armour 1½–2in; engine twin General Motors 6–71 Diesel, 12-cylinder 375hp; 29mph; 18ft 6in x 8ft 11in x 10ft 3in.

54. Medium Tank, M3A4: This version was identical to the M3, but fitted with the Chrysler A-57 Multibank 370hp engine. This consisted of five automobile engines coupled together on a common drive shaft, and was devised by Chrysler to alleviate the shortage of Continental engines. The hull was lengthened by 14inches to 19ft 8in overall to accommodate the longer engine. Longer chassis and track were also necessary. Side doors were eliminated. 64,000lbs; crew 6; 75mm gun, 37mm gun, 3 MG; armour 1½–2in; engine Chrysler A–57 Multibank 30-cylinder 370hp; 26mph; 19ft 8in x 8ft 11in x 10ft 3in.

55. Medium Tank, M3A5: As for M3A3, but with riveted instead of welded hull; side doors welded up or eliminated on late production models. All late production vehicles had the longer 75mm M3 gun irrespective of model. 64,000lbs; crew 6; 75mm gun, 37mm gun, 3 MG; armour 1½–2in; engine twin General Motors 6–71 Diesel 12-cylinder 375hp; 29mph; 18ft 6in x 8ft 11in x 10ft 3in.

56. M3A4 with experimental suspension (original HVSS)

57. MEDIUM TANK T6

Due to the restricted traverse of the main armament of the Medium M3 it was intended to supplant this vehicle as soon as possible, by a tank mounting a 75mm gun in a full-traversing turret and utilising as many Medium M3 parts as possible. Design work was begun in 1940 and a prototype machine was produced by 16 September, 1941. Designated Medium Tank T6 the vehicle had a cast hull and turret, and mounted a short 75mm M2 gun in the turret. With modifications this vehicle was standardised as Medium Tank M4 in October 1941. 30tons; crew 5; 75mm gun, 4 MG; armour 1-½in; engine Wright Radial 9-cylinder 400hp air-cooled; 26mph; 18ft 6in x 8ft 8in x 9ft 7½in.

58. T6 Side view

MEDIUM TANK M4 SERIES

The M4 series was the most widely produced, most widely used, and most important of all tanks in service with American, British, and Allied forces in World War II. Popularly known by its British name of Sherman, the M4 was produced simultaneously by several different manufacturers, the various models differing from each other principally by their engines. Initially the engine was a Continental R-975 air-cooled radial type, but an ever-persistent shortage of this Wright-built power unit, forced the adoption of alternative engines thus giving rise to the main production variants. A further difference was that the M4A1 had a cast hull, whereas the other types were welded. A major design change before production began was the elimination of the hull doors of the prototype T6; this gave a stronger structure and simplified production. It was realised that the cast turtle-shaped hull of the T6 would present further production problems, as casting facilities at the heavy engineering plants would not be able to cope with the production figures set for this vehicle. Accordingly, a simpler box-like welded hull was designed which was within the less sophisticated production capabilities of plants without casting facilities or experience. The Medium Tank M4 had the same basic chassis as the M3 medium, with vertical volute suspension, rear engine and front drive. The 75mm M3 gun was mounted in a simple cast turret and provided with a gyrostabiliser as in the M3. A number of changes were made during production, with the result that later types differed from the earlier models. These changes included the lower front nose plate, which on the earlier models consisted of three pieces bolted together; later production models had one-piece casting. Introduction of sand-shields over the suspension, and the fitting of horizontal volute suspension distinguished later types of the M4 series.

59. MEDIUM TANK M4 (SHERMAN I) (above, early production model)

Standardised in October 1941, this vehicle had a welded hull, cast turret, 75mm Gun M3 in the M34 gun mount. Early vehicles had a three-piece bolted differential housing, and vision slots (these were later eliminated) for the driver and hull gunner. Earlier models had the track return roller mounted at the top centre of the bogie unit. Later production models of the M4 had the 75mm gun in the M34A1 gun mount, a combination rolled and cast front hull, and a cast one-piece sharp-nosed differential housing. Sand shields were also fitted. This late version when in service with the British Army was known as Sherman Hybrid I. 66,500lbs; crew 5; 75mm gun, 3 MG; armour 1–2in; engine Continental R975-C1 9-cylinder 400hp air-cooled; 24mph; 19ft 4in x 8ft 7in x 9ft.

60. M4 with three-piece nose

61. M4 with cast one-piece nose

62. MEDIUM TANK M4AI (SHERMAN II) (above, early production model)

Standardised in December 1941, this was similar to the M4 but had a cast hull which was curved to present less flat surfaces to a direct hit from any angle. It had the three-piece differential housing and vision slots in the front armour. The 75mm gun M3 was in a M34 gun mount. Very early models had the track return rollers at the top centre of the bogie unit, and the ports in the front hull for the twin fixed bow machine-guns. Later production models used the M34AI gun mount, additional periscopes replacing vision slots for the driver; the track return rollers were at the rear of the bogie unit. It had a cast one-piece round-nosed differential housing and sand shields. Some of the late production vehicles had appliqué armour attached to the turret sides or on the hull sides for extra protection. Some of them were also fitted with gun travelling locks. 66,500lbs; crew 5; 75mm gun, 3 MG; armour I–2in; engine Continental R975-CI 9-cylinder 400hp air-cooled; 24mph; 19ft 2in x 8ft 7in x 9ft.

63. M4AI with the three-piece nose.

64. M4AI, late production model with cast one-piece nose.

65. MEDIUM TANK M4A2 (SHERMAN III) (above, early production model)

Standardised in December 1941. This version was similar to the M4, with welded hull and cast turret, but was powered with twin General Motors 6–71 diesel engines. The early production model had the 75mm gun M3 in the M34 gun mount and vision slots in the front armour plate. It had the three-piece bolted differential housing and retained the twin fixed bow machine-guns. The track return roller was at the top of the bogie unit. On later models the return rollers were to the rear of the bogie mount. Some early models also had the cast one-piece differential housing, this type of housing being used exclusively on the late production M4A2s, which were fitted with a M34AI gun mount, appliqué armour on the turret and hull, and hatch guard plates welded in front of the driver's position. A gun travelling lock was mounted on the front and sand shields were fitted. Very late production version had 47 degree front armour plate and larger doors for the driver. The differential housing was a cast one-piece sharp nose type. 69,000lbs; crew 5; 75mm gun, 3 MG; armour I–2in; engine twin General Motors 6–71 Diesel 12-cylinder 410hp, liquid-cooled; 29mph; 19ft 5in x 8ft 7in x 9ft.

66. Late production M4A2.

67. MEDIUM TANK M4A3 (SHERMAN IV) (above, early production model)

This vehicle was standardised in January 1942, and was similar to the M4 with welded hull and a cast turret, but this version was fitted with a 500hp Ford tank engine. This was an 8-cylinder liquid-cooled V-type engine designed specifically for tanks. The early production model was equipped with the M34 gun mount, vision slots in the front armour and a cast one-piece round-nosed differential housing. The vertical volute spring suspension had the later model bogie with the return roller at the rear. On later production models the vision slots were replaced by persicopes for the driver and this model had sand shields fitted. The very late production model of the M4A3 had the 75mm gun in a M34AI gun mount, a vision cupola for the tank commander and introduced a small oval hatch over the loader's position. It was equipped with 47 degree front armour plate on the hull, had larger driver's doors and a cast one-piece sharp-nosed differential housing. A gun travelling lock was also fitted on the front plate. Some late versions of the M4A3 were provided with 75mm ammunition racks which had liquid filled containers on either side to prevent fire in case the side of the vehicle was pierced. This was referred to as wet stowage. Vehicles fitted with this device were designated M4A3W. All M4s (76mm) series were equipped with wet stowage. 68,500lbs; crew 5; 75mm gun, 3 MG; armour I–2in; engine Ford GAA-III, 8-cylinder 500hp, liquid-cooled; 25mph; I9ft 4½in x 8ft 7in x 9ft.

68. Late production M4A3

69. MEDIUM TANK M4A4 (SHERMAN V) (above, early production model)

This vehicle was standardised in February 1942, and was generally similar to the M4, but was powered by the Chrysler 5-line water-cooled tank engine. This consisted of five conventional car engines, geared together to operate as a single unit. To obtain sufficient clearance for this power unit, the hull was extended 6in, and a modified vertical volute spring suspension was used. A longer track with 83 shoes was required, as compared to 79 shoes for other models. Early models mounted the 75mm gun M3 in an M34 gun mount, had vision slots in the front armour, and a three-piece bolted differential housing. The late 1943 production model had the M34 gun mount replaced with an M34AI mount. The vision slots were eliminated and periscopes were installed

for the drivers. The three-piece bolted differential housing was still retained. 71,000lbs; crew 5; 75mm gun, 3 MG; armour I–2in; engine Chrysler 5-line 30-cylinder 425hp, water-cooled; 25mph; I9ft I0½in x 8ft 7in x 9ft.

70. Late production M4A4.

7I. MEDIUM TANK M4A6

Like the M4A4, this vehicle had a lengthened hull to permit the installation of the Ordnance RD-1820 air-cooled diesel engine. Tracks of 83 shoes were used. This vehicle had the combination rolled and cast upper hull with a cast one-piece sharp-nosed differential housing. The 75mm gun was mounted in an M34AI gun mount, the suspension was the vertical volute spring, and sand shields were fitted. The dimensions of the engine necessitated bolstering the floor and top plates of the hull, reducing ground clearance and restricting traverse of the gun. Production difficulties and the increased demands for tractors resulted in cancellation of production of this version. A total of 75 of these vehicles were built from October 1943 to February 1944. Some of the M4A6 models had appliqué armour on the hull sides to protect the 75mm ammunition racks. 71,000lbs; crew 5; 75mm gun, 3 MG; armour I–2in; engine Ordnance RD-1820 9-cylinder 497hp; 25mph; I9ft I0½in x 8ft 7in x 9ft.

72. M4A3 with 32½in detachable grousers

Experimental Suspensions

Wider tracks were obtained by fitting extended end connectors (better known as grousers) these provided better traction in mud and under winter conditions, and were widely used in the European theatre of operations. Experiments were made with the suspension of the M4 to improve the riding qualities of the vehicle, and to provide a more stable firing platform. From the various tracks and suspensions that were experimented with, was evolved the horizontal volute spring suspension (HVSS). This had wider tracks with centre line guides, horizontal springs, shock absorbers, and rubber tyred road and idler wheels. This suspension was standardised and incorporated into later production M4 series, replacing the vertical volute spring type.

73. M4AI with TI6 half-track suspension units.

74. M4A2 with 24in tracks and torsion bar suspension.

Office of the Chief of Ordnance – Detroit
Neg. No. 3498   1-13-44   Development Branch
Allis – Chalmers Horizontal Spring Suspension – Side View.
Vehicle – M4A4 Medium Tank.

75. M4A4 with Chalmers horizontal spring suspension.

76. M4A4 fitted with early form of horizontal spring suspension.

77. M4A3 fitted with horizontal spring suspension and 23in track. This became the standardised type.

78. MEDIUM TANK M4E6

To provide greater firepower for the medium tanks, the Ordnance Department initiated a project for the development of a 76mm high velocity tank gun in July 1942, and the completed gun, the TI which had been designed to use the existing 3-inch armour-piercing round was standardised in September 1942 as the 76mm Gun MI. Mounted in the standard turret of a Medium Tank M4AI, the trials of this adaption proved impracticable, and further trials were later made with a turret that had been designed for the Medium Tank, T23. This pilot model was designated M4E6. Though the tests of the M4E6 proved satisfactory, the Armored Command recommended that quantity production of this gun tank be deferred until it had thoroughly tested pilot models and determined their tactical suitability; the Ordnance Department was instructed to procure no more than twelve Sherman tanks mounting the 76mm gun. Due to the lack of interest the entire project was later dropped and was not revived until August 1943, when Headquarters Armored Command recommended the procurement of 1,000 medium tanks armed with the 76mm gun. The first production tanks mounting the 76mm gun built as a result of this recommendation were completed in January 1944. In February 1944, standardisation was recommended and approved of Medium Tanks, M4, M4A1, M4A2 and M4A3 with the 76mm gun. The designation 'wet' was added in May 1945 to indicate adoption of this modification for the ammunition stowage.

79. Experimental mounting of the 76mm gun T1 in a M4A1 medium tank.

MEDIUM TANK, M4 (76mm)

This version was provided with the 76mm gun M1A1 or M1A2 (these guns differed in that the M1A2 had the muzzle end threaded for the attachment of a muzzle brake). This weapon was mounted with a stabiliser in a power-operated 360° traverse turret and the gun could be elevated from —10 degrees to +25 degrees. The 76mm gun used 3in ammunition with muzzle velocity, maximum range and armour penetration considerably greater than that of 75mm ammunition. The 3in APC projectile M62 fired from the 76mm gun had a range of 16,100 yards and could penetrate 4in of face-hardened armour at 1,000 yards. A commander's vision cupola was mounted above the turret hatch equipped with six prismatic vision blocks of 3in laminated bullet-resistant glass that afforded a wide view. A travelling clamp was provided on the front of the hull to support the gun barrel when travelling in non-combat zones. Water protected ammunition racks were provided. 70,000lbs; crew 5; 76mm gun, 3 MG; armour 1½–2½in; engine Continental R975-C1 9-cylinder 400hp, air-cooled; 24mph; 20ft 4in x 8ft 9½in x 9ft 9in.

80. MEDIUM TANK M4A1 (76mm) (SHERMAN IIA)

The first production version of this vehicle mounted a 76mm gun M1A1 in a turret similar to that of the Medium Tank, T23, a pistol port being added for the loader.' A vision cupola was provided for the commander with a gun ring hatch over the loader's position. Vertical volute spring suspension was replaced on later models by the horizontal volute spring suspension, a small oval hatch replaced the gun ring over the loader's position, and the 76mm gun M1A1 was replaced with the M1A1C or M1A2 with a muzzle brake. 70,000lbs; crew 5; 75mm gun, 3 MG; armour 1½–2½in; engine Continental R975-C1 9-cylinder 400hp air-cooled; 24mph; 20ft 4in x 8ft 9½in x 9ft 9in.

81. M4A1 (76mm) with horizontal volute spring suspension.

82. MEDIUM TANK M4A2 (76mm) (SHERMAN IIIA)

This version was armed with the 76mm M1A1C or M1A2 mounted in the later cylindrical 76mm turret with a vision cupola for the commander and a small oval loader's hatch. The hull had a 47 degree front armour plate and cast one-piece sharp nosed differential housing. The suspension of the later models was of the horizontal volute spring type. British designation of late model was Sherman IIIAY. 72,800lbs; crew 5; 76mm gun, 3 MG; armour 1½–2½in; engine General Motors Twin 6–71 Diesel 12-cylinder 410hp, water-cooled; 29mph; 20ft 8in x 8ft 9½in x 9ft 9in.

83. M4A2 (76 mm) with horizontal volute spring suspension.

84. MEDIUM TANK M4A3 (76mm) (SHERMAN IVA)

First production models were armed with a 76mm gun MIAI in turret similar to that of the Medium Tank, T23. A vision cupola was provided for the commander and a gun ring over the loader's position. This vehicle had a 47 degree front armour plate with the cast one-piece sharp nosed differential housing. Fitted with vertical volute spring suspension and sandshields. The final production version had the wide track horizontal volute spring suspension with a small oval hatch replacing the gun ring over the loader's position. The gun was a 76mm MIAIC or MIA2 with muzzle brake. 71,100lbs; crew 5; 76mm gun, 3 MG; armour 1½–2½in; engine Ford GAA-III 8-cylinder 500hp, liquid-cooled; 26mph; 20ft 7½in x 8ft 9½in x 9ft 9in.

85. M4A3 (76mm) HVSS

86. MEDIUM TANK M4 (105mm HOWITZER) SERIES (above, M4A4EI)

Design studies for the mounting of the 105mm howitzer in the turret of the M4 Medium Tank had been recommended in 1941, and work on this project was started at the Aberdeen Proving Ground in March 1942. In November 1942 two Medium Tanks,

M4A4 were modified to mount the 105mm howitzer in combination with a .30 calibre machine-gun, these pilot models were designated M4A4EI. Further modifications were made with two M4 vehicles designated M4E5. Changes were suggested by the Armored Force Board after tests, and these vehicles so modified were standardised as M4 (105mm How) and M4A3 (105mm How) in July, 1943. Production of these vehicles began in February and May 1944, respectively. This modification of the Medium Tank M4 and M4A3 was designed to combine the firepower of a 105 howitzer with the performance of a medium tank and to replace the 75mm Howitzer Motor Carriage in Battalion Headquarters Companies of Medium Tank Battalions. The 105mm Howitzer M4 was mounted in a combination gun mount M52 with one coaxial .30cal machine-gun. Other armament was as for M4 and M4A3 Medium Tanks. Howitzer rounds carried totalled 66.

87. Medium Tank, M4E5: Test vehicle for 105mm Howitzer.

88. MEDIUM TANK M4 (105mm HOWITZER) (SHERMAN IB)

This version had a gun ring hatch for the commander and a small oval hatch over the loader's position. The differential housing was the cast one-piece sharp nosed type and the front armour was set at 47 degrees. Early models were fitted with the vertical volute spring suspension and sandshields, on later production the suspension was changed to the wide track horizontal volute type. British designation for this late production vehicle was Sherman IBY. 66,500lbs; crew 5; 105mm Howitzer, 3 MG; armour 1½–2in; engine Continental R975-CI 9-cylinder 400hp, air-cooled; 24mph; 19ft 4in x 8ft 7in x 9ft 2⅛in.

89. M4 (105mm) HVSS

90. MEDIUM TANK M4A3 (105mm HOWITZER) (SHERMAN IVB)

This version had a vision cupola for the commander and a small oval hatch over the loader's position. In common with all Shermans mounting the 105mm howitzer there were two ventilators on the turret top. This variant also had the 47 degree front armour and the cast one-piece sharp nosed differential housing. Suspension was of the vertical volute spring type with sand shields, this suspension being changed on the final production models to the wider track horizontal volute spring type. 68,500lbs; crew 5; 105mm Howitzer, 3 MG; armour 1½–2in; engine Ford GAA-III 8-cylinder 500hp, liquid-cooled; 26mph; 19ft 4½in x 8ft 7in x 9ft 2¹¹⁄₁₆in.

91. M4A3 (105mm Howitzer) HVSS

92. ASSAULT TANK M4A3E2

In early 1944, with the scheduled second front fast approaching, it was apparent that there existed an immediate need for an assault tank in the European theatre of operations for the close support of infantry. As the heavy tank T26E1 had not yet been accepted and in any case would not be ready in time to meet this demand, changes were made with the standard M4A3 to produce a compromise design able to withstand the heavy punishment an assault tank could expect. Designated M4A3E2, this reworked version of the M4A3 had rolled armour of 12in thickness welded to the sloping front plate of the hull and to the upper sideplates of the hull, a thicker final drive casting was used, and a new turret was installed with an armour thickness of 6in, this was provided

with a gun mount shield of 7in thick. Standard suspension and tracks were used, with extended end connectors. Powered by the Ford GAA engine, this vehicle with increased armour weighed about 42tons. Armed with the 75mm gun M3, this was replaced on some vehicles in the field with the 76mm gun, this being carried out by the Ninth Army Ordnance to increase the hitting power of this vehicle. The procurement of 254 M4A3E2 assault tanks was authorised in March 1944, and these were produced at the Grand Blanc Tank Arsenal, May–June 1944. 84,000lbs; crew 5; 75mm gun, 3 MG; armour 4½–5½in; engine Ford GAA-III, 8-cylinder 500hp, liquid-cooled; 22mph; 20ft 7in x 9ft 3½in x 11ft 2⅞in.

93. M4A3E2 (76mm)

94. M4 WITH SPECIAL DEVICES

Rocket Launchers T34 (Calliope): This consisted of 60 unit 4.6in rocket projector mounted on a frame above tank turret, the two bottom rows of 12 tubes could be jettisoned.

Rocket Launcher T34E1: As for T34, but with two bottom rows of 14 tubes. Mounted on M4A1.

95. Rocket Launcher T34E2: This device consisted of 60 7.2in rockets, with the firing tubes arranged in three units, the top unit of two banks of 18 tubes each, the lower two in two banks, six tubes to a bank.

Rocket Launcher T39: This launcher held 20 7.2in rockets; it was of box construction with opening and closing doors.

96. Rocket Launcher T40 (MI7): Mounted on the M4A1, this consisted of a box type frame. The rockets could be fired single or automatic. The device could be jettisoned from within the tank by means of hydraulic controls.

97. Rocket Launcher T40 (Short version): This device was similar

to the T40, but with shorter tubes, and was mounted on a modified M4A2. The primary gun of the tank was removed and replaced by an installation which contained the elevation mechanism for the launch. The tank was further modified by an access door in the side.

98. Rocket Launcher T72: Similar to the Rocket Launcher device T34, but with 60 short tubes containing 4.6in rockets.

99. Rocket Launcher T73: The T73 device was elevated independently of the tank turret. Approximately 10ft long it was of box construction, and carried ten 7.2in rockets.

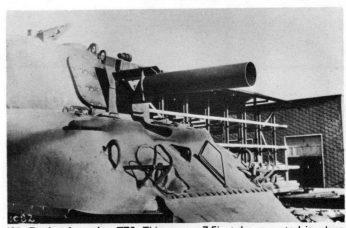

100. Rocket Launcher T76: This was a 7.5in tube mounted in place of the 75mm gun. It was reloaded from inside the tank and had an open section forward of the turret through which the gases escaped during firing. The launcher was capable of elevation and traverse as a normal gun turret and fired a 7.2in rocket.

101. Rocket Launcher T76EI: This device was similar to the Rocket Launcher T76, and was mounted on the M4A3 (76mm) replacing the 76mm gun. This vehicle is also equipped with a T73 rocket launcher on the turret and a dozer blade.

102. Rocket Launcher T105: Mounted in the turret of a M4A1, this was a similar device to the Rocket launcher T76 but was of box construction.

103. Multiple Rocket Launcher T99: This device consisted of two box type launcher containers mounted either side of the turret. Each box held 22 4.5in rockets. Small charges were used to jettison the launchers after use.

104. T31 Demolition Tank: This experimental tank used the M4 chassis with horizontal volute spring suspension and a specially

designed turret. A howitzer was mounted in the centre of the turret face, with two machine-gun ball mounts, and two T94 rocket launchers were mounted each side of the turret.

105. Mine Exploder TIE3 (MI) (Aunt Jemima): Developed in 1943 and put into limited production, this device consisted of two roller units, each of five 10ft diameter steel discs driven by roller chain from tank drive sprocket. Mine exploder, TIE6 was a similar device, but with serrated edges to the discs.

106. Mine Exploder TIE6

107. Mine Exploder TIE4: Developed as a more manoeuvrable version than the previous disc type devices. This 1944 development consisted of 16 discs 48in in diameter individually mounted through rubber torsion elements in a single heavy frame unit pushed by a modified M4 tank and suspended by a heavy curved articulated boom.

108. Mine Exploder T3: Development of the T3 device was begun in 1942 and was based on the British Scorpion flail device. This consisted of two booms extending forward from the tank with a rotating shaft fitted with chains to beat the ground as the vehicle advanced. Power for the rotor was obtained from an outboard auxiliary engine.

Mine Exploder, T3EI: This was developed in 1943, and was a lighter version of the Mine Exploder T3, with the rotor power derived from the main tank engine.

I09. Mine Exploder T3E2: The experimental model was a further development of the Mine Exploder T3 series, with the rotor replaced by a steel drum and rotor power derived from two outboard auxiliary engines.

II0. Improvised Flail: This flailing equipment was used in the Pacific area and was constructed by the US Marines and Navy Construction Engineers (Seabees).

III. Mine Excavator T5E3: Approved for limited procurement in June 1944, this device was developed from Mine Excavator models T5, T5E2 and T6E2, and was intended for clearing mines on beaches or sandy soil. The entire device could be jettisoned when required and was interchangeable with the tank bulldozer blade.

II2. Mine Exploder T8: This experimental device consisted of a series of vertical plunger rods mounted on a pivoted frame in front of the vehicle, geared to strike the ground as the vehicle moved forward. Tested in 1944, only one pilot model was built.

II3. Mine Exploder T9EI: This consisted of a heavy, drum type roller mounted on a framework and attached to the front of a medium tank. Spuds cast in the roller were intended to penetrate the ground and detonate buried mines. Two versions built, the T9 and T9EI. A lighter roller was tested on the T9EI. Project was cancelled in September 1944 due to poor performance.

II4. Mine Exploder TII (mine destroyer and demolition vehicle): This was an experimental device mounted on the front of an M4A4, and consisted of six mortar discharger on a elevatable frame. It was intended for launching spigot mortar bombs against mine-fields, to explode the mines by blast, or for use against obstacles.

II5. M4 (Doozit): Vehicle equipped with T40 Rocket Launcher (Short version) and dozer-blade, carried on the blade was a wooden platform of explosives for placing against concrete obstacles.

116. M3-4-3 Flamethrower: Supplied as a kit for fitting in the field when necessary, this consisted of a flame projector that was installed in place of the bow machine-gun and a 22 gallon fuel tank located in the right sponson.

117. Close-up of the Flamethrower

118. POA-CWS 75-HI Flamethrower: This was a Pacific theatre improvisation using a US Navy Mk I flamethrower with the projector tube fitted inside the barrel of an old 75mm M3 gun. Used in the M4, M4AI and M4A3 series of M4 tanks, sixty two vehicles were adapted for this equipment.

119. Anti-Personnel Tank Projector EI: Developed in 1945, this consisted of four small special-purpose flamethrowers which were mounted externally on tanks to ward off enemy troops attempting to attack the vehicle by means of bombs or magnetic mines. Each unit was controlled electrically from within the vehicle by a push-button switch and could be fired singly or simultaneously.

120. Flamethrower T33: Under development during May–June 1945, this device consisted on the M4A3E2 medium tank chassis equipped with a special turret in which were coaxially mounted a 75mm M6 aircraft gun and a flame projector E.20. The flame fuel and propellant gas was carried inside the vehicle.

121. MI9 Swimming Device: Used in conjunction with wading equipment, this American device consisted of air-tight metal boxes filled with plastic foam for buoyancy, fitted around the tank. These held the vehicle well above the water so that the gun could be fired as the tank approached the shore. On reaching the shore the device was blown off by small charges. Used in the Pacific.

122. Sherman with Wading Equipment: Used by both British and American armoured forces, this consisted of kits for waterproofing the vehicle and metal cowls to fit over the engine and exhaust system. Various types existed, adapted to fit the various production models.

123. Sherman Prong: Also known as the Cullin Hedgerow device after Sergeant Culin of the US Army who devised this piece of equipment, it was fitted to the front of the vehicle to facilitate breaking through the thick hedges of the Bocage country in Normandy. Variations of this device were in use with both British and American forces.

124. M4 Tankdozer: This was the normal Sherman gun tank equipped with the MI or MIA dozer blade. The latter was intended for vehicles with HVSS.

125. MEDIUM TANK M7

This was the T7E2 light tank recategorised as a medium tank in August 1942. By this time it had been redesigned with a 75mm gun and other detail changes. A total of 3,000 vehicles were ordered but after standardisation the entire project was cancelled (February 1943) in order to concentrate on the Medium Tank M4 series.

126. MEDIUM TANK T20

At the suggestion of the Ordnance Department, development of a medium tank to supplant the M4 was begun in early 1942. Various pilot models were built or projected, armed with the 75mm automatic gun, 76mm gun or 3in gun and fitted with horizontal volute spring suspension or torsion bar suspension. Powered with a Ford 470hp GAN V-8 tank engine. The pilot model T20 was completed in June 1943 and was armed with the 76mm MI gun. The suspension was the early horizontal volute spring type with shock absorbers on the front and rear bogies. It was equipped with a Torquematic transmission. On trials considerable trouble was experienced with this newly designed transmission. As a result the tests were discontinued and only one pilot model was built. 65,758lbs; crew 5; 76mm gun, 3 MG; armour 1½–2½in; engine Ford GAN V-8 470hp, water-cooled; 25mph; 18ft 10in x 9ft 10in x 8ft.

127. Medium Tank T20E3: Development of the models armed with the 75mm automatic gun and 3in gun were cancelled, and the second pilot model was completed with torsion bar suspension and independently sprung wheels. Designated Medium Tank, T20E3, this vehicle like the T20 was equipped with the 76mm MI gun and powered with the Ford GAN engine with Torquematic transmission. Difficulties were encountered with the transmission similar to that of the T20 and defects in the suspension resulted in only one vehicle being built. 67,500lbs; crew 5; 76mm gun, 3 MG; armour 1½–2½in; engine Ford GAN V-8 470hp, water-cooled; 35mph; 18ft 10in x 9ft 10in x 8ft.

128. MEDIUM TANK T22

Two pilot models were completed by Chrysler in June 1943 as alternative versions of the T20. These vehicles were similar to the Medium Tank T20, except that a 5-speed mechanical transmission was used instead of the Torquematic. Like the T20 these vehicles were equipped with the early type of horizontal volute spring suspension and armed with the 76mm MI gun. One of these models later converted by installing a new turret and an automatic loading 75mm gun was designated Medium Tank T22EI. Unsatisfactory transmission arrangements and the need for larger calibre guns led to the cancellation of these vehicles in December 1944. 69,000lbs; crew 5; 76mm gun, 3 MG; armour 1½–2½in; engine Ford GAN V-8 470hp, liquid-cooled; 25mph; 20ft ¼in x 9ft 10in x 7ft 9in.

129. Medium Tank T22EI

130. MEDIUM TANK T23 (above, pilot model)

First pilot T23 was completed in January 1943, and these vehicles were the first to be completed in the T20 series. They differed from the other T20 series in using the electric drive transmission manufactured by General Electric. They were also fitted with the vertical volute spring suspension similar to that used on the Medium M4 Tank. The armament consisted of the 76mm MI gun. As with the T20 and T22 series, projects were initiated for development of vehicles armed with the 75mm automatic and 3in guns. Designated T23EI and T23E2 respectively, these projects were cancelled without development. After tests of the pilot vehicle T23, production was authorised for 250 of these vehicles. The production model differed in several ways from the pilot vehicle: 76mm MI gun was replaced with model MIAI, a vision cupola was provided for the commander, and the gun ring hatch mounting the .50 calibre AA machine-gun was moved to the loader's position. Production commenced in November 1943 and continued through to December 1944, but none were shipped overseas. Though this vehicle did not see active service, features tried and developed in the T20-T23 series were incorporated into M4 vehicles, in particular the T23 type turret and 76mm gun, HVSS and the simplified 47° hull front. Research work on these vehicles also played a big part in the development of the T25 and T26 Medium Tanks. 73,500lbs; crew 5; 76mm gun, 3 MG; armour 1½–2½in; engine Ford GAN V-8 470hp, liquid-cooled; 35mph; 19ft 8⅜in x 9ft 10½in x 8ft 4in.

131. Medium Tank T23 Production model

132. Medium Tank T23E3: The Armored Board while finding the T23 satisfactory in manoeuvre, found it over-heavy, with weight inequably distributed, with excessive ground pressure, and doubted the reliability of the electric control mechanism. They requested ten T23s for further trials in an attempt to overcome these shortcomings. First of these ordered was designated T23E3. This vehicle was built using the torsion bar suspension and 19in track, while the second, T23E4 was to have horizontal volute spring suspension and 23in centre guided tracks. This later vehicle was subsequently cancelled. The T23E3, completed by Chrysler in August 1944, had a turret taken from a production T23 and torsion bar suspension taken from a Medium Tank T25EI. The power train, armament and armour in this vehicle was essentially the same as the T23. The turret basket was eliminated permitting an increase in the 76mm ammunition stowage from 64 to 84 rounds. In July 1943, standardisation was proposed of the T23E3 as the Medium Tank M27 and the T20E3 as the Medium Tank M27BI. However approval was denied and no additional vehicles were produced. 75,000lbs; crew 5; 76mm gun, 3 MG; armour 1½–3in; engine Ford GAN V-8 470hp, liquid-cooled; 35mph; 19ft 2⅛in x 10ft 4in x 8ft 4⅝in.

133. MEDIUM TANK T25

In September 1942 when the T20 design was drawn up the Ordnance Department suggested that a 90mm gun be developed for future mounting in tanks of this series. By March 1943 such a weapon had been produced and mounted for tests in a Medium Tank T23E3. In April 1943, Army Service Forces gave approval for the procurement of 50 trials vehicles based on the T23E3, but mounting the 90mm gun. Of these, 40 were to have the same basic armour characteristics as the T23E3 and would be designated Medium Tank T25, while the other 10 vehicles were to have increased armour protection, these being designated Medium Tank, T26. Two T25 pilot tanks were constructed by Chrysler. The first was delivered in January 1944 and the second in April 1944, these vehicles were equipped with the horizontal voluted spring suspension and a 23in track; the hull differed from the T23 by having a longer, narrower hatch opening for the driver and a ribbed roof to provide great strength to carry the heavy turret. Development of the two pilot models indicated that the T25 would weight 40½tons and the T26 approx 45tons, to keep within the set weight limits, a change was made from electric drive to Torquematic transmission in these vehicles and they were redesignated Medium Tanks T25EI and T26EI. 82,000lbs; crew 5; 90mm gun, 3 MG; armour 1½–3½in; engine Ford GAF V-8 470hp, water-cooled; 30mph; 18ft 6⅜in x 10ft 11in x 8ft 10½in.

134. Medium Tank T25EI: Design studies of the electric drive Medium Tank T25, had indicated that the vehicle would have a weight exceeding 80,000lbs. To reduce this weight, the tank was redesigned to use a Torquematic transmission. This vehicle was equipped with a torsion bar suspension and a 19in centre guided track. Built at the Fisher Tank Division of General Motors the first vehicle was completed in January 1944. Production continued through May 1944 and reached a total of 40 tanks. Since major interest had now shifted to the development of the T26 series of tanks, no further vehicles were produced. However the 40 vehicles produced served as a basis for numerous experimental projects. 77,590lbs. crew 5; 90mm gun 3 MG; armour ½–3in; engine Ford GAF V-8 470hp, water-cooled; 30mph; 19ft 4½in x 10ft 4in x 9ft 1⅜in.

135. MEDIUM TANK T26EI

The design of this vehicle, the T26, was originally based on the use of the electric drive. Development closely followed that of the Medium Tank T25. One inch of additional armour was provided and consequently a heavier torsion bar suspension and 24in track, instead of the 19in, was found necessary. Since the weight of this vehicle was estimated at 45tons it was found desirable to incorporate the Torquematic instead of the electric drive, the T26 then being redesignated Medium Tank T26EI. The ten scheduled production vehicles were completed as Medium Tanks T26EI. Field and engineering tests were carried out with these ten vehicles, as a result of which many modifications were carried out. The turret platform was eliminated, a muzzle brake was fitted to the 90mm gun, the differential and cooling system redesigned, the suspension was strengthened, and changes were made in the electrical system. In June 1944 the T26EI was redesignated as Heavy Tank T26EI. 86,500lbs; crew 5; 90mm gun, 3 MG; armour 2–4in; engine Ford GAF V-8 470hp, liquid-cooled; 25mph; 22ft 4½in x 11ft 2in x 9ft 1⅜in.

136. Medium Tank T26 (pilot model)

137. HEAVY TANK M6 (TIE2)

While no heavy tanks had been developed prior to 1940, the need for vehicles of this class had been considered in 1939, and development of heavy tank TI was recommended and approved in May 1940. Tentative specifications called for a vehicle weighing about 50tons, with a speed of 25mph, with 3in armour, mounting one 3in high-velocity gun and one 37mm gun in a turret as the main armament. Power was to be supplied by the Wright Whirlwind G-200 engine of 925hp with Hydramatic or automatic transmission. In February 1941 approval was given to build four variations of the basic model to test alternative forms of transmission and hull form to select the best for the production vehicles. These were: TIEI, with cast hull and electric drive; TIE2, with cast hull and torque converter drive; TIE3, with welded hull and torque converter drive; and TIE4 with welded hull, 4 diesel engines and twin Torquematic transmission. This latter model was subsequently cancelled since the diesel installations would have involved protracted development time. The first pilot vehicle to be completed was the TIE2, in December 1941. Trials with this vehicle at the Aberdeen Proving Ground showed the need for a complete redesign of the brakes and cooling system. After modifications had been completed, the TIE2 was standardised during May 1942 as the Heavy Tank M6. Meanwhile the TIE3 had been completed and tested and this was also standardised in May 1942 as the Heavy Tank M6AI, the only external difference between these two models being the welded hull of the latter. The TIEI was the last pilot model to be completed and was not ready for trials until June 1943. Standardisation was not approved for the TIEI, though it became semi-officially known as the M6A2, and was generally referred to as such. Though it had been originally planned in 1941 to produce 5,500 of these vehicles this was reduced in September 1942, to 115 by the new Army Supply Program. Meanwhile the Armored Force had been testing the pilot models and reported that they considered the M6 unsatisfactory, being too heavy, undergunned, poorly shaped, and requiring improvements to the transmission. Because of these deficiencies and consequent tactical limitations they could see no requirements for heavy tanks of this type. In March 1943, therefore the Ordnance Department cut back production requirements to only 40 vehicles. As built these consisted of 8 M6s, 12 M6AIs, and 20 M6A2s. The Heavy Tank M6 series was declared obsolete in late 1944. 126,500lbs; crew 6; 1 3in, 1 37mm gun, 4 MG; armour 1–3½in; engine Wright G-200 9-cylinder 800hp, air-cooled; 22mph; 24ft 9in x 10ft 2½in x 9ft 10in.

138. Heavy Tank M6AI (TIE3)

139. Heavy Tank M6A2 (TIEI)

140. TIEI fitted with 90mm gun: In early 1944 an experimental mounting of the 90mm gun T7 on the TIEI was made, using a turret based on that of the Heavy Tank M26, with the hull stowage rearranged for 90mm ammunition. Project cancelled in March 1944.

141. Heavy Tank M6A2EI: In anticipation of demands for assault tanks from the European theatre of war, one M6A2 was modified with a new heavy turret and 105mm gun, TI5EI. It was planned to convert I5 M6A2 vehicles with this gun and use the remaining 5 vehicles as spare parts. However as no interest was shown in this project, it was terminated in September 1944. This vehicle was later used in weapon development tests for the heavy tank T29.

142. HEAVY TANK T26E3 (M26 GENERAL PERSHING)
Standardisation of Heavy Tank M26 culminated the developments conducted over several years with the Medium Tank T20 series, which included Medium Tanks, T20, T22, T23, T25, T26 and variations. Engineering and service tests resulted in modifications to the ten pilot T26EI Heavy Tanks, these being intended for incorporation in production vehicles. To avoid confusion between the modified vehicles and the ten pilot models, production vehicles were redesignated Heavy Tanks, T26E3, and classified as a limited procurement type. Production of these vehicles began in November 1944. Additional trials were conducted by the Armored Force Board with the production vehicles to determine the adequacy of these modifications and the vehicles were certified as battle worthy in January 1945, and were standardised as

Heavy Tank M26 in March 1945. 92,000lbs; crew 5; 90mm gun, MG; armour 2–4in; engine Ford GAF V-8 470hp; liquid-cooled; 20mph; 20ft 9½in x 11ft 6½in x 9ft 1⅜in.

143. M26.

144. Heavy Tank M26EI: This designation was applied to the M26 mounting a 90mm gun T54, which fixed ammunition, using a longer cartridge case. The gun had a concentric recoil mechanism, and the ammunition stowage in the vehicle was modified. Two pilot models were built.

145. Heavy Tank T26E2 (M45): A project for mounting a 105mm howitzer in Medium Tank T23 was begun in early 1944. Later, this project was switched to the development of a 105mm howitzer installation for the Medium Tank T26EI. Design work was begun in June 1944. a new turret and gun mount were developed, and ammunition stowage in the vehicle redesigned. General arrangements of the turret and gun mount assembly were similar to that in Heavy Tank T26E3, except that the gun mount was equipped with a gyrostabiliser and, because of the lighter weight of the piece, the armour thickness of the turret front and gun shield was increased to maintain equilibrium of the turret. On successful completion of tests, the T26E2 was classified for limited procurement, and production was begun in July 1945. 93,000lbs; crew 5; 105mm Howitzer, 3 MG; armour 2½–5in; engine Ford GAF V-8 470hp, liquid-cooled; 20mph; 20ft 9in x 11ft 6in x 9ft 1in.

146. Heavy Tank T26E4: The Heavy Tank, T26E4 was essentially the same as the Heavy Tank M26 except that the high velocity 90mm T15E2 gun replaced the 90mm M3 gun. This was chambered to fire fixed ammunition, and was installed in a Heavy Tank T26E1. Changes in the basic vehicle included heavier elevating mechanism, modification of the gun cradle, installation of an equilibrator system, use of a counterweight to balance the turret in traverse, and redesign of ammunition stowage. This tank was designated Heavy Tank, T26E4 in March 1945, and was classified as limited procurement.

147. Heavy Tank T26E5: The success of the Medium Tank M4A3E2 with heavy frontal armour suggested the use of heavier armour on the M26. Classified limited procurement, 27 of these vehicles were manufactured, differing from the standard Heavy Tank M26 essentially only in the following respects: new armour front hull casting, with a maximum thickness of 6in, a new turret casting with a frontal thickness of 7½in, a gun mount shield with a maximum thickness of 11in, increased equilibrator capacity, and other minor changes. With these changes the vehicle weighed about 51tons. Unit ground pressure was reduced by the use of the 23in track with 5in extended end connectors. In May 1946 all T26/M26 series vehicles were reclassified as medium tanks. 98,750lbs; crew 5; 90mm gun, 3 MG; armour 2–6in; engine Ford GAF V-8 500hp, liquid-cooled; 22mph; 20ft 9in x 11ft 6in x 9ft 1in.

148. M26 with T99 Multiple Rocket Launcher: Tested in 1945, this device consisted of a total of forty-four 4.5in rockets carried in jettisonable launcher frames.

149. ASSAULT TANK T14

Design studies for an assault tank had been begun in December 1941, and at a meeting in late March, 1942, of the British and United States Tank Commission, an agreement was reached to provide 8,500 of these heavily armoured tanks, as a requirement for the British Government. This vehicle was to use all possible components of the M4 medium tank with the main armament either a 75mm or 6pdr gun. Armour was to be a maximum thickness of 3in on the hull and 4in on turret. The vehicle was to weigh about 46tons and have a speed of 18mph. The power plant was to be the Ford V-8 engine with provision for later use of the Ford V-12. Two pilot vehicles were made. Tracks and suspension were similar to that of the Heavy Tank T6, with skirting plates. The power train was identical to that of the Medium Tank M4, except for final drive gear ratios. Because of track and suspension difficulties and the lack of interest, this project was cancelled in late 1944. 93,930lbs; crew 5; 75mm gun, 3 MG; armour 2–3in; engine Ford GAZ V-8 liquid-cooled 470hp; 24mph; 20ft 9⅜in x 10ft 3in x 8ft 1¹⁄₁₆in.

150. SUPER-HEAVY TANK T28

Developed as a heavy armoured assault tank, armed with a high velocity 105mm gun for attacking heavily fortified positions. The hull was a cast structure, two-thirds the length of the track assemblies and set towards the rear. The turtle shaped superstructure featured a vision cupola for the commander surmounted by an AA machine-gun on a ring mount and a jib at the rear for loading ammunition into the fighting compartment. The 105mm T5E1 gun was mounted on the hull front, in a ball shaped mantlet of 12in armour, with a limited traverse of 10° left and right, and an elevation of 10° to +20°. Each track assembly was a twin unit made up of two complete HVSS units, the outer of which on each side could be disconnected and removed to reduce the vehicle's weight and width for transportation. The two detached track units could then be linked together, side by side to form a dumb unit which could be towed by the parent vehicle or attendant prime mover. As the main armament was not turret mounted the designation of this vehicle was changed to 105mm Gun Motor Carriage T95 in March 1945. Five pilot models were ordered, but were reduced to two when the war in Europe ended. After preliminary tests by the makers, Pacific Car & Foundry, the first completed pilot model was sent to the Aberdeen Proving Ground for trials during December 1945, followed by pilot model No 2 in January 1946. Due to the successful development of the Heavy Tank T29 which mounted the same calibre gun in a turret with 360° traverse, all work on the T28/T95 project was terminated in October 1947. 190,000lbs; crew 8; 105mm gun, 1 MG; armour 2–12 in; engine Ford GAF V-8 410hp, liquid-cooled; 8mph; 36ft 6in x 14ft 5in x 9ft 4in.

151. T28 with assembled outboard tracks in towing position.

152. HEAVY TANK T29

Development of the T29 was authorised in September 1944 as an attempt to develop a heavy tank able to meet potential requirements for attacks on fortified positions and heavily armoured enemy tanks. The hull with torsion bar suspension was similar to that of the Heavy Tank T26E3, but lengthened to take the massive cast turret mounting a 105mm T5E2 gun with twin cal. 50 coaxial machine-guns. The turret with an 80in base ring was driven by a 5hp traversing mechanism. Installed in the turret was a crew of 4, with the tank commander located in the turret bulge. The vehicle was powered by a Ford V-12 engine with cross-drive transmission. With the cessation of hostilities, production was limited to a batch of pilot models only, for testing and development. These were delivered during 1947. 139,000lbs; crew 6; 105mm gun, 4 MG; armour 2–4in; engine Ford GAC V-12 770hp, liquid-cooled; 22mph; 25ft x 12ft 6in x 10ft 7in.

153. HEAVY TANK T30

This was a parallel design to the T29, evolved and produced at the same time and within the same programme. Principal difference was the installation of a Continental 810hp air-cooled engine in place of the Ford unit, and the mounting of a 155mm T7 gun in place of the 105mm weapon. A power rammer was provided for loading the gun, which fired separate ammunition, as well as a power hoist for handling. Twelve machines were authorised for construction, two of which were later diverted to the Heavy Tank T34 programme. 145,000lbs; crew 6; 155mm gun, 3 MG; armour 2–4 in; engine Continental AV-1790-3, 12-cylinder 810hp, air-cooled; 22mph; 24ft 2$\frac{9}{16}$in x 12ft 6in x 10ft 6$\frac{7}{8}$in.

154. HEAVY TANK T32

This was an improved version of Heavy Tank T26E3 (M26) designed to provide better armour protection without impairing the performance or reliability. With a lengthened T26E3 as the

basis, the design incorporated increased armour of 5in on the hull front at 54°, 3in on the hull sides, 8in on the turret front and 6in on the turret sides. It was first proposed to use the 90mm M3 gun as in the T26E3, this was replaced by the 90mm gun T15E1. The engine was uprated to 750hp, and cross-drive transmission replaced the Torquematic transmission of the T26E3. Four pilot models were ordered in February 1945, two of which were modified by having welded hull fronts instead of cast; these were redesignated Heavy Tank T32E1. The bow machine-gun was eliminated on T32E1. 120,000lbs; crew 5; 90mm gun, 3 MG; armour 2–5in; engine Ford GAC 12-cylinder 770hp, liquid-cooled; 22mph; 23ft 2$\frac{3}{8}$in x 12ft 4$\frac{1}{4}$in.

155. HEAVY TANK T34

Using the chassis of the Heavy Tank T30, this vehicle was very similar, the only difference being that the primary armament was the 120mm gun, T53, an anti-aircraft weapon that had been modified for tank installation. The 120mm gun was mounted in a T30 turret which had been reworked with 4in of additional armour applied to the rear to counter balance the weight of the T53 gun. Ammunition stowage was adapted for 120mm rounds. 141,000lbs; crew 6; 120mm gun, 3 MG; armour 2–4in; engine Continental AV-1790-3, 12-cylinder, 810hp air-cooled; 22mph; 24ft 2$\frac{9}{16}$in x 12ft 6in x 10ft 6$\frac{7}{8}$in.

156. LIGHT TANK T1

The first light tank to meet post 1919 requirements for a light tank not over 5tons weight capable of being transported in trucks. Produced in 1927 by Cunningham, this vehicle had a weight of 7.5 tons and was armed with a 37mm gun and coaxial .30 cal machine-gun in a turret that was placed at the rear of the hull, the engine being situated in the front that extended beyond the track. 15,000lbs; crew 2; 37mm gun, 1 MG; armour 0.25–0.375in; engine Cunningham V type 8-cylinder 105hp; 20mph; 12ft 6in x 5ft 10$\frac{1}{2}$in x 7ft 1$\frac{1}{2}$in.

157. Light Tank TIEI (MI): In 1929 the Cunningham firm produced a modified version of the TI. Built to the US Ordnance design, a batch of four were built designated TIE4. This vehicle was later standardised as the Light Tank MI, but this was later revoked. The protruding front was eliminated on this version. I5,000lbs; crew 2; 37mm gun, I MG; armour ⅜in; engine Cunningham V type 8-cylinder IIOhp, water-cooled; I7mph; I2ft 8½in x 5ft I0½in x 7ft I⅜in.

160. Light Tank TIE4: The final model of the TI series, TIE4 was produced in 1932 by the US Ordnance Department, and with this version came a radical change in design. The engine, power train, and final drive were reversed, thus placing the engine at the rear and the final drive in front. The turret though retaining the same armament as the previous models was now mounted in the centre of the vehicle. The suspension was based on that of the British Vickers-Armstrong 6ton Tank Mk 'E' 8.6tons; crew 3; 37mm gun I MG; armour ⅜–⅝in; engine Cunningham V type 8-cylinder I40hp, water-cooled; 20mph; I5ft 5in x 7ft 2¾in x 6ft 6¾in.

158. Light Tank TIE2: Also built during 1929 by Cunningham was a third variant called TIE2, with this model previous defects of the TIEI were corrected, the armour made heavier and the engine horsepower increased. I7,800lbs; crew 2; 37mm, I MG; armour ⅜–⅝in; engine Cunningham V type 8-cylinder I32hp, water-cooled; I8mph; I2ft I0½in x 6ft 2¾in x 7ft 7in.

161. Light Tank TIE5: Produced in 1932 this was a TIEI fitted with controlled differential in place of clutch brake steering.

Light Tank TIE6: This was the final modification of the Light Tank TI series, and consisted of a rebuilt TIE4 with the hull raised, and with an American La France engine of 240hp replacing the Cunningham version. I9,900lb; crew 3; 37mm gun I MG; armour ⅜–⅝in; engine American La France 240hp, water-cooled; 20mph; I5ft x 6ft 8in x 6ft 6in.

159. Light Tank TIE3: The next model of the TI series, the TIE3 was a modification of one of the TIEI vehicles. Basically similar to the previous marks this vehicle had an improved suspension, this being changed from link to spring hydraulic. Dimensions as for TIEI, but fitted with Cunningham V-8 engine of I32hp. Modified by the Ordnance Department in 1931.

162. TRACK DEVELOPMENT CHASSIS TI
This was an experimental vehicle built by Cunningham during 1928 to an Ordnance Department design for a One-Man Tank. It was also used to test a special type of flexible track made of band saw steel. Each track consisted of two steel bands 4½in wide, lined with

commercial belting. These were clipped together by steel grousers that also acted as track guides. 1.5tons; crew 1; 1 MG; armour 5–9mm; engine Ford Model A, 4-cylinder 42hp, water-cooled; 19.5mph; 8ft 8in x 4ft 9in x 5ft 1½in.

vehicle armed with a .30 calibre machine-gun in a front sponson. The chassis was similar to the Light Tank T2 but with modified suspension. Aluminium was used at points of low vulnerability, such as bottom plate, top plate of crew compartment, track rollers, differential case, etc. 7.08tons; crew 2; 1 MG; armour ¼–⅜in; engine Ford V type 83hp, water-cooled; 35mph; 11ft 3in x 6ft 9½in x 4ft 6in.

163. LIGHT TANK T2

Information gathered during the development of the T1 series of Light Tanks proved invaluable in the development of the Light Tank T2, the design of which was started in 1933. Based on Light Tank T1E4, the pilot model built at Rock Island Arsenal appeared in 1934. Armed with two calibre .30 and one calibre .50 machine-guns, it was powered with a Continental aircraft engine of 260hp. Suspension was the Vickers double leaf spring articulating bogie type fitted with rubber jointed track. Crew 4; 3 MG; armour ⅜–⅝in; engine Continental aircraft radial 260hp, air-cooled; 27mph; 13ft 4½in x 7ft 9½in x 6ft 9in.

166. LIGHT TANK T6

Produced in 1939 at the Rock Island Arsenal, this experimental turretless vehicle resembled the British Carden-Loyd Mk VI Machine-Gun Carrier. Two Buick engines, each of 140hp were located at the rear. The suspension consisted of a pair of front volute spring bogies and connected trailing idler and single rear bogie. Crew 3; armour ¾–1in; engine Two Buick type Vertical-overhead valve, each 140hp; 30mph; 12ft 5½in x 7ft 11in x 5ft 2¾in.

164. Light Tank T2E1: Produced at the Rock Island Arsenal in 1934–5, this version was basically similar to the Light Tank T2, but was fitted with volute spring suspension instead of the double leaf spring articulating bogie type. It was also equipped with rubber block tracks. Fitted with a new type of turret, nine of these vehicles were manufactured and standardised in 1938 as the Light Tank M2A1. 9.4tons; crew 4; 3 MG; armour ⅜–⅝in; engine Continental Aircraft Radial 260hp, air-cooled; 46mph; 13ft 5¼ x 7ft 4½in x 6ft 9in.

Light Tank T2E2 (M2A2): Produced in 1932, this was similar to T2E1, but was fitted with two turrets. Standardised as Light Tank M2A2.

167. Light Tank M2A1: Developed from Light Tank T2E1. 18,790lb; crew 4; 3 MG; armour ½–⅝in; engine Continental Radial 250hp, air-cooled; 45mph, .CC 20mph; 13ft 7in x 7ft 10in x 7ft 5in.

165. LIGHT TANK T3

Produced in 1936 at the Rock Island Arsenal, this was a turretless

168. Light Tank M2A2: Developed from Light Tank T2E2. Experimental model fitted with Guiberson Diesel engine became designated M2A2E1. 19,100lb; crew 4; 3 MG; armour ½–⅝in; engine Continental Radial 250hp, air-cooled; 45mph .CC 20mph; 13ft 7in x 7ft 10in x 7ft 9in.

169. Light Tank M2A2E2: This was a Light Tank M2A2 with modified suspension, thicker armour and other modifications. 21,500lb; crew 4; 3 MG; armour ⅝–1in; engine Continental Radial 250hp, air-cooled; 38mph, CC 20mph; 13ft 9in x 8ft 1½in x 6ft 10¾in.

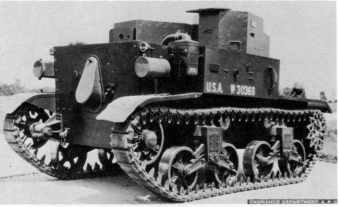

170. M2A2E2 rear view.

171. Light Tank M2A2E3: Developed in 1938, this vehicle was similar to M2A2E2 but had modified suspension with trailing idler and was equipped with a GM diesel engine. Crew 4; 3 MG; armour ⅝–1in; engine GM Diesel 165hp; 30mph, CC 20mph; 12ft 1in x 8ft 1½in x 6ft 10¾in.

172. Light Tank M2A3: Produced at the Rock Island Arsenal during

1938, the M2A3 was an outgrowth of the M2A2, having a longer wheelbase, repositioned bogie units, increased armour thickness, a hexagonal cupola on the left turret (instead of the round type on the M2A2), and other various modifications. The M2A3 series were the last of the light tanks to be equipped with twin turrets. Experimental test vehicles of the M2A3 series were: M2A3E1 with Guiberson 9-cylinder radial air-cooled diesel; M2A3E2, a vehicle fitted with experimental Electrogear transmission. 9.5tons; crew 4; 3 MG; armour ⅝–⅞in; engine Continental Radial 250hp, air-cooled; 38mph; CC 25mph; 14ft 6½in x 7ft 9¼in x 7ft 5in.

173. M2A3 Front view.

Light Tank M2A3E3: Developed at the Rock Island Arsenal in 1940, this experimental tank was fitted with a GM Diesel engine and a reworked suspension with trailing idler wheel. 10.75tons; crew 4; 3 MG; armour ⅝–⅞in; engine GM Diesel type V 250hp, water-cooled; 38mph; 14ft 10in x 7ft 9¼in x 7ft 5in.

174. Light Tank M2A4: Developed at the Rock Island Arsenal and standardised in 1939 as the M2A4, this was the final development in the M2 light tank series. Basically similar to the M2A3, a single turret with a 37mm gun replaced the twin turrets of the earlier vehicles. Additional .30cal machine-guns were carried in side sponsons. Maximum armour thickness was further increased and the engine compartment was redesigned. Used in the early Pacific campaigns, M2A4s were supplied to Great Britain, where they were used for training. Prototype differed from production vehicles in that no cupola was fitted, nor was there armour protection for the 37mm recoil cylinders. 11.5tons; crew 4; 37mm gun, 4 MG; armour ⅜–1in; engine Continental radial 7-cylinder 250hp, air-cooled; 34mph, CC 25mph; 14ft 7in x 8ft 4in x 8ft 2½in.

175. M2A4 Prototype vehicle.

177. M3 with welded turret and riveted hull.

178. M3 with rounded, welded, homogeneous turret.

179. M3 with cast/welded turret and welded hull.

176. **LIGHT TANK M3 (STUART I)** (above, all-riveted model)
Standardised in July 1940, the M3 was based on the Light Tank M2A4 but had heavier armament and other improvements. Principal changes included the use of a trailing idler wheel to carry the additional weight, lengthened rear superstructure and redesigned engine compartment, armoured against aircraft attack. Numerous improvements were made during the production period, so that the final M3s were vastly different from the first. The first production models were of a riveted construction with a seven-sided turret; this was followed by a model with a welded seven-sided turret, and then a rounded, welded, homogeneous turret. The final model was entirely welded. A gyrostabiliser to permit accurate firing of the 37mm gun while the tank was in motion, was incorporated in 1941. As a result of battle experience in North Africa additional fuel capacity was provided by two jettisonable fuel tanks. Fitted with sponson machine-guns fired by the driver, these were sometimes blanked off. Equipped with the Continental Radial 7-cylinder engine, some vehicles were fitted with the Guiberson T-1020 Diesel. Supplied to the US Army and to the Allies under Lend-Lease these tanks were designated, General Stuart, by the British forces. The diesel engined version was known as Stuart II. 12.3tons; crew 4; 37mm gun, 5 MG; armour 1–1½in; engine Continental Radial 250hp, air-cooled; 35mph, CC 15–20mph; 14ft 10in x 7ft 4in x 8ft 3in.

180. Stuart I in Canadian service.

181. M3 with Mine Exploder T2: 1942 experiment with T2 mine exploder on boom rigged in front of the tank.

182. Light Tank M3 Experimentals (above, M3E3): Four experimental variations of the M3 were made: M3E1 was the M3 fitted with a Cummins HBS Diesel engine; M3E2 was a test vehicle for twin Cadillac engines and Hydramatic transmission. M3E3 was the M3E2 fitted with turret basket; this vehicle became the prototype of the M5 Light Tank. M3E4 was the designation given to the vehicle used to test Straussler Flotation Equipment.

183. M3 in British service, showing modifications that included smoke dischargers and sand shields. On this vehicle the sponson machine-guns have been blanked off.

184. Light Tank M3A1 (Stuart III): Standardised in August 1941, this was the M3 modified to include a gyrostabiliser, power traverse for the turret, and a turret basket. The turret was similar to that of the final version of the M3, but with no cupola. The side sponson machine-guns were blanked off. Stuart IV as for M3A1 but fitted with Guiberson diesel engine. 12.7tons; crew 4; 47mm gun, 4 MG; armour 1–1½in; engine Continental radial 250hp, air-cooled; 34mph, CC 15–20mph; 14ft 10in x 7ft 4in x 7ft 6in.

185. M3A1 with Satan Flame Gun: Used by the USMC, the 37mm gun was removed and replaced by a flame-projector and Canadian Ronson flamethrower equipment.

186. M3A1 (Stuart III) fitted with British wading equipment.

187. Light Tank M3A3 (Stuart V): Final production variant of the M3 light tank series was the M3A3 (the M3A2 that was to be similar to the M3AI but with welded hull was not put into production). Light Tank M3A3 was standardised in August 1942, and included changes in the turret, hull and sponsons. The driver's compartment was enlarged, the hatches being moved to the top plate, the sponsons were redesigned, and elimination of the sponson guns provided space for two additional fuel tanks, engine air cleaners, and added ammunition stowage. The turret was redesigned with a bulge at the rear to provide space for a radio set. Sand shields were fitted over the suspension. I2.3tons; crew 4; 37mm gun, 3 MG; armour I–I½in; engine Continental radial 250hp, air-cooled; 34mph, CC I5–20mph; I6ft 6in x 8ft 3in x 7ft 6½in.

188. LIGHT TANK M5 (STUART VI)
Standardised in February 1942, this was designed as a modification of Light Tank M3AI, to use twin Cadillac engines and Hydramatic transmission. The hull was fabricated of welded, homogeneous armour plate with the reinforced front plate, extended sponsons and streamlined effect subsequently adopted for Light Tank M3A3. To accommodate the twin Cadillac engines, the rear engine covers were stepped up. The welded, power-operated turret and integrated turret basket was similar to that of the Light Tank M3AI, Gyrostabiliser was fitted for the 37mm gun. I5tons; crew 4; 37mm gun, 2 MG; armour I2–67mm; engine Twin Cadillac each I2Ihp; 40mph; I4ft 2¾in x 7ft 4¼in x 7ft 6½in.

I89. M5, with Cullin hedgerow device: Metal prongs fitted to the front of the vehicle, for cutting through undergrowth and hedges.

190. LIGHT TANK M5AI
The M5AI was designed and standardised in September 1942 and replaced the Light Tank M5 in production. Principal change was the use of an improved turret with a radio bulge at the rear. This was similar to that in use on the Light Tank M3A3. Larger access hatches for the driver and co-driver, improved mount for the 37mm gun, and improved vision devices were other changes. In addition there was better water-sealing on the hatches, and an escape hatch added in the hull floor. A later modification was the provision of a detachable shield or fairing on the turret side to protect the AA machine-gun mount. 33,907lb; crew 4; 37mm gun, 3 MG; armour I2–67mm; engine Twin Cadillac each I2Ihp; 40mph; I5ft I0½in x 7ft 6in x 7ft I0½in.

I9I. M5AI with E7–7 Flame gun: Flamethrowing equipment replaced the main armament; fuel and equipment stowed in hull.

192. M5AI with E9–9 Flame Gun: This was based on the British Crocodile, and consisted of a flame-projector replacing the hull machine-gun, fuel and air bottles carried in a trailer.

193. M5AI with T39 Rocket launcher: This device held 20 7.2in rockets and was of a box-type construction.

194. Light Tank M5AIEI: Test vehicle, fitted with 18in wide offset steel tracks.

195. LIGHT TANK T7E2
Designed as a replacement for the M2A4 and M3 series of light

tanks in early 1941. Thicker armour (38mm) and a lower silhouette were the main requirements. Four prototypes were put in hand at the Rock Island Arsenal, the T7EI, T7E2, T7E3 and T7E4. The T7EI was to be all-riveted and with HVSS but was cancelled before completion. T7E2 was of all-cast construction, T7E3 was to be all-welded with Cadillac engines. Subsequently only the T7E2 was proceeded with, but changing requirements, and the need for a heavier calibre gun took it out of the light tank class. The T7E2 was reclassified and standardised as the Medium Tank M7. 51,000lb; crew 5; 57mm gun, 2 MG; armour 1¼–1½in; engine Wright R975 400hp, air-cooled; 35mph, CC 18mph; 17ft 7in x 9ft 2in x 7ft 4in.

196. LIGHT TANK T9EI (M22 LOCUST)
Development of this vehicle arose from a military requirement for an airborne tank. Design studies were submitted by General Motors Corporation, the Marmon-Herrington Co, and J. Walter Christie. The Marmon-Herrington design, using the Lycoming 6-cylinder air-cooled engine and Marmon-Herrington suspension and track, was accepted. The first pilot model, the T9 was delivered in the Autumn of 1941. Though performance was satisfactory, modifications were indicated. Design studies of an improved model, the T9EI, were begun in February 1942. The front of the hull was reshaped, the bow machine-gun being eliminated. The turret power traverse and gyrostabiliser were also removed to decrease the weight. The turret and turret basket were removable for air transportation. Accepted for production, the T9EI was standardised in limited standard classification as Light Tank M22 in August 1944. A large number of these vehicles were supplied to the British under Lend-Lease, some of them being lifted in British Hamilcar gliders in the Rhine crossing operations on March 24, 1945, by the British 6th Airborne Division. 16,400lb; crew 3; 37mm gun, 1 MG; armour ¾–1in; engine Lycoming 6-cylinder 162hp, air-cooled; 35mph; 12ft 11in x 7ft 3¾in x 5ft 8½in.

197. Light Tank T9

198. Light Tank M22

199. M22 in British service.

200. LIGHT TANK T24

Development of this vehicle was begun in April 1943 to provide an improved light tank with greater accessibility, increased flotation and mobility, and armed with a heavier weapon than the 37mm gun then in use. The design of this tank was based on the use of the aircraft lightweight type 75mm gun, T13E1 with concentric recoil mechanism, twin Cadillac engines and Hydramatic transmission which was in successful use with the Light Tank M5. The torsion bar suspension was adapted from the Gun Motor Carriage, M18. Two pilot models were recommended and approved, and these were built by the Cadillac Motor Car Division. The first pilot was delivered in October 1943 and proved successful on trials. It was immediately authorised that 1,000 Light Tanks T24 be procured (this was later raised to 5,000). Standardisation of T24 as Light Tank M24 took place in July 1944.

201. Light Tank T24E1: This was the T24 fitted with a Wright R-975 air-cooled engine and torque convertor transmission to compare performance against the T24 equipped with Cadillac engines and Hydramatic transmission. To install the Wright engine the rear deck of the vehicle was raised and the louvres modified. The picture shows the vehicle with a longer gun and muzzle brake that was later fitted.

202. LIGHT TANK M24 (CHAFFEE)

Owing to the late start in production, the M24 saw only limited service during World War II. A small number of them were supplied to Britain in 1945 and remained in service for a short time after the war. In British service the M24 was known as the Chaffee, named after General A. R. Chaffee the founder of the US Armored Forces. The M24 had been designed as the basis of a Light Combat Team, the chassis serving as a universal mount for various self-propelled guns, cargo carriers, and recovery vehicles, so simplifying maintenance and production. 40,500lb; crew 5; 75mm gun, 3 MG; armour 1–2½in; engine twin Cadillac 110hp each; 35mph, CC 25mph; 18ft x 9ft 4in x 8ft 1in.

203. M24 fitted with Dozer-blade T4.

204. M24 with swimming device M20.

RESTRICTED

205. M24 with deep-water fording kit.

206. COMBAT CAR TI

Four Medium Tanks T3 were delivered in 1932 to the US Cavalry and were designated Combat Car TI. These differed from the Medium Tank T3 in that the 37mm gun was replaced by a .50cal machine-gun. 10.5tons; crew 3; 2 MG; $\frac{1}{2}-\frac{5}{8}$in; engine Liberty V-12 338hp, water-cooled; 46mph on wheels, 27mph on tracks; 18ft x 17ft 4in x 7ft 6in.

207. COMBAT CAR T2

Produced in 1931 by the Rock Island Arsenal, this was a convertible type and had originally been built as the T5 Armored Car, in which form it ran on road wheels or as a semi-tracked vehicle. As Combat Car T2 it was fitted with full tracks in its tracked form. 18,470lb; crew 3; 3 MG; armour $\frac{3}{8}$–1in; engine Continental radial 156hp, air-cooled; 41mph on wheels, 27mph on tracks; 14ft 10$\frac{3}{4}$in x 7ft 5in x 6ft 10in.

208. Combat Car T2EI: Produced by the Rock Island Arsenal in 1932, this was the T2 with the hull modified to install a larger Continental engine and to redistribute the weight. Crew 3; 3 MG; engine Continental radial 200hp, air-cooled; 41mph on wheels; 27mph on tracks; 12ft 3in x 6ft 6in x 6ft 10in.

209. COMBAT CAR T4

Built at the Rock Island Arsenal in 1933, this was an Ordnance Department version of the Combat Car TI. Adapted for wheel or track running it was smaller than the TI. 9.6tons; crew 4; 3 MG; engine Continental radial 250hp, air-cooled; 52mph on wheels, 26mph on tracks; 16ft 1in x 7ft 7in x 6ft 7in.

210. Combat Car T4 on wheels.

211. Combat Car T4EI: This was the Combat Car T4 modified, fitted with a new type of turret, which was later adopted for Combat Cars. The front of the vehicle was reshaped and fitted with side sponson .30cal machine-guns. Another machine-gun was mounted in the front hull plate. 20,000lb; crew 3; 6 MG; armour ½in; engine Continental radial 264hp, air-cooled; 44mph on wheels, 29mph on tracks; 16ft 1in x 7ft 7in.

212. Combat Car T4E2: Similar to Combat Car T4E1, but with turret replaced by barbette superstructure. Data as for T4E1 Medium Tank.

213. Combat Car T4E2 rear view.

214. COMBAT CAR T5
Developed concurrently with Light Tank T2E1 with essential parts common to both machines, the T5 was fitted with twin turrets and vertical volute suspension. Built at Rock Island Arsenal during 1934 it was tested with a Guiberson diesel engine and became the T5E3. 9.7tons; crew 4; 3 MG; engine Continental radial 264hp, air-cooled; 36mph; 13ft 4in x 7ft 6in x 6ft 8in.

215. Combat Car T5E1: Reworked T5, with barbette superstructure substituted for turrets, developed at Rock Island Arsenal during 1934–35. 13,850lb; crew 4; 6 MG; armour ⅜–½in; engine Continental radial 257hp, air-cooled; 45mph; 13ft 4in x 8ft 1in x 7ft 6in.

216. Combat Car T5E1 rear view.

217. Combat Car T5E2 (Combat Car M1/Light Tank M1A2): Produced at Rock Island Arsenal in 1936, this vehicle was basically similar to Light Tank T2E1. Fitted with a new type of turret mounting two machine-guns, it was standardised as Combat Car M1. Redesignated in 1940 as Light Tank M1A2. 9.7tons; crew 4; 3 MG; armour ½–⅝in; engine Continental radial 250hp; air-cooled; 45mph; 13ft 7in x 7ft 10in x 7ft 5in.

221. Combat Car MIE3: This was the Combat Car MI fitted with experimental continuous band rubber track, and later with rubber block tracks, 1939. Trials only.

218. COMBAT CAR T7

This was a new model designed and built at Rock Island Arsenal in 1938. It was basically a Combat Car MI hull with lengthened chassis and featured a wheel and track capability similar to the Christie vehicles. The road wheels were fitted with pneumatic tyres. 11tons; crew 4; 3 MG; armour $\frac{5}{8}-\frac{1}{2}$in; engine Continental radial 250hp, air-cooled; 53mph on wheels, 24mph on tracks; 16ft 8in x 8ft 7$\frac{1}{2}$in x 8ft 1in.

219. Combat Car T7 on wheels.

COMBAT CAR MIEI

Combat Car MI equipped with Guiberson 250hp engine in 1937. Trials only.

222. Combat Car MIAI: This was Combat Car MIE2 fitted with constant mesh transmission, turret offset to the right, and radio added, 1938.

Combat Car MIAIEI: The MIAI fitted with a Guiberson diesel engine, 1938. Limited service.

223. Combat Car M2 (Light Tank MIAI): As Combat Car MIAI, but with improved turret and fixed with Guiberson T1020 diesel engine. Trailing idler was introduced on this model. This vehicle was redesignated Light Tank MIAI in 1940.

220. Combat Car MIE2: Produced at the Rock Island Arsenal in 1937 this was the Combat Car MI with modified engine space and rear bogie moved back 11in. Rear of hull was reshaped for better access and to increase fuel capacity. 19,530lb; crew 4; 4 MG; armour $\frac{1}{2}-\frac{5}{8}$in; engine Continental radial 250hp, air-cooled; 45mph; 14ft 7in x 7ft 9$\frac{3}{4}$in x 7ft 5in.

MARMON-HERRINGTON TANKS

During the period from 1935 to 1941, the firm of Marmon-Herrington built a series of tanks for export, some of them being procured by the US Army and Marine Corps. These vehicles ranged from light turretless two-man tanks that were based on commercial tractor components produced by the firm, to three- and four-man tanks of the more conventional design. The turretless vehicles were known as the CTL series and were all basically similar in design, with variations in the engine, armour thickness and suspension. The armament consisted of from one to three machine-guns in ball mounts on the front hull plate. The suspension was of the leaf spring type with four small road wheels and a rubber track reinforced with steel cable.

227. CTL-3 front view.

224. CTL-I: Built in 1935 for trials with the Persian Army. One ball-mounted machine-gun on the right of the front hull plate. CTL-ID was similar but with a 6-cylinder 85hp Ford engine. 8,975lb; crew 2; I MG; armour ¼in; engine Ford 12-cylinder 110hp; 30mph; 10ft 8in x 6ft 4in x 5ft 5½in.

228. CTL-3A: Built in 1938, this version was similar to the CTL-3, but was equipped with strengthened and braced suspension. The front of the superstructure was bevelled to the sides and the front centre ball mount eliminated.

225. CTL-2: This was similar to the CTL-I, but with solid road wheels, ⅜in thickness of armour and an increased weight of 9,565lb. CTL-20 similar but with a 6-cylinder 85hp Ford engine.

229. CTL-3M: Built for the US Marine Corps in 1939–40, this vehicle was basically similar to the CTL-3A, but was equipped with volute spring suspension.

CTL-4: This model was the same as the CTL-3, but was equipped with a Ford 6-cylinder 95hp engine.

226. CTL-3: Similar in design to the CTL-I and 2, but with spoked road wheels, ½in armour thickness armed with a .50cal and two .30cal machine-guns in the front hull plate. The weight was increased to 10,155lb. This model was built for the US Marine Corps in 1937. CTL-3D similar but with 6-cylinder 85hp Ford engine.

230. CTL-6: Built for the US Marine Corps in 1940–1, this version was basically the CTL-3M with the front plate faired away and the rear of the hull raised. Fitted with steel tracks.

231. CTVL: Built for Mexico in 1937, this was a modified version of the CTL series with a built-up superstructure, armed with two ball-mounted machine-guns in a redesigned front plate. 4tons; crew 2; 2 MG; armour .5in; engine Ford 8-cylinder 85hp; 30mph; 11ft x 6ft 3in x 5ft 3in.

232. CTM-3TBD: This three-man tank was basically the CTL-6 model with a modified superstructure to mount a turret. Armed with two .50cal machine-guns in addition to the three hull-mounted guns. Produced for the US Marine Corps in 1941 the CTM-3TBD was powered with a diesel engine.

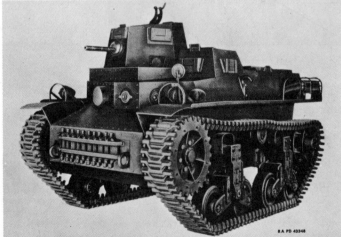

233. CTLS-4TAC (Light Tank TI6): Designed and built in 1941 by Marmon-Herrington for export to China and the Dutch East Indies,

this was an improved model based on the CTL series featuring the vertical volute suspension. The CTLS while retaining the three machine-gun ball mounts on the front hull plate, had in addition a small rotating turret armed with a machine-gun. Two versions of this model were built: the CTLS-4TAC with left-hand drive and the turret offset to the right, and the CTLS-4TAY with right-hand drive and the turret offset to the left. An armoured hatch was supplied for the driver. When these countries were overrun by the Japanese, 240 of these vehicles were taken over by the US War Department and distributed to American troops for training under the US Army designation Light Tank TI6. 8.4tons; crew 2; 2 or 3 MG; armour ½in–1in; engine Hercules 6-cylinder 124hp, water-cooled; 11ft 6in x 6ft 10in x 6ft 11.

234. CTLS-4TAC front view.

235. CTMS-ITBI: This was an enlarged version of the CTM-3BD model with modified vertical volute spring suspension, the addition of an extra return roller and wider steel tracks. It was equipped with a larger turret mounting a 37mm gun in an armoured sheath. The machine-gun ball mounts were retained on the hull front. Known as the Dutch Three-Man Tank, this vehicle was built in 1942 for the Dutch East Indies and was later supplied to Cuba, Ecuador, Guatemala and Mexico. 12.5tons; crew 3; 37mm gun, 2 or 3 MG; armour ½in; engine RLXD 6-cylinder 152hp, water-cooled; 25mph; 13ft 9¾in x 7ft 8in x 8ft 1⅞in.

236. MTLS-IGI4: Originally ordered for the Dutch East Indies and known as the Dutch Four-Man Tank, this was the largest of the tanks built by Marmon-Herrington. Though the hull design was similar to that of the CTMS-ITBI, it was longer and deeper and was fitted with wider tracks. The two-man turret was equipped with twin 37mm guns, with a .30cal machine-gun mounted on the right side of the turret plate. In addition a AA machine-gun socket mount was provided at the rear of the turret and ball mounts on the hull front. Crew 4; 2 37mm guns; 2 to 4 MG; armour ½–1in; engine Hercules 6-cylinder 240hp, liquid-cooled; 26mph; 16ft 1in x 8ft 8½in x 9ft 2¼in.

237. CHRISTIE MI932

Further development of the MI928 as a private venture design by Christie. Also had features (hull and transmission) based on the Medium Tank T3. Demonstrated to US Army in 1932, but rejected by them. Had duraluminium wheels with pneumatic tyres; double skin hull, inner thickness of duraliminum and outer thickness of steel. Gun (not fitted) to be installed in nose rather than a turret. 5tons; crew 3; armour 12mm(max); engine (Hispano Suiza V-12 gasoline) 750hp; 60mph (tracks), 120mph (estimated maximum) (wheels); 22ft (approx) x 7ft (approx) x 5.66ft.

MI932 Flying Tank: Adaptation of the MI932 with addition of detachable biplane wings and tail boom with free rotating propeller. Theory was for the vehicle to use its very high wheeled speed to become airborne for short hops. Alternative scheme was for vehicle to be slung under low flying aircraft for release to glide to earth, the tracks being set running before release. Vehicle was not tested in its flying form. Basic MI932 subsequently sold to Russian War Department.

238. CHRISTIE MI935A

Further private venture design built as a prototype only and also

contemplated for airborne use. Followed normal Christie layout but was shorter and lighter than before and had cupolas to accommodate the crewmen. Designed to mount a 75mm gun in the nose. 4tons; armour 12mm(max); engine (gasoline) 450hp; 60mph (tracks), 90mph (wheels); 15ft (approx) x 6.5ft x 5.5ft.

239. Christie MI935B: Lengthened version of the MI935A and believed to be that vehicle in rebuilt form. Also contemplated for the airborne role but never so used. Cupolas for crewmen and mock-up of long calibre 75mm gun in front barbette. Details as MI935A except 5.5tons; engine (gasoline V-12) 750hp; 65mph (tracks), 90mph (wheels); length 21ft.

240. CHRISTIE MI936

Prototype of an advanced design produced as a private venture and intended to give a sustained cross-country speed of over 60mph on tracks only (no provision for driving on wheels only). Contemplated for air-dropping from aircraft but never so used. The vehicle was unarmed – with provision for a gun in the nose – and had thin armour and unprotected suspension units. The specially tuned Christie-Curtiss aero engine gave a rating of 300hp. Rapid acceleration, reaching 60mph in 100ft. Sold in Britain (Nuffield Mechanisation and Aero Ltd) in 1937 and became basis of AI3 series design, the first British fast cruiser tank. 6tons; crew 2; engine (gasoline) 300hp; 60mph; 17.5ft x 6.5ft x 5.5ft.

241. Christie MI937: MI936 modified to give optional armament layout. Nose gun position taken by driver (in cupola) and space left in hull top for fitting barbette or light turret. Fitted with Curtiss-Wright aero engine of 430hp. Taken to England by Christie in 1937 for demonstration to the War Office in the form in which it was eventually handed over to the British.

242. CHRISTIE MI938 (T-I2)
Development of the MI936/MI937 vehicle with similar suspension but reshaped roomier hull. Used aluminium to reduce weight wherever possible. Uprated Wright engine gave top speed of 80mph cross-country. No guns or turret fitted. Details as MI936 except weight 4.5tons; engine 450hp; 80mph.

243. CHRISTIE MI942A (above) AND MI942B
A Christie design which was produced in mock-up hull form only on the chassis of the Christie MI941 Bigley Gun Motor Carriage, a prototype self-propelled gun produced the previous year. Vehicle had a fixed barbette with proposed armament of one (37mm?) gun and six MG, two each side, one forward, and one at rear. This vehicle was never completed with steel body or the designed armament and the project was dropped. Length I8ft (approx), width 7ft (approx). Other details as MI938(T-I2).

N.B.—Contemporary design, the MI942B was not actually built and existed in scale model form only. Essentially this was the Christie MI936 or MI937 attached to a wooden glider or transport plane and forming, in effect, the undercarriage. This allowed the aircraft to operate from short unprepared strips using the traction of the tank for added power or basic power. Christie also postulated a release system for the tank when carried by a powered aircraft, in similar fashion to his earlier airborne tank ideas.

244. Disston Tractor Tank (final model): Developed in 1933 by the Disston Safe Company, this was an open armoured superstructure designed to be dropped and bolted over a commercial Caterpillar tractor, model 35 or 40, to convert it into a cheap form of tank. Armed with a Colt machine-gun in the front plate and a 37mm gun in the open top. It weighed 6.8tons, carried a crew of 3 (7 could be carried when required) had an armour thickness of $\frac{1}{4}$in to $\frac{1}{16}$in and a speed of 4.6mph. In 1934 a second version was produced, this had improved armour protection and was equipped with a revolving turret armed with a 37mm gun on a high angle mount for anti-aircraft fire. The front machine-gun was now mounted in a armoured housing. This version was later furnished with track extension attachments for the front idler wheels, by this device the tracks were extended to the level of the nose of the vehicle. Three of the Disston tanks were sold to Afghanistan in 1934. Similar vehicles were later built in Australia and New Zealand.

T26 tanks advance, September 1941.

Tank-borne infantry advance on T34 tanks, Ukranian Front, 1944.

T34/85 tanks attack, Odessa, 1944.

U.S.S.R.

INTRODUCTION

As in other countries various projects for tracked armoured vehicles were worked out in Russia prior to the actual practical realisation of the tank in 1915–16. An early design was Mendeleev's 'Armoured Land Cruiser' perfected in 1915 after several year's work. Mendeleev was a naval architect who proposed to use a submarine engine and naval guns on a large tractor chassis. This vehicle was not actually built, though Mendeleev went on to design (but not build) an improved replacement.

In the summer of 1914 an engineer called Porokovskikov designed a small tracked vehicle with Pedrail-type tracks and small jockey wheels each side to assist in steering. Named Vezdekhod ('Go anywhere'), this was intended as an infantry assault vehicle for crossing ground under fire. Turtle-shaped, it had provision for a small machine-gun turret. The vehicle did well in tests during 1915 but the Russian War Department decided against production, partly due to the industrial limitations of what was then still a very backward country.

Further early 'tank' ideas included a 'Land Cruiser' on a roller chassis, and the 'Tsar' tank, a 'big wheel' project which was actually built as a prototype in 1915, but proved impractical owing to its great size and shape. A promising design of 1916 was the Reno-Russkiy, a vehicle not unlike the French Schneider tank. It was designed by the Renault agents in Moscow but was never actually built.

After news of the British use of tanks on the Western Front, the Russian War Department made some attempt to sponsor an official tank design, and a new model of the Vezdekhod was undertaken. This had the Pedrail type of track, plus wheels for road running and steering. A prototype was built but no production followed.

The first tanks in Russia were actually British and French, purchased direct for the Imperial Government; a total of 32 Mk V and Medium Mk 'C' tanks came from Britain and 100 Renault FTs came from France in 1918. By 1919 many of these had been captured by the Bolsheviks and later they acquired even more tanks when the British Expeditionary Force withdrew from Russia leaving its few tanks behind.

In late 1919 the Soviet War Council decided to build a tank for the newly established Red Army and chose a French Renault FT as the basis for a new design. The resulting vehicle — the KS (Krasno-Sormova) — was an almost exact replica of the Renault FT though it differed mechanically in having parts (eg, a Fiat engine) bought from foreign suppliers. A further 14 KS tanks were built to supplement the 100 or so ex-Allied tanks now in Red Army hands. The order was completed by 1922.

The KS — sometimes referred to as the 'Russkiy-Renault' — set the pattern for major Soviet tank development over the next fifteen years. This was simply to copy the best features of foreign designs, purchasing samples from abroad, and producing close copies (with or without licence) of the most suitable types. Given the relatively primitive state of Russian industry in the 1920s and 1930s, this was a very shrewd measure: it meant reducing development time to a minimum and directing limited engineering resources to good effect.

Before this pattern was fully established however, there were some attempts to build indigenous designs. A notable vehicle was the Zhitonoski light tank which was an ultra-miniature, 7ft long one-man vehicle. It was armed with a machine-gun and the crewman drove in the prone position. Trials proved that it was of limited tactical value, being uncomfortable and offering the driver only a limited view ahead owing to his low position. The Central Armoured Force Comand instituted a couple of prize competitions in the 1919–21 period calling for various types of tank with all-round traverse and amphibious capability. At least two designs were accepted but the Central Armoured Force Command was abolished before any prototypes could be built, and the projects lapsed.

Instead, attention was turned to developing an improved version of the KS type a proved and well-tried design. With a new engine and lengthened and improved suspension, the MS–I tank was evolved out of the KS. It was virtually a direct copy of the Renault development of the FT the NC–27, and was standardised for the Red Army as the T–18. With a transverse engine the T–18 was actually slightly lighter and roomier than the KS. Production started in 1928, after which slightly improved and heavier models were evolved, the MS–2 and MS–3.

From the T–18 was developed a longer, wider vehicle, the T–12, which was intended as a Medium version of the T–18 Tested in 1930, the vehicle proved unreliable and was dropped.

The First Five Year Plan, started in 1929, included measures for mechanising the Red Army and providing a range of tanks in the various tactical categories. Tank groups were to be established specifically to support infantry divisions. A number of new designs appeared, most of them based on the MS–I (T–18) design. A tankette with one-man crew and machine-gun armament (the T–17), two light tanks (T–19 and T–20) a bigger light tank (the T–21) and a two-man tankette (the T–23) were all built and tested but none proved worth proceeding with. A heavy tank the TG also proved a failure. The most promising of the spate of new 'Five Year Plan' designs was the T–24 a heavier light tank which once again utilised a Renault NC–27 type of suspension but which had a 45mm gun and turret. About 25 of the T–24s were built in 1930 for trials but the generally poor designs had many mechanical shortcomings.

Coincident with these 'home-grown' designs and adaptions of existing models, a purchasing commission visited Britain and there purchased examples of several Vickers designs together with licences for production in the Soviet Union. Medium tanks Mk II, Carden-Loyd tankettes, Vickers amphibious tanks, 6ton light tanks and tractors were included. The deal proved significant. It gave the Soviets a basic starting point for a series of light to medium tanks based on sound design principles and some details of the vehicles were also passed to the Germans who had a secret training arrangement with the Russians at the Kazan Tank School. Thus some features of Vickers and Carden-Loyd designs also appeared in early German tanks (eg PzKpfw I) in the 1930s.

Other moves in 1930 involved a licence agreement for engines with the German firm of BMW and a mission to America where rights to manufacture the Christie fast tank were acquired from its designer, J. Walter Christie.

In February 1931 after evaluation of the new foreign types, the Vickers 6tonner was adopted and was designated T–26. The Carden-Loyd tankette was designated T–27 and the Christie type was designated BT–I (fast tank). These three types were out into production later in the year, the BT only in small numbers. The T–19 and the subsequent Russian designs (T–20 to T–24 etc.) already described, were dropped completely as they did not match the efficiency and ease of assembly of the Vickers designs. Several new tank factories were opened up in the 1930s (about 30 eventually) and a massive build-up of Russian armoured strength now began.

The T–27 tankette was supplemented from 1932 by the T–37, a developed version of the Vickers Light Amphibious Tank and this in turn was supplemented by a further development, the T–38. Meanwhile the BT–2 became the definitive production of the BT (fast tank) series. Over the next few years the BT series developed up to the BT–7, details of individual models being given in the reference section.

In the new tank programme the first vehicle of wholly Russian design was the Medium T–28 which appeared in 1932. This copied many features from the contemporary British 16tonner and also from the Grosstraktor tanks then being secretly planned at Kazan by the Germans. Some T–28s were still in service in 1941, having been up-armoured as a result of experience in the Russo-Finnish War of 1939–40. The T–28, slabsided and slow, was obsolete when encountered by the Germans and proved no match for the invaders.

The last standard design arising from the First Five Year Plan was a heavy tank, the T–32. This was a very close copy in size and layout of the British 'Independent' tank of 1929. It featured a main turret and four auxiliaries. In 1933–34 an improved version of the design, the T–35, was produced. These vehicles, again completely outmoded in concept, were still in service in 1941. The multi-turret idea stemmed from the premise that such a vehicle could engage several targets simultaneously and act as a self-contained mobile fortress.

During the 1930s, Soviet armoured power was greatly increased. By about 1935–36, it was estimated that the Red Army had more than 10,000 AFVs of all types and possessed by far the largest tank force in the world.

In the late 1930s efforts were turned to improving the quality of Russian tanks. Several experimental prototypes were built in the 1930s all based on existing designs. Among these were the T–29, a Christie suspension version of the T–28 the T–III medium tank, and the BT–7M and the BT–IS, the latter two being much developed versions of the original BT series. Produced in 1937–38, these were important links in the development of what was to become Russia's greatest tank, the T–34. Both the BT–7M and the BT–IS featured sloped armour instead of the vertical or slightly angled hull plates of earlier vehicles. This idea was taken a stage further in two designs of 1938–39, the A–20 and the A–30. These vehicles featured hulls with sloped armour all round, and with side sponsons over-hanging the tracks. Christie suspension was retained. A further development, designed in 1938–39, was the T–32 which had increased armour, a turret to take a 76mm gun, and dispensed with the track-or-wheel facility of the earlier Christie-based vehicles.

From the T–32 came the T–34, a design with many mechanical improvements and wider tracks and better suspension. Prototypes were completed in early 1940 and the early trials proved highly satisfactory. The type was rushed into production, and with war now declared in Europe every effort was made to get the T–34 into service. Meanwhile the Germans had remained ignorant of the potent new tank and after the invasion of Russia in May 1941, met it for the first time in June. Until then German Panzer Divisions had encountered little difficulty in the attack and claimed to have destroyed 17,500 Russian tanks in the first 6 months. The T–34 was still not met in force however, until September, 1941, and it was soon proved able to outshoot, outrun, and outlast, any German tank. In short it rendered all German tanks obsolete. The T–34, therefore had a profound effect on subsequent developments in the AFV field. It led directly to the heavy-gun Tiger tank and the Panther, which copied many T–34 designs features including sloped armour and low ground pressure. Over 40,000 T–34 variants were produced during World War II, the many models being shown and listed in the reference pages. The T–34 was arguably the most successful and revolutionary tank design to have appeared until that time, setting many new trends for the future. It lent itself to mass production and it was simple to maintain and operate.

In the heavy tank category two new multi-turret designs, the T–100 and SMK were built in small numbers to replace the T35. Ready in 1940, they were used on the Finnish front but proved too bulky to be wholly successful. At Stalin's suggestion the basic design was changed to give a single turret, a shorter hull, and thicker armour. The resultant vehicle was the KV (Klimenti Voroshilov) produced in 1940. This again was developed through several variants and proved to be an excellent design, bigger and better armed than the heaviest German tanks of 1941.

From the KV series was developed the IS (Stalin) design. This mounted a huge 122mm gun and appeared in 1942. Like the KV series, the IS series was also developed. In May 1945 the most formidable Stalin tank model appeared the IS–3. This had sloped armour all round and a ballistically excellent turret of 'inverted frying pan' shape. At this period the IS–3 was the most powerfully armed tank in full production and gave the Soviet Army superiority over all other big powers' tanks. By 1944 the T–34 had also been considerably updated and in its latest form had a 85mm gun (T–34/85) making it the most powerful of medium tanks.

VEZDEKHOD ARMOURED TRACKLAYER

Projected in 1914 just after the outbreak of war as an armoured vehicle for storming trenches. (Vezdekhod means 'Go Anywhere'.) Prototype built early 1915. The track consisted of a full-width single band with steering by tiller-operated pivoted wheels outside the track. A petrol engine drove a rear roller inside the track. The armoured turtle-shaped hull enveloped the tracks. Central traversing turret was envisaged but not fitted. Effective design but not adopted by the army. Abandoned in December 1915. 5tons (approx); crew 2; engine (gasoline) 20hp. No other details known.

I. Ex-British Mk V tank in Russian service: For vehicle details see British section. In 1918–1919 a British force was sent to Russia to help Tsarist forces fight the Bolsheviks. When the British withdrew the tanks were left behind. In 1919 many of these were captured by the Reds and became the first Soviet tanks. The Mk V was known as the 'Ricardo' to the Soviets. Also captured were a few Medium Mk B Whippets (for vehicle details and picture see British section).

Ex-French Renault FT in Russian service, 1919: For vehicle details see French section. These vehicles were provided for the Tsarist forces by the French. In 1919 they fell into Soviet hands.

2. KS ('RUSSKIY-RENAULT') LIGHT TANK

Direct copy of captured French Renault FT built at Krasno-Sormova (KS). Prototype completed in August 1920. Limited production in 1922 (15 vehicles). Italian engine and American gearbox (from factories set up in Russia), but otherwise similar to Renault FT. Details as Renault FT (see French section) except: 37mm gun or 2 MG; armour 8–16mm; engine (gasoline) 45hp.

ZHITONOSKI TANKETTE

Private venture design for a one-man vehicle with prone driver/gunner. Maxim MG in limited traverse barbette in the nose. Licence-built Italian engine as in KS tank. (Zhitonoski means 'Shield Bearer'.) Though ingenious this vehicle was too much for one man to handle. It was not adopted by the authorities though 16 were built for trials. 2.25tons; crew 1; 7.62mm MG; armour 10mm; engine (gasoline) 40hp; 15mph.

3. KS (MS–23 'RUSSKIY-RENAULT') LIGHT TANK

Late production version of the KS, built 1923, with detail changes and provision of both a 37mm gun and MG turret. 15 built. Details as original KS.

4. MS–I (T–18) LIGHT TANK

First entirely indigenous Soviet design by the War Department tank bureau which had been set up in 1923. The MS–I was based in layout on the KS with a similar hull and turret, but new, more compact engine compartment, new transverse engine and transmission, and entirely new sprung suspension. In production 1928–31 (960 built, including later models). (MS stood for 'Maliy Soprovozdieniya', meaning 'small accompanying tank', i.e., infantry support.) 5.4tons; crew 2; 37mm gun and MG; armour 6–22mm; engine(gasoline) 35hp; 10.6mph; 11.8ft x 5.75ft x 6.90ft.

5. MS–2 LIGHT TANK

Later production model of MS–I with detail changes and uprated engine. Basic details as MS–I.

6. MS–3/MS–3A LIGHT TANKS

Final production version of MS series. As MS–I but with redesigned hull front to give full-width glacis. More powerful engine (6-cylinder instead of 4); higher speed, increased weight; MG in each side of turret. Basic details as MS–I.

7. T–I2 MEDIUM TANK
Experimental vehicle designed as an enlarged version of the MS series and with similar layout. Weighed I9tons and had 45mm gun. Mechanically unreliable and abandoned after trials.

8. T–I7 TANKETTE
Prototype one-man vehicle with fixed superstructure and MG armament only. 2-cylinder air-cooled engine. Suspension similar to MS series. Unsatisfactory.

9. T–I9/T–20 (above)/T–2I LIGHT TANKS
Experimental prototypes similar to the MS series but with modified suspension based on the contemporary French Renault NC–27 type (see French section). The T–20 also had an uprated engine and clutch and brake steering.

I0. T–23 TANKETTE
Lightweight version of the T–I8 (MS series), developed from the MS–3 and with similar hull form. Turret suppressed in favour of fixed superstructure and MG armament. Details as for MS series but weight reduced to 3.5tons and speed increased to 28mph. Prototype only.

II. TG HEAVY TANK (above, on wheels)
Experimental heavy tank. (TG stood for 'Tank Grotte', or heavy tank.) A very advanced design with low silhouette and high power : weight ratio. Pneumatic-servo steering. Unreliable transmission. 25tons; crew 5; 75mm gun and 4 MG; engine (gasoline) 300hp; 25mph.

I2. TG (on tracks)

I3. T–24 MEDIUM TANK
Developed from T–I2 (see above) but with many added refinements and improvements. Intended as a possible replacement for the MS series. Very well armed and armoured. Limited production was terminated owing to mechanical faults in design (25 were completed). I8.5tons; crew 3; 45mm gun and 3 MG; armour I0–25 mm approx; engine (gasoline) 300hp; I4mph.

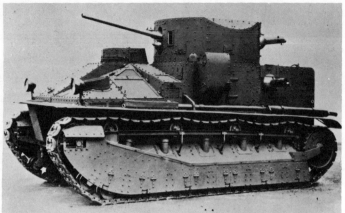

14. **Vickers Medium Tank, export model for Russia:** In 1930 the Soviet War Department made numerous overseas purchases, mainly from Britain, and obtained licences to build Vickers designs in the Soviet Union. Major buys were the Medium Mk II (known as 'English Workmen' to the Russians, Vickers 6 tonners (developed into the T–26 series, see below), Carden-Loyd Mk VI tankettes (developed into the T–27 series, see below), and Carden-Loyd amphibious tanks (developed into the T–37 series, see below). For details of all these vehicles see British section. The Russian export models of the Vickers Medium Tank had detail changes to make their performance stand up to the extremes of the Russian climate.

15. **English Workman (front view)**

16. **T–27/T–27A (above)/T–27B LIGHT TANKS**
Licence-built version of the Carden/Loyd Mk VI tankette with

changes which included a lengthened rear compartment, widened superstructure, and full-width head cover for the crew. Russian GAZ truck engine and transmission components. Three production models, the A and B featuring successive minor internal and external detail improvements. Over 4,000 were built, production ceasing in 1941. All-riveted construction. Could be carried slung under a heavy bomber aircraft. Put to various utility uses after withdrawal from first-line service. 1.7tons; crew 2; 7.62mm MG; armour 4–9 mm; engine (gasoline) 22hp; 28mph; 8.5ft x 6ft x 4.5ft.

17. **T–37/T–37A/T–37(V) (above)/T–37M LIGHT AMPHIBIOUS TANKS**
Based on Carden-Loyd A4EII amphibious tank purchased from Britain. Fitted with heavier suspension than original Vickers design. Prototype was designated T–33. T–37A (from 1935) had original balsa wood side floats omitted and combined welded/riveted construction. (V) model was a commander's tank with radio fitted and carried 'handrail' type aerials on the superstructure. T–37M was the final production model. Production terminated in 1936 but vehicles were still in service until 1942. 3.5tons; crew 2; 7.62mm MG; armour 4–9mm; engine (gasoline) 40hp; 20mph; 12.25ft x 6.5ft x 5.5ft.

18. **T–33 prototype**

19. **T–33 second prototype**

20. T–37

2I. T–37A

22. T–38 (above)/T–38M–2 LIGHT AMPHIBIOUS TANK
Improved amphibious type with lower hull, numerous mechanical and transmission changes, and turret and engine positions transposed. T–38M–2 had uprated engine and detail changes. In service until I942. 3.28tons; crew 2; 7.62mm MG; armour 4–9mm; engine (gasoline) 40–50hp; 28–40mph; I2.35ft x 7.65ft x 5.33ft.

23. T–38M–2

24. T–38M armed with a 20mm gun

25. T–26 SERIES LIGHT TANK (above, T–26A–I)
The T–26 was a licence-built version of the Vickers 6ton light tank Models A and B (see British section), examples of which were purchased in 1930 along with the lighter types. This successful design had all-riveted construction, and air-cooled rear engine, and twin turrets (Model A) or a single turret (Model B). Russian-built early versions were exact copies of the original Vickers design apart from armament changes. Later models, however, were wholly Russian developments of the original design. 'A' series models were as follows:
T–26A–I: Original Vickers vehicle (6 purchased) with Vickers MGs.
T–26A–2: Russian-built vehicle with air-cooled 7.62mm MGs.
T–26A–3: As A–2 but with I2.7mm gun in right turret.
T–26A–4: As A–2 but with 27mm gun in right turret. Infantry support tank.
T–26A–5: As A–2 but with 37mm gun in right turret. Infantry support tank.
8.5tons; crew 3; 2 MG or MG and heavier gun (see above); armour 6–I5mm; engine (gasoline) 88hp; 22mph; I5.76ft x 7.85ft x 6.75ft.

26. T–26A–4

27. T–26A–4V Commander's Tank: The original version of the T–26 commander's tank had the left turret removed. More common was the T–26A–4V or A–5V which retained both turrets. All models had the distinctive 'handrail' type frame aerial. Details as T–26A.

OT–26 Flamethrowing Tank: Flamethrower version of T–26A with left turret removed and flame gun fitted in right turret. Some used in Russo-Finnish war, 1939.

30. T–26B SERIES LIGHT TANK (above, T–26B–I)
A new model with single turret and high velocity gun developed for the use of mechanised cavalry. Based on Vickers 6ton Model B. One prototype was built, however, based on the T–26A with a 37mm gun in the left turret and the right turret removed. This was unsatisfactory and the actual T–26B models had a larger central turret, utilising the turret design from the BT tanks then being introduced. Aside from small details, hull and mechanics were as the T–26A. 'B' series models were as follows:

T–26B–I: Cylindrical turret with 37mm gun in cylindrical mantlet in early production vehicles. Later vehicles had a 45mm gun in a cast mantlet.

AT–I: Experimental tank glider with biplane wings at sides and twin boom tail, all designed to be detached on landing. Basic vehicle was a T–26B–I.

28. OT–26 with flush-top turret

T–26B–2: Improved model of mainly welded construction, and with hull storage boxes. Turret had larger overhang with gun counterweight inside. Welded mantlet. Some vehicles had a ball-mounted MG in the turret rear.

29. OT–26A with stepped-top turret

3I. T–26B–I(V) Commander's Tank: This was the basic B–I model fitted with radio in the turret rear and with a frame aerial round the turret. Similar in appearance was the T–26B–2(V) which had the same turret but the welded hull and other changes of the B–2 model.

32. T–26B–2(V)

33. T–26B–2(V) in Chinese service

34. OT–I30 Flamethrowing Tank: Flamethrower version of either T–26B–I, T–26B–2, or T–26B–I(V) (frame aerial replaced by whip aerial in latter case). In service 1939–4l. (25).

35. OT–I30, second version

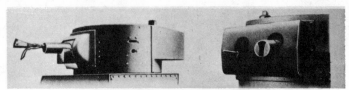

36. The two OT–I30 models, flame guns compared

37. T–26S SERIES LIGHT TANK

Final production version of the T–26, this model was a considerable redesign. Thicker armour, welding throughout, and rounded-off superstructure were major features, and many had a ball MG in the turret rear. Often known as the T–26C. Late production model was also called the T–26E, having its 45mm stabilised in elevation. Some T–26B–2 tanks were modernised to T–26S standard by addition of the new turret. l0.3tons; 45mm gun plus 2 MG; armour l0–25mm; height 7.65ft. Other details as T–26A.

38. T–26B–2, reworked to T–26S standard

39. OT–I33 Flamethrowing Tank: This was a flamethrower version of the T–26S. Flame projector was fitted in place of the 45mm gun and the two MGs, front and rear, were retained. Fuel for flames carried in turret. In service 1939–42.

AT–I Artillery Tank: This was a close-support version of the T–26B–I with the 45mm gun replaced by a short low velocity 76.2mm howitzer.

40. T–46 LIGHT TANK
This was an intended replacement for the T–26 series in which the Christie type suspension of the fast BT tanks was married to the T–26 hull. Apart from increased speed and the well-known Christie capability of running on wheels or tracks, it was similar in all respects to the T–26. It was abandoned, however, after only a few had been built, as offering no worthwhile improvement over the T–26. I0.2tons; crew 3; 35mph; length I8ft. Other details as T–26A.

4I. T–4I LIGHT AMPHIBIOUS TANK
Very light (3.2tons) design intended to replace the T–37. Proved

unsatisfactory on trials, however, and only the prototype was built.

42. T–30 LIGHT AMPHIBIOUS TANK
Prototype light tank intended to replace earlier designs. It had a 20mm aircraft cannon and coaxial 7.62mm MG. It was replaced by an improved but similar design, the T–40, and no production took place. Details generally as T–40.

43. T–50 LIGHT TANK
Designed to replace the T–26, this vehicle had torsion bar suspension, a cast turret, cupola for the commander, and much improved shape with thicker armour. A diesel engine was fitted. It saw only limited service, however, since production ceased after 65 had been built owing to its excessively complicated production requirements. I3.5tons; crew 4; 45mm gun plus 2 MG; armour I2–37mm; engine (diesel) 300hp; 32.5mph; I7ft x 8.Ift x 6.6ft.

44. T–40 LIGHT AMPHIBIOUS TANK (above, T–40A)
Built as a replacement for the amphibious tanks T–27, T–37A, and T–38 series, this was virtually an improvement on the T–30 design and intended to overcome the complications of the T–50 by utilising automobile components wherever possible to simplify production. Flotation tanks were built into the hull and there was torsion bar suspension. Production models were:
T–40: Original type with squared off blunt nose.
T–40A: Improved type with streamlined nose and folding trim vane.

45. T–40S: Improved (1942) production model with thicker armour on hull sides, front, and turret, and with rear propeller removed. This was non-amphibious. It was externally similar to the T–40A except for the absence of trim vane and propeller.
6.2tons; crew 2; 12.7mm or 20mm gun plus MG; armour 10–14mm; engine (gasoline) 85hp; 26mph; 14ft x 7.65ft x 6.48ft (figures for T–40A, other models differ slightly).

46. T–60 LIGHT TANK
Completely new model to replace all existing types of obsolescent light tank in service, this vehicle was based on the T–40 chassis but was intended from the start to be non-amphibious. It had the same general layout as the T–40, with similar suspension, but the armament was a 20mm aircraft cannon and the armour was increased. Turret was inspired by Swedish Landsverk designs. Over 6,000 T–60 series vehicles were built by 1943 when production ceased. 5.75tons; crew 2; 20mm gun and MG; armour 7–25 mm; engine (gasoline) 85hp; 27mph; 13.1ft x 7.5ft x 6.65ft.

47. T–60A Light Tank: Improved production model (early 1942) of the T–60. It had thicker frontal armour (35mm), solid disc wheels instead of the earlier spokes, and differed dimensionally from the T–60 by a few inches.

48. T–70 LIGHT TANK
Produced to overcome the limitations of armour and firepower apparent in the T–60, this vehicle utilised the basic T–60 chassis with drive changed to the front. Hull armour was increased and there was a new welded turret. Twin truck-type engines were fitted (the T–60 had a single) giving much greater power. Designed for mass-production by the automotive industry, 8,226 were built when production ended in 1944. The later production model was the T–70A which was virtually identical to the original design except for thicker turret armour and a squared off turret rear with reinforced corners. 9.05tons; crew 2; 45mm gun plus MG; armour 10–60mm; engine (gasoline) 2 x 70hp; 32mph; 15.28ft x 7.68ft x 7.5ft.

49. T–70A

50. T–80 LIGHT TANKS
Based closely on the T–70, this vehicle had extra welded-on hull armour and a new turret, wider and more heavily armoured and with a cupola. There was possibly an extra crew member. Few were built as light tanks were discontinued in the Soviet Army in 1944, their role being taken over largely by Lend-Lease American half-tracks. Apart from thicker armour, details as for T–70.

51. BT–I MEDIUM TANK

Copied from the Christie M–1931 (T–3) tank (see American section) which was brought from the USA by a Soviet Purchasing Mission. This vehicle had the original Christie capability of running either on its tracks or on its road wheels as required. Construction was all-riveted and turret was exactly similar to M–1931 with twin MGs. Engine was a copy of the Liberty engine in the Christie vehicle. Limited production. 10.2tons; crew 3; 2 7.62mm MG; armour 6–13mm; engine (gasoline) 343–400hp; 40–69mph; 18ft x 7.33ft x 6.33ft.

52. BT–2 MEDIUM TANK

Developed from BT–I and very similar except for a new turret with 37mm gun and ball-mounted MG. First major production type and still in service in 1940. Details as BT–I except for heavier armament and IItons weight.

53. BT–2 on wheels

54. BT–3 (above)/BT–4 MEDIUM TANKS

BT–3 was a modified version of the BT–2 with solid disc wheels instead of the spoked type of earlier vehicles. The 37mm gun was replaced by a 45mm gun. Production was limited. The BT–4 was a prototype with hull features of the BT–3 but with the single turret replaced by the twin turret arrangement of the T–26A series light tanks (qv). It was not put into production. All other details for both vehicles as for BT–I.

55. BT–3 Bridgelayer: 1937 conversion of BT–3 with gun removed and wooden folding bridge carried on front of hull. Prototype only.

BT–3 Flamethrowing Tank: 1939 conversion of BT–3 with the original turret replaced by OT–I33 turret. Prototype only.

56. BT–5 MEDIUM TANK

Major production model evolved from initial BT series. Enlarged cylindrical turret, 45mm gun, coaxial MG, new engine derived from aero type, improved vision devices, and stronger suspension. Similar variant was the BT–5A which was a close-support tank with a 76.2mm howitzer replacing the 45mm gun. II.5tons; crew 3; 45mm gun plus MG; armour 6–13mm; engine (gasoline) 350hp; 40–69mph; 18ft x 7.33ft x 7.25ft. Other users: Finland, Germany (captured vehicles).

57. BT–5(V) Commander's Tank: This was identical to the BT–5 except for the frame aerial round the turret and the provision of a radio in the rear turret overhang.

58. BT–7 MEDIUM TANK (above, BT–7–2)
Further improvement on the BT–5 with a new conical turret (BT–7–2) in all but the earliest vehicles (BT–7–I). Thicker front armour, all-welded construction, a more powerful aero-type engine, a ball-mounted MG in the turret rear (in some vehicles), new gearbox, and extra fuel and ammunition stowage were other features. The BT–7 was the major service type in the 1939–41 period. A similar vehicle was the BT–7A close support tank which had a 76.2mm howitzer replacing the 45mm gun. Dispensed with wheel running ability and car type steering. 13.8tons; crew 3; 45mm gun plus 2 MG; armour 6–22mm; engine (gasoline) 450hp; 45mph; 18.65ft x 7.98ft x 7.5ft. Other users: Finland, Germany (captured vehicles).

59. BT–7–I(V) Commander's Tank: BT–7 fitted with the turret from the BT–5(V), complete with frame aerial sockets. Shown here with tracks removed.

60. BT–7M MEDIUM TANK
Based on the BT–7 chassis but with considerable redesign to take V-2 diesel engine and a full-width sloped front glacis plate instead of the faired nose of earlier BTs Turret from T–28 with two ball-mounted MGs and 76.2mm gun. Also called the BT–8. Limited production. Retained wheel/track running ability.

6I. BT–IS MEDIUM TANK
Final development of the BT series, this vehicle was built as a prototype only and was based on the BT–7M but was given sloped side armour as well as the sloping glacis. It retained the conical turret of the BT–7–2 and had removable side skirts. This was an important development vehicle in the evolution of the T–34 tank and was the first Soviet tank with all-sloped armour. 15.6tons; crew 3; 45mm gun plus MG; armour 6–30mm; engine (diesel) 500hp; 40mph; 18.98ft x 7.5ft x 7.5ft.

62. T–28 MEDIUM TANK
Designed with high firepower as a major attack type. Inspired by British A6 and similar German Nb Fz designs. Centrally mounted main turret and two auxiliary MG turrets in front. Suspension copied from Vickers type (vertical springing) as on Vickers Medium Tank. Prototype had 45mm gun; production vehicles had 76.2mm low velocity gun. Later vehicles sometimes had a 45mm gun in the right auxiliary turret in place of MGs. In service until 1941. 28.5tons; crew 6; 76.2mm plus 3 MG; armour 10–30mm; engine (gasoline) 500hp; 23mph; 18ft x 9.20ft x 9.25ft.

63. T–28 Prototype

66. T–28B MEDIUM TANK
This was the original T–28A, modified with a turret basket, visors for the driver, and — in most cases — a longer and more powerful L/26 76.2mm gun.

64. T–28A MEDIUM TANK
This was an improved production model, mainly with changes to the suspension and with slightly thicker front armour.

67. T–28C MEDIUM TANK
Existing T–28Bs given increased armour (up to 80mm) on hull front and turrets as a result of early experience in Russo-Finnish war. Also fitted with a longer L/26 gun in main turret. Distinguished by high plain armour screens round the turret. Used against the Germans in 1941.

OT–28 Flamethrowing Tank: A conversion produced in small numbers.

68. T–29–5 EXPERIMENTAL MEDIUM TANK
An attempt to marry Christie suspension to the T–28 medium tank chassis. The resulting design had the Christie type wheel and track capability. Details generally as for T–28.

65. T–28(V) Commander's Tank: This was a radio-fitted version of the T–28 which had a frame aerial round the turret sides.

69. T–29 EXPERIMENTAL MEDIUM TANK

Further refinement of the Christie idea, this time with ability to run at the same speed on wheels or tracks. Prototype only. 28.5tons; crew 5–6; 76.2mm gun plus 4–5 MG; armour 40mm (max.); engine (gasoline) 500hp; 35mph. Other details as T–28.

70. T–III(T–46–5) MEDIUM TANK

Prototype utilising Christie suspension with small road wheels. Powered by diesel engine, armoured to 60mm maximum and armed with a 45mm gun. It was intended to run on tracks or wheels in the original Christie fashion. Over-complex suspension and inferior ballistic shape led to its rejection in favour of the A–20 and A–30 designs. 28tons; crew 4; 45mm gun plus 2 MG; armour 60mm (max.); engine (diesel) 300hp; 28mph.

71. A–20 MEDIUM TANK

Developed from the BT–IS as an alternative design to the T–III and to meet the same requirements for a new medium tank. Weight limit set was 20tons. Wheel and track running facility with Christie suspension. Fully sloped armoured hull on basic BT–7M chassis and turret of rolled armour plate. Prototype only leading to the development of A–30. 19.8tons; crew 4; 45mm gun plus 2 MG; armour 15–60mm, engine (diesel) 450hp; 40mph; 17.85ft x 8.85ft x 7.85ft.

A–30 MEDIUM TANK

A–20 further modified with 76.2mm gun replacing the 45mm gun. Unsatisfactory, but it led to the T–32 design. Details as A–20 except weight, 20.86tons.

72. T–32 MEDIUM TANK

Redesign for a medium tank based on experience with the A–20/A–30 prototypes. Wheel and track running ability and steering wheel steering were abandoned in favour of tracks only with lever and brake steering. Tracks were widened and the hull shape was improved. Enlarged turret allowed the installation of a 76.2mm gun. 19tons; crew 4; 76.2mm gun plus 2 MG; armour 30–60mm; engine (diesel) 450hp; 38mph; 17.85ft x 8.85ft x 7.85ft.

T–34/76A MEDIUM TANK

Production design based on the T–32 prototype. Pilot models were produced early in 1940. Thicker armour than the T–32 and many detail improvements. The 76.2mm gun was standard: short calibre (L/30) on early vehicles but a longer (L/40) version in most vehicles. This became the major USSR tank of World War II with many production models and special variants (see subsequent details). Full production commenced in June 1940. Being the most advanced design of its time it gave the Red Army an immediate tank superiority over the Germans. Fully sloped armour, simple to build, unsophisticated fittings, easy to maintain, and with a very low silhouette. Early vehicles had a second MG in a turret ball mount. Unarmoured ball mount for hull MG. 26.3tons; crew 4; 76.2mm gun plus 2 or 3 MG; armour 14–45mm; engine (diesel) 500hp; 31mph; 21.6ft x 9.8ft x 8ft.

73. T–34/76A, with welded turret, L/30 76.2mm gun

74. T–34/76A with cast turret L/30 76.2mm gun

75. T–34/76B MEDIUM TANK
Second production model of the T–34 with a rolled plate turret
mounting, an L/40 76.2mm gun and other detail changes. Commander's models had radio, and stowage boxes on the track
covers. Late production vehicles had a cast instead of welded
turret and many had all-steel wheels instead of rubber-tyred
wheels, owing to rubber shortage. Details as for T–34/76A except
for weight 28tons.

76. T–34/76B ATO–4I Flamethrowing Tank: with armoured fuel tank
on hull rear and flame projector in place of hull MG. Limited
production.

77. T–34/76C MEDIUM TANK
Third production model with new enlarged turret and twin hatches
replacing the large single hatch of previous models: Improved
spudded tracks, an armoured sleeve for the hull MG, and better
vision devices (including twin instead of single episcopes in the
driver's hatch) were among the changes. Details as T–34/76A
except weight 30tons and speed 30mph.

78. T–34/76D MEDIUM TANK
Much improved production model with entirely new hexagonal

turret and wide mantlet/mount for gun. This turret eliminated th
shot trap from rear of turret. Increased fuel tankage includin
provision for external jettisonable tanks (later retro-fitted on earlie
models). Details as earlier models except 30.9tons; armour 18–7
mm; 3Imph.

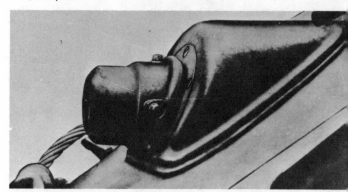

79. T–34/76D ATO–42 (OT–34) Flamethrowing Tank: 1944 develop
ment from ATO–4I with fuel tank of double the ATO–4I capacity
carried inside the tank. Identical to basic model except for pro
minent flame gun in place of hull MG.

80. T–34/76E MEDIUM TANK
As T–34/76D but with added cupola and all-welded constructior
and cooling improvements.

8I. T–34/76F MEDIUM TANK
As T–34/76D but with cast instead of welded turret. Mechanica
improvements including five-speed gearbox. Production terminatec
after I00 vehicles in favour of T–34/85. Details as T–34/76D.

82. T–34/76F with commanders cupola

83. T–34/76F with mine-rollers

86. T–34/85–II

84. T–43 MEDIUM TANK

Much improved development of T–34/76D with cupola on turret, five-speed gearbox, increased frontal armour, and mechanical changes. Limited production owing to introduction of upgunned model, the T–34/85. Details are T–34/76D except 31.5tons; armour 18–110mm; length 22.5ft.

87. T–34/85, with mine-rollers

NOTE: T–34 variants continued in service until 1970 and beyond. There were also self-propelled gun versions, beyond the scope of this book. Total T–34 series production (all variants) to 1945 was nearly 40,000. By early 1960s it had reached nearly 55,000. Other users: Poland (from late 1944). Czechoslovakia, Republic of China, East Germany, Egypt, Syria, Libya, North Korea, Jugoslavia, Israel, Hungary, Cuba (all post 1945).

85. T–34/85 MEDIUM TANK (above, T–34/85–I)

Upgunned version of the T–34 featuring a completely new and enlarged turret with 85mm gun to match improved firepower of later German tanks. Turret was modified from that developed from the KV–85(qv). Gun was based on an AA gun already in service on a field carriage. In service in 1944, it was produced in increasing numbers until the end of war and beyond. (In 1947 a further improved model was put into production which became known as the T–34/85–II, the original being distinguished as the T–34/85–I.) 31.5tons; crew 5; 85mm gun plus MG; armour 18–75 mm; engine (diesel) 500hp; 31mph; 24.6ft x 9.8ft x 7.8ft.

88. T–44 MEDIUM TANK

Designed in 1944 and in production in 1945. Total redesign of medium tank concept with lower silhouette, transverse rear engine, reduced depth hull, torsion bar suspension, enlarged turret, thicker armour, and hull MG deleted. Early vehicles had a similar 85mm gun to the T–34/85; later vehicles had a 100mm gun. Mechanical defects led to limited production. Eventually replaced (postwar) by T–54 series. 31–34tons (depending on gun); crew 4; 85mm or 100mm plus 2 MG; armour 15–120mm; engine (diesel) 512hp; 32mph; 25ft or 26.5ft x 10.2ft x 7.85ft.

89. T–32 (M–II) HEAVY TANK

Multi-turreted vehicle inspired by British Independent Tank (see British section). Complementary to T–28 medium tank. Developed from TG heavy tank design. Massive slab sides completely covering suspension. Five turrets: main with 76.2mm gun, two with 7.62mm MGs, and two with 37mm guns. Each large calibre gun also had a coaxial MG. Limited production before replacement by improved model, the T–35. 44.8tons; crew 10; 76.2mm gun, 2 37mm gun, 6 MG; armour 11–25mm; engine (gasoline) 345hp; 18mph; 30.5ft x 10.5ft x 10ft.

90. T–35 HEAVY TANK

Replaced the T–32 and generally similar but with many detail improvements. More powerful engine, increased ammunition stowage, reduced side skirts, thicker armour, and provision of radio (with prominent frame aerial) were new features. Production was limited to about 30 vehicles. Retrospective improvements included replacement of 37mm guns by 45mm guns in auxiliary turrets; one or two vehicles were fitted as flamethrowers, and late vehicles had conical main turrets. T–35s were used in the Russo-Finnish War and again in the opening stages of the German invasion of Russia, June 1941, where many were destroyed. Guns and/or turrets were reduced in some vehicles with corresponding reduction in crew. 45tons; crew 10; 76.2mm gun, 2 45mm guns, 6 MG; armour 11–35mm; engine (gasoline) 500hp; 18mph; 31.5ft x 10.5ft x 11.25ft.

91. T–35: Late production vehicle with conical slope-sided main turret. This vehicle had more welding in its construction.

92. T–35, Commander's model

93. T–100 HEAVY TANK

Replacement for the T–35 designed once more on the multi-turret principle. Originally to have three turrets but one deleted to reduce bulk and allow thicker armour. Torsion bar suspension with small road wheels 76.2mm gun in main turret with 45mm gun in lower turret with traverse from side to side only. Cast armour. Few prototypes constructed. Combat-tested in Finland in 1939, it proved to be excessively large and unwieldy. Work on the T–100 was abandoned in 1940 in favour of the KV. 56tons; crew 6; 76.2 mm gun, 45mm gun, 3 MG; armour 30–60mm; engine (gasoline) 400hp; 18.7mph. 29.3ft x 9.75ft x 10.7ft.

94. SMK (SERGIUS MIRONOVITCH KIROV) HEAVY TANK

Produced concurrently with the T–100 as a slightly lighter type. Used in Finland but proved too unwieldy and abandoned as a project. Externally almost identical to the T–100. 45tons; crew 7; 76.2mm gun, 45mm gun, 3 MG; armour 30–60mm; engine (gasoline) 400hp; 20mph; 31.5ft x 10.5ft x 10.5ft.

95. KV-I (KLIMENTI VOROSHILOV) HEAVY TANK
Redesign based closely on the T–100/SMK vehicles but with the second turret eliminated and dimensions reduced accordingly. Torsion bar suspension, but features otherwise similar to the earlier vehicles. Prototypes were tested under combat conditions in the Russo-Finnish War. Fitted with same diesel engine and many detail components in common with the T-34. Very powerful and successful design which saw much further development (see variants below). Welded turret and cast mantlet. Early vehicles had the short (L/30) 76.2mm gun; later vehicles had the L/40 gun. 46.35tons; crew 5; 76.2mm plus 3 MG; armour 30–77–75 + 25mm; engine (diesel) 550hp; 22mph; 22.6ft x 10.65ft x 8.75ft.

96. KV-IA: Improved 1940 production model with L/40 gun as standard and bolted/welded mantlet; new resilient wheels. Details as KV-I.

97. KV-IB: Uparmoured version with 25–35mm additional armour on hull front and sides. Extra armour bolted on turret sides. This was the 1941 production type.

98. KV-IB (cast turret): 1942 production vehicle with new cast turret replacing the earlier welded type. Added hull armour as for original KV-IB.

99. KV-IC: 1942 production model with improved cast turret having thicker (120mm) armour and extra side armour (total of 130mm), and engine uprated to 600hp. New wider tracks. Details as for KV-I except weight 47tons and differences noted above.

100. KV-Is: Lightened version of KV-IC produced in small numbers in 1942-3 to increase speed (s stood for 'skorostnoy' meaning fast). Appliqué armour largely omitted but appearance otherwise similar to KV-IC. Details as KV-I except weight 42.5tons; armour 60mm (max.); 25mph.

101. KV-85: Produced in 1943, this had a bigger cast turret than previous models and the 85mm gun. Most were converted from KV-Is by the addition of the new turret. Limited production owing to introduction of new improved types with better weapons. Details as KV-I except where noted. 46tons.

102. KV–2A: Close support version of the KV produced in 1940 concurrently with the KV–I. Early models had a 122mm howitzer but most had a 152mm howitzer, mounted in a very large, high turret. Proved most unwieldy and of limited tactical value and was withdrawn at an early stage. 53tons; crew 6; 152mm howitzer plus 2 MG; armour 35–100mm; engine (diesel) 550hp; 16mph; 22.3ft x 10.93ft x 12ft.

KV–2B: Improved version of KV–2, based on the KV–IB chassis. Had an assymetric mantlet, otherwise similar to the KV–2A. One or two were fitted for flamethrowing. Details as KV–2A except weight 57tons; height 13.7ft.

KV–2–I: Experimental prototype with 85mm gun replacing the 152mm Howitzer. Not put in service, produced in 1943. Another vehicle was similarly fitted with a 122mm gun.

103. IS–85 (above)/IS–100/IS–I (IOSEPH STALIN) HEAVY TANK
Virtual redesign of the KV to allow fitting of a larger diameter turret and so permit mounting of even bigger guns to counter increasing firepower of German tanks. Original design was chosen

from 21 new designs for future types in late 1943. As built the early vehicles had a 85mm gun (IS–85) but these were later replaced by vehicles with a 100mm gun (IS–100). The Stalin was the most powerful gun tank, in terms of firepower, in Europe at the time of its first appearance. Chassis similar to KV but with idlers, sprockets, and return rollers lowered to allow superstructure to overhang the tracks and so accommodate larger turret. Cast hull front with streamlined front superstructure. In 1944 the small number of IS–Is with 100mm guns were replaced by later vehicles armed with 122mm guns in a larger turret. 44tons; crew 4; 85mm or 100mm or 122mm gun plus 4 MG; armour 19–120mm; engine (diesel) 513hp; 23mph; 27.3ft x 10.25ft x 8.9ft.

104. IS–I was the definitive production version with 122mm gun.

105. IS–2 HEAVY TANK
Improved production model with reduced weight and better shape to hull. Sloping streamlined glacis plate. Minor turret changes. Major production type (2,250 built). Details as IS–I.

106. IS–3 HEAVY TANK
Complete redesign of Stalin tank to give lower silhouette, improved ballistic shape to hull, maximum shot deflection, and low 'inverted frying pan' turret. Most advanced heavy tank of its time and a major influence on subsequent British and American designs. In service early 1945. 45.8tons; crew 4; 122mm gun plus 2 MG; armour 24–120mm; engine (diesel) 519hp; 23mph; 32.75ft x 10.5ft x 8.9ft.
NOTE: Several self-propelled guns were produced on the KV or IS series chassis. Other users: (Stalin series) Poland, Czechoslovakia, Egypt, Syria, Libya, East Germany (all post-1945).

MISCELLANEOUS COUNTRIES

The following section deals with countries that, prior to 1940, equipped their armoured units with tanks that were either purchased or built under licence from major armament producers like Vickers-Armstrongs, Renault, Fiat, Skoda, Ceskomoravaska Kolben Danek or Landsverk. Some of these vehicles were modified by the users to suit their own requirements. Only in a few instances did some of these countries build prototype vehicles to their own designs or (as in the case of Argentina) a limited batch of production vehicles. After the outbreak of World War II many of these nations declared for either the Allied or German sides and subsequently they received additional equipment from the major combatants. In the case of the nations (mostly Latin-American states) within the Allied sphere of influence, the majority of the equipment was supplied by the United States.

The following summary lists the various tank types used by these countries but fuller details of these vehicles are given in the relevant main sections of the book.

1

2

3

4

5

6

7

8

9

10

11

12

13

14

17

15

18

19

16

20

21

25

22

26

23

27

24

28

29

32

30

33

31

34

35

39

36

40

37

38

41

42

45

43

46

47

44

48

49

51

50

52

	User country	Type	Maker	Country of origin	Approx. date in service	Remarks
I.	**Afghanistan**	Disston Tractor Tank	Disston Tractor Co	USA	1936	Based upon the 'Caterpillar 30' tractor
		CV.33	Ansaldo	Italy		Two-man tankette
	Albania	3000 B	Fiat	Italy	1929	Two-man light tank
	Arabia	Light Tank Mk II	Vickers — R.O.F.	Gt. Britain	1933	Two-man light tank
		Carden-Loyd Mk VIB	Vickers-Armstrongs	Gt. Britain		Two-man tankette
2.	**Argentina**	Carden-Loyd M1934	Vickers-Armstrongs	Gt. Britain	1938	Two-man light tank Twelve vehicles acquired
3.		Nahuel		Argentina	1942–3	Four-man medium tank produced in Argentina. Production ceased after 16 machines were manufactured 35tons; 1 75mm gun, 2 MG; 25mph
4.	**Austria**	CV.33	Ansaldo	Italy	1935	Two-man tankette Austrian designation: Kleinkampfwagen M.1933 rearmed with Austrian Schwarzlose MG
5.	**Belgium**	FT	Renault	France	1920–2	Two-man light tank Seventy-five vehicles acquired. Armed with either a 37mm gun or MG.
6.		Carden-Loyd M1934	Vickers-Armstrongs	Gt. Britain	1935	Two-man light tank Forty-two vehicles acquired — High conical turret — Armed in Belgium with a 13.2mm Hotchkiss air-cooled MG Belgian designation: T15
7.		AMC-35 (ACGI)	Renault	France	1937	Three-man medium tank Twelve vehicles acquired — Fitted with a Belgian-made turret housing a 47mm A/Tk gun and a 13.2mm MG. Belgian designation: Auto-mitrailleuse du Corps de Cavalerie
	Bolivia	FT M1917-M1918	Renault	France		Two-man light tank

	User country	Type	Maker	Country of origin	Approx. date in service	Remarks
	Brazil	Carden-Loyd Mk VIB	Vickers-Armstrongs	Gt. Britain	1930	Two-man tankette
		6ton	Vickers-Armstrongs	Gt. Britain	1930	Three-man light tank
		FT M1918	Renault	France	1923	Two-man light tank
8.		CV.33	Ansaldo	Italy		Two-man tankette — Fitted with a 13.2mm MG
9.		M3 Stuart	American Car & Foundry	USA	1942	Four-man light tank
		M4 Sherman	Chrysler and others	USA	1944	Five-man medium tank
10.	Bulgaria	CV.33	Ansaldo	Italy	1935	Two-man tankette
11.		6ton Mk 'E'	Vickers-Armstrongs	Gt. Britain	1938	Three-man light tank, single turret type — Eight vehicles acquired
	Chile	Carden-Loyd Mk VIB	Vickers-Armstrongs	Gt. Britain	1931	Two-man tankette
	China	FT M1918	Renault	France	1927	Two-man light tank — delivered to Chang Tso Lin
		T-27		Russia		Two-man tankette
12.		T–26B		Russia		Three-man light tank, single turret type
13.		6ton Mk 'E'	Vickers-Armstrongs	Gt. Britain	1936	Three-man light tank single turret type — Sixteen vehicles acquired
		6ton Mk 'F'	Vickers-Armstrongs	Gt. Britain	1936	Three-man light tank, single turret type — Four vehicles acquired — fitted with a radio equipment housed in turret rear overhang
14.		Carden-Loyd M1931	Vickers-Armstrongs	Gt. Britain	1935	Two man light amphibious tank Twenty-nine vehicles acquired
		Carden-Loyd M1936	Vickers-Armstrongs	Gt. Britain	1936	Two-man light tank, fitted with radio equipment — four vehicles acquired
15.		CV.33	Ansaldo	Italy	1936	Two-man tankette
		CTLS-4TAC	Marmon-Herrington	USA	1940	Two-man light tank Right hand turret type
		CTLS-4TA	Marmon-Herrington	USA	1940	Two-man light tank Left hand turret type Both 4TAC and 4TA orders were taken over by US Ordnance Department and redesignated: Light Tank T16
16.		M3A3 Stuart	American Car & Foundry	USA	1943	Four-man light tank
17.		M5 Stuart	Cadillac and others	USA	1944	Four-man light tank
18.	Cuba	M4 Sherman	Chrysler and others	USA	1943–4	Five-man medium tank
		CTMS-ITBI	Marmon-Herrington	USA	1942	Three-man light-medium tank
		M3 Stuart	American Car & Foundry	USA	1942–3	Four-man light tank
	Denmark	3000 B	Fiat	Italy	1920	Two-man light tank
		NC.2 (NC.31)	Renault	France	1932	Two-man light tank One vehicle acquired for trials
		Carden-Loyd 'Patrol'	Vickers-Armstrongs	Gt. Britain	1934	Two-man small tank One vehicle (second model) acquired for trials
	Ecuador	CTMS-ITBI	Marmon-Herrington	USA	1942–3	Three-man light-medium tank
		M3 Stuart	American Car & Foundry	USA	1944	Four-man light tank
19.	Egypt	Light Tank Mk III	Vickers — ROF	Gt. Britain	1937	Two-man light tank
		Light Tank Mk VIB	Vickers — ROF	Gt. Britain	1938	Three-man light tank
		Medium Tank Mk II	Vickers	Gt. Britain	1937	Five-man light-medium tank
	Eire	Mark V*		Gt. Britain	1920	World War I heavy tank
20.		Vickers Mk C	Vickers	Gt. Britain	1930	Five-man tank one vehicle acquired for trials
		L-60	Landsverk	Sweden	1938	Three-man light tank Three vehicles acquired
	Esthonia	Mark V		Gt. Britain	1919	World War I heavy tank
		FT M1917	Renault	France	1924	Two-man light tank
		TKS	PZI	Poland	1934	Two-man tankette
	Ethiopia	3000 A	Fiat	Italy	1925	Two-man light tank one vehicle acquired
		3000 B	Fiat	Italy	1930	Two-man light tank three vehicles acquired
	Finland	FT M1917-M1918	Renault	France	1921	Two-man light tank
		Carden-Loyd 'Patrol'	Vickers-Armstrongs	Gt. Britain	1933	Two-man small tank
		Carden-Loyd Mk VI*	Vickers-Armstrongs	Gt. Britain	1933	Two-man tankette one vehicle acquired

	User country	Type	Maker	Country of origin	Approx. date in service	Remarks
21.		Carden-Loyd M1933	Vickers-Armstrongs	Gt. Britain		Two-man light tank one vehicle acquired
22.		6ton Mk 'E'	Vickers-Armstrongs	Gt. Britain		Three-man light tank, single turret type — Twenty-seven vehicles delivered by 1939 — Armament fitted in Finland
23.		BT (illustrated) T-26, T-27, T-28, T-33, T-37, T-38, T-50, T-60, T-34, KV-I.		Russia		Russian tanks of various types captured during the two Russo-Finnish Wars
	Greece	FT	Renault	France	1920	Two-man light tank
		NC.I (NC.27)	Renault	France		Two-man light tank
		NC.2 (NC.3I)	Renault	France		Two-man light tank
		3000 B	Fiat	Italy		Two-man light tank
		6ton Mk 'E'	Vickers-Armstrongs	Gt. Britain	1931	Three-man light tank Two vehicles were acquired, either of single and twin turret types
24.		CV.33/35	Ansaldo	Italy	1941	Two-man tankette — captured vehicles
	Guatemala	CTMS-ITBI	Marmon-Herrington	USA	1942	Three-man light medium tank
		M3 Stuart	American Car & Foundry	USA	1945	Four-man light tank
	Iran (Persia)	FT	Renault	France	1924	Two-man light tank
		CTL-I	Marmon-Herrington	USA	1935	Two-man tankette, turretless One vehicle acquired for trials
25.		AH-IV-P	CKD/Praga	Czech.	1935–6	Two-man small tank Fifty vehicles acquired
26.		TNH-P	CKD/Praga	Czech.	1935–7	Three-man light tank Export version of the (LT)TNH design Fifty vehicles acquired
	Latvia	Mark V		Gt. Britain	1930	World War I heavy tank
		Medium Mk B	MCWF	Gt. Britain	1930	World War I medium tank
		FT	Renault	France	1939	Two-man light tank
		3000 B	Fiat	Italy	1930	Two-man light tank
		Carden-Loyd M1936	Vickers-Armstrongs	Gt. Britain	1938	Two-man light tank Eighteen vehicles acquired
27.	Lithuania	FT M1917-M1918	Renault	France	1925	Two-man light tank
		Carden-Loyd M1933	Vickers-Armstrongs	Gt. Britain	1934	Two-man light tank Eighteen vehicles acquired
28.		Carden-Loyd M1936	Vickers-Armstrongs	Gt. Britain	1937	Two-man light tank Eighteen vehicles acquired
29.		LTL	CKD/Praga	Czech.	1938–40	Three-man light tank Export version of the (LT)TNH design Twenty-one vehicles acquired
		L-I0	Landsverk	Sweden		Four-man light medium tank not confirmed
30.	Mexico	CTVL	Marmon-Herrington	USA	1938	Two-man light tank — turretless
31.		CTMS-ITBI	Marmon-Herrington	USA	1941	Three-man light medium tank
		M3 Stuart	American Car & Foundry	USA	1943	Four-man light tank
		M4 Sherman	Chrysler and others	USA	1945	Five-man medium tank
32.	Netherlands	FT M1918	Renault	France	1928	Two-man light tank Two vehicles acquired for trials
33.		Carden-Loyd Mk VI	Vickers-Armstrongs	Gt. Britain		Two-man tankette Five vehicles acquired
34.	Netherlands East Indies	Carden-Loyd M1936 'Dutchman'	Vickers-Armstrongs	Gt. Britain		Two-man light tank Twenty-four vehicles acquired Some were armed with two machine-guns in turret
35.	Netherlands West Indies (Guiana)	Carden-Loyd M1931	Vickers-Armstrongs	Gt. Britain		Two-man light amphibious tank
		CTMS-ITBI	Marmon-Herrington	USA	1942	Three-man light medium tank
		MTLS-IGI4	Marmon-Herrington	USA	1942	Four-man medium tank
36.		CTLS-4TAC	Marmon-Herrington	USA	1942	Two-man light tank These vehicles were originally ordered for shipment to the Netherlands East Indies, they were finally delivered in Dutch Guiana

#	User country	Type	Maker	Country of origin	Approx. date in service	Remarks
	Peru	LTP	CKD/Praga	Czech.	1938	Three-man light tank / Twenty-four vehicles acquired / Export version of the (LT)TNH design
	Portugal	NC2 (NC31)	Renault	France	1931	Two-man light tank / Acquired for trials
		Carden-Loyd Mk VI	Vickers-Armstrongs	Gt. Britain	1931	Two-man tankette / Six vehicles acquired
		6ton Mk 'E'	Vickers-Armstrongs	Gt. Britain	1931	Three-man light tank / Two vehicles acquired, single and twin turret types
	Rumania	FT M1917	Renault	France	1920	Two-man light tank
		S-IIa (T-II)	Skoda — CKD/Praga	Czech.	1938	Four-man light tank
37, 38.		R-I	CKD/Praga	Czech.	1941–2	Two-man small tank / Thirty-five vehicles acquired
39.		TNH	CKD/Praga	Czech.	1936–7	Four-man light tank / PzKpfw 38 (t) delivered by Germany
40.		R-35 (ZM)	Renault	France	1939	Two-man light tank
41.	Spain	FT M1917-M1918	Renault	France	1920	Two-man light tank
42.		Trubia Tank	Trubia	Spain	1926	Three-man light tank / Designed by Captain Ruiz de Toledo
		Trubia A-4 Tank	Trubia	Spain		Improved version
43.		Landesa	Landesa	Spain		Based upon an agricultural tractor
44.		T-26		Russia	1936	Various models supplied to Loyalists during Spanish Civil War
45.		PzKpfw I Ausf. A	Henschel and others	Germany	1936	Two-man tank — Supplied to Nationalists during Spanish Civil War
46.		Verdeja		Spain	1940	Three-man light tank designed by Captain Verdeja. 6tons; I 45mm gun and 2 MG; armour 7–15mm — equipped with radio
		PzKpfw II	MAN and others	Germany		Two-man light tank
		PzKpfw III	Daimler-Benz and Others	Germany	1940–4	Five-man medium tank
		PzKpfw IV	Krupp and others	Germany		Five-man medium tank / Various models supplied by Germany
	Switzerland	FT M1917	Renault	France	1920	Two-man light tank / One vehicle acquired for trials
47.		Carden-Loyd M1934	Vickers-Armstrongs	Gt. Britain	1935	Two-man light tank / Six vehicles acquired
48.		LTH	CKD/Praga	Czech.	1939	Three-man light tank / Twenty-four vehicles acquired (assembled in Switzerland) / Armed with an Oerlikon 24mm cannon / Swiss designation: Pzw 29 (Praga)
	Thailand (Siam)	Carden-Loyd Mk VI	Vickers-Armstrongs	Gt. Britain	1930	Two-man tankette with head covers / Thirty vehicles acquired
		Carden-Loyd M1931	Vickers-Armstrongs	Gt. Britain	1934	Two-man light amphibious tank
		Carden-Loyd Mk VI*	Vickers-Armstrongs	Gt. Britain	1935	Two-man tankette with complete over-head covering / Thirty vehicles acquired
49.		6ton Mk 'E'	Vickers-Armstrongs	Gt. Britain	1935	Three-man light tank, single turret type / Ten vehicles acquired in 1933 / A second order was placed later
	Turkey	FT	Renault	France		Two-man light tank
		BT-2		Russia	1936	Three-man light-medium tank
		Light Tank Mk VIB	Vickers — ROF	Gt. Britain		Three-man light tank
		R-35 (ZM)	Renault	France	1940	Two-man light tank
		PzKpfw III	Daimler-Benz and others	Germany	1943	Five-man medium tank
50.		PzKpfw IV Ausf H	Krupp and others	Germany	1943	Five-man medium tank
	Yugoslavia	FT M1917	Renault	France	1921	Two-man light tank
51.		NC.I (NC.27)	Renault	France	1928	Two-man light tank
52.		S-Id	Skoda	Czech.	1938	Two-man light tank, turretless
		R-35 (ZM)	Renault	France	1940	Two-man light tank

BIBLIOGRAPHY

Andronikov, I. G. and Mostovenko, V. D., *Die roten Panzer* (Munich, 1963)

Barnes, G. M., *Weapons of World War II* (New York, 1947)

Brophy, Miles and Cochrane, *The Chemical Warfare Service: From Laboratory to Field* (Washington, 1959)

Chamberlain, P. and Ellis, C., *The Sherman* (London, 1968, New York, 1969)

Chamberlain, P. and Ellis, C., *British and American Tanks of World War II* (London and New York, 1969)

Chamberlain, P. and Ellis, C., *British and German Tanks of World War I* (London and New York, 1969)

Chamberlain, P. and Ellis, C., *German Heavy Tanks* (London, 1970)

Chamberlain, P. and Ellis, C., *Sherman Tank 1941–1945 (Production Models)* (London, 1970)

Chamberlain, P. and Ellis, C., *Soviet Combat Tanks, 1939–1945* (London, 1970)

Chamberlain, P. and Ellis, C., *The Churchill Tank* (London, 1971)

Chase, D., *A History of Combat Vehicle Development* Private Manuscript U.S.A.

Duvignac, A., *Histoire de L'Armée Motorisée* (Paris, 1948)

Fuller, J. F. C., *Tanks in the Great War 1914–1918* (London, 1920)

Guderian, H., *Panzer Leader* (London, 1952, 1971)

Hara, T. and Takenchi, A., *Japanese Tanks and Fighting Vehicles* (Tokyo, 1961)

Hara, T. and Eimori, D., *Japanese Tanks and Armoured Vehicles* (Tokyo, 1961)

Heigl, F., *Taschenbuch der Tanks* (Munich, 1926, 1927)

Heigl, F., Icks, R. J., Hacker, O. H., Merker, O. and von Zezschwitz, G. P., *Taschenbuch der Tanks* Parts I and II (Munich, 1935)

Heigl, F. and von Zezschwitz, G. P., *Taschenbuch der Tanks, Part III* (Munich, 1938)

Hunnicutt, R. P., *A.F.V. Data Book* (San Mateo, 1965)

Hunnicutt, R. P., *Pershing: A History of the Medium Tank T.20 Series* (California, 1972)

Icks, R. J., *Tanks and Armoured Vehicles* (New York, 1945)

Jones, R. E., Rarey, G. H. and Icks, R. J., *The Fighting Tanks since 1916* (Washington, 1933)

Liddell Hart, B. H., *The Tanks: The History of the Royal Tank Regiment* (London, 1959)

Magnuski, J., *Wozy Bojowe* (Warsaw, 1960, 1964)

Martel, G. le Q., *In the Wake of the Tank* (London, 1931)

Martel, G. le Q., *Our Armoured Forces* (London, 1945)

Milsom, J., *Russian Tanks, 1900–1970* (London and Harrisburg, 1970)

Mostovenko, V. D. and Magnuski, J., 'Historia Rozwoju Radzieckich Czolgow' (The History of Soviet Tanks) in *Wojskowy Przeglad Techniczny* (Warsaw, 1968–1969)

Mostovenko, V. D., *Tanki* (Tanks) (Moscow, 1955)

Nehring, W., *Panzer Und Motor* (Potsdam, 1936)

Ogorkiewicz, R. M., *Armoured Forces* (London and New York, 1970)

Pafi, B., Falessi, C. and Fiore, G., *Corazzati Italiani 1939–45* (Rome, 1968)

Petter, D., *Der Deutschen Kampfwagen im Weltkriege 1914–1918* (Berlin, 1932)

Postan, M. M., Hay, D. and Scott, J. D., *Design and Development of Weapons* (London, 1964)

Pugnani, A., *Storia della Motorizzatione Militare Italiana* (Turin, 1951)

Senger und Etterlin, F. M. von., *German Tanks of World War II* (London and Harrisburg, 1969)

Stern, A. G., *Tanks 1914–1918 The Log-Book of a Pioneer* (London, 1919)

Sueter, M., *The Evolution of the Tank* (London, 1937)

Thomson, H. C. and Mayo, L., *Procurement and Supply: Ordnance Department, United States Army in World War II: The Technical Services* (Washington, 1960)

Anonymous/Official Publications:

Armoured Fighting Vehicles (Vickers-Armstrongs, Chertsey, 1945)

Automotive Historical Records: Tanks and Combat Records, Vol III (Aberdeen Proving Ground, Maryland, 1944)

Carden-Loyd Light Tank (Vickers-Armstrongs, London, 1931)

Canadian Armoured Vehicles Data Book (Department of Munitions, Ottawa, 1943–5)

Design Record, Canadian Developed Military Vehicles of World War II Vols. II and III (Department of Munitions, Ottawa, 1950)

Handbook on German Military Forces (War Department, Washington, 1945)

Handbook on Japanese Military Forces (War Department, Washington, 1944)

Illustrated Record of German Army Equipment Vol. III: Armoured Fighting Vehicles (War Office, London, 1947)

Japanese Tanks and Anti Tank Warfare Special Series No 34 (War Department, Washington, 1945)

Kennblatter Fremdengerat Kraftfahrzeug (War Department, Berlin, 1941–2)

Mechanization (Vickers-Armstrongs, London, 1930)

Modern Ordnance Material (U.S. Raritan Arsenal, 1943)

The Story of the 79th Armoured Division (1945)

Standard Military Motor Vehicles (War Department, Washington, 1943)

Summary of German Tanks (S.H.A.E.F., 1944)

Weekly Tank Notes (War Office, London, 1918–19)

CONVERSION TABLES

in:cm

in	0	1	2	3	4	5	6	7	8	9
	cm	cm	cm	cm	cm	cm	cm	cm	cm	cm
0		2.54	5.08	7.62	10.16	12.70	15.24	17.78	20.32	22.86
10	25.40	27.94	30.48	33.02	35.56	38.10	40.64	43.18	45.72	48.26
20	50.80	53.34	55.88	58.42	60.96	63.50	66.04	68.58	71.12	73.66
30	76.20	78.74	81.28	83.82	86.36	88.90	91.44	93.98	96.52	99.06
40	101.60	104.14	106.68	109.22	111.76	114.30	116.84	119.38	121.92	124.46
50	127.00	129.54	132.08	134.62	137.16	139.70	142.24	144.78	147.32	149.86
60	152.40	154.94	157.48	160.02	162.56	165.10	167.64	170.18	172.72	175.26
70	177.80	180.34	182.88	185.42	187.96	190.50	193.04	195.58	198.12	200.66
80	203.20	205.74	208.28	210.82	213.36	215.90	218.44	220.98	223.52	226.06
90	228.60	231.14	233.68	236.22	238.76	241.30	243.84	246.38	248.92	251.46
100	254.00	256.54	259.08	261.62	264.16	266.70	269.24	271.78	274.32	276.86

cm:in

cm	0	1	2	3	4	5	6	7	8	9
	in	in	in	in	in	in	in	in	in	in
0		0.394	0.787	1.181	1.575	1.969	2.362	2.756	3.150	3.543
10	3.937	4.331	4.724	5.118	5.512	5.906	6.299	6.693	7.087	7.480
20	7.874	8.268	8.661	9.055	9.449	9.843	10.236	10.630	11.024	11.417
30	11.811	12.205	12.598	12.992	13.386	13.780	14.173	14.567	14.961	15.354
40	15.748	16.142	16.535	16.929	17.323	17.717	18.110	18.504	18.898	19.291
50	19.685	20.079	20.472	20.866	21.260	21.654	22.047	22.441	22.835	23.228
60	23.622	24.016	24.409	24.803	25.197	25.591	25.984	26.378	26.772	27.164
70	27.559	27.953	28.346	28.740	29.134	29.528	29.921	30.315	30.709	31.102
80	31.496	31.890	32.283	32.677	33.071	33.465	33.858	34.252	34.646	35.039
90	35.433	35.827	36.220	36.614	37.008	37.402	37.795	38.189	38.583	38.976
100	39.370	39.764	40.157	40.551	40.551	40.945	41.339	42.126	42.520	42.913

ft:m

ft	0	1	2	3	4	5	6	7	8	9
	m	m	m	m	m	m	m	m	m	m
0		0.305	0.610	0.914	1.219	1.524	1.829	2.134	2.438	2.743
10	3.048	3.353	3.658	3.962	4.267	4.572	4.877	5.182	5.486	5.791
20	6.096	6.401	6.706	7.010	7.315	7.620	7.925	8.229	8.534	8.839
30	9.144	9.449	9.753	10.058	10.363	10.668	10.972	11.277	11.582	11.887
40	12.192	12.496	12.801	13.106	13.411	13.716	14.020	14.325	14.630	14.935
50	15.239	15.544	15.849	16.154	16.459	16.763	17.068	17.373	17.678	17.983
60	18.287	18.592	18.897	19.202	19.507	19.811	20.116	20.421	20.726	21.031
70	21.335	21.640	21.945	22.250	22.555	22.859	23.164	23.469	23.774	24.079
80	24.383	24.688	24.993	25.298	25.602	25.907	26.212	26.517	26.822	27.126
90	27.431	27.736	28.041	28.346	28.651	28.955	29.260	29.565	29.870	30.174
100	30.479	30.784	31.089	31.394	31.698	32.003	32.308	32.613	32.918	33.222

m:ft

m	0	1	2	3	4	5	6	7	8	9
	ft	ft	ft	ft	ft	ft	ft	ft	ft	ft
0		3.281	6.562	9.842	13.123	16.404	19.685	22.966	26.247	29.527
10	32.808	36.089	39.370	42.651	45.932	49.212	52.493	55.774	59.055	62.336
20	65.617	68.897	72.178	75.459	78.740	82.021	85.302	88.582	91.863	95.144
30	98.425	101.71	104.99	108.27	111.55	114.83	118.11	121.39	124.67	127.95
40	131.23	134.51	137.79	141.08	144.36	147.64	150.92	154.20	157.48	160.76
50	164.04	167.32	170.60	173.88	177.16	180.45	183.73	187.01	190.29	193.57
60	196.85	200.13	203.41	206.69	209.97	213.25	216.53	219.82	223.10	226.38
70	229.66	232.94	236.22	239.50	242.78	246.06	249.34	252.62	255.90	259.19
80	262.47	265.75	269.03	272.31	275.59	278.87	282.15	285.43	288.71	291.99
90	295.27	298.56	301.84	305.12	308.40	311.68	314.96	318.24	321.52	324.80
100	328.08	331.36	334.64	337.93	341.21	344.49	347.77	351.05	354.33	357.61

miles:km

miles	0	1	2	3	4	5	6	7	8	9
	km	km	km	km	km	km	km	km	km	km
0		1.609	3.219	4.828	6.437	8.047	9.656	11.265	12.875	14.484
10	16.093	17.703	19.312	20.921	22.531	24.140	25.750	27.359	28.968	30.578
20	32.187	33.796	35.406	37.015	38.624	40.234	41.843	43.452	45.062	46.671
30	48.280	49.890	51.499	53.108	54.718	56.327	57.936	59.546	61.155	62.764
40	64.374	65.983	67.593	69.202	70.811	72.421	74.030	75.639	77.249	78.858
50	80.467	82.077	83.686	85.295	86.905	88.514	90.123	91.733	93.342	94.951
60	96.561	98.170	99.779	101.39	103.00	104.61	106.22	107.83	109.44	111.04
70	112.65	114.26	115.87	117.48	119.09	120.70	122.31	123.92	125.53	127.14
80	128.75	130.36	131.97	133.58	135.19	136.79	138.40	140.01	141.62	143.23
90	144.84	146.45	148.06	149.67	151.28	152.89	154.50	156.11	157.72	159.33
100	160.93	162.54	164.15	165.76	167.37	168.98	170.59	172.20	173.81	175.42

km:miles

km	0	1	2	3	4	5	6	7	8	9
	miles	miles	miles	miles	miles	miles	miles	miles	miles	miles
0		0.621	1.243	1.864	2.486	3.107	3.728	4.350	4.971	5.592
10	6.214	6.835	7.457	8.078	8.699	9.321	9.942	10.562	11.185	11.805
20	12.427	13.049	13.670	14.292	14.913	15.534	16.156	16.776	17.399	18.019
30	18.641	19.263	19.884	20.506	21.127	21.748	22.370	22.990	23.613	24.233
40	24.855	25.477	26.098	26.720	27.341	27.962	28.584	29.204	29.827	30.447
50	31.069	31.690	32.311	32.933	33.554	34.175	34.797	35.417	36.040	36.660
60	37.282	37.904	38.525	39.147	39.768	40.389	41.011	41.631	42.254	42.874
70	43.497	44.118	44.739	45.361	45.982	46.603	47.225	47.845	48.468	49.088
80	49.711	50.332	50.953	51.575	52.196	52.817	53.439	54.059	54.682	55.302
90	55.924	56.545	57.166	57.788	58.409	59.030	59.652	60.272	60.895	61.515
100	62.138	62.759	63.380	64.002	64.623	65.244	65.866	66.486	67.109	67.729

lb:kg

lb	0	1	2	3	4	5	6	7	8	9
	kg	kg	kg	kg	kg	kg	kg	kg	kg	kg
0		0.454	0.907	1.361	1.814	2.268	2.722	3.175	3.629	4.082
10	4.536	4.990	5.443	5.897	6.350	6.804	7.257	7.711	8.165	8.618
20	9.072	9.525	9.979	10.433	10.886	11.340	11.793	12.247	12.701	13.154
30	13.608	14.061	14.515	14.969	15.422	15.876	16.329	16.783	17.237	17.690
40	18.144	18.597	19.051	19.504	19.958	20.412	20.865	21.319	21.772	22.226
50	22.680	23.133	23.587	24.040	24.494	24.948	25.401	25.855	26.308	26.762
60	27.216	27.669	28.123	28.576	29.030	29.484	29.937	30.391	30.844	31.298
70	31.751	32.205	32.659	33.112	33.566	34.019	34.473	34.927	35.380	35.834
80	36.287	36.741	37.195	37.648	38.102	38.555	39.009	39.463	39.916	40.370
90	40.823	41.277	41.730	42.184	42.638	43.091	43.545	43.998	44.453	44.906
100	45.359	45.813	46.266	46.720	47.174	47.627	48.081	48.534	48.988	49.442

kg:lb

kg	0	1	2	3	4	5	6	7	8	9
	lb	lb	lb	lb	lb	lb	lb	lb	lb	lb
0		2.205	4.409	6.614	8.818	11.023	13.228	15.432	17.637	19.842
10	22.046	24.251	26.455	28.660	30.865	33.069	35.274	37.479	39.683	41.888
20	44.092	46.297	48.502	50.706	52.911	55.116	57.320	59.525	61.729	63.934
30	66.139	68.343	70.548	72.752	74.957	77.162	79.366	81.571	83.776	85.980
40	88.185	90.389	92.594	94.799	97.003	99.208	101.41	103.62	105.82	108.03
50	110.23	112.44	114.64	116.84	119.05	121.25	123.46	125.66	127.87	130.07
60	132.28	134.48	136.69	138.89	141.10	143.30	145.51	147.71	149.91	152.12
70	154.32	156.53	158.73	160.94	163.14	165.35	167.55	169.76	171.96	174.17
80	176.37	178.57	180.78	182.98	185.19	187.39	189.60	191.80	194.01	196.21
90	198.42	200.62	202.83	205.03	207.23	209.44	211.64	213.85	216.05	218.26
100	220.46	222.67	224.87	227.08	229.28	231.49	233.69	235.89	238.10	240.30

1 imperial ton = 2240 lb
1 short (U.S.) ton = 2000 lb
1 tonne (metric) = 2205 lb

VEHICLE INDEX

1. Select Index of Tank Names

Although official designations were given to all tanks, they were — and still are — more commonly referred to by shortened, or more popular names; thus the U.S. Medium tank M4 is far more famous as the Sherman. This index is therefore intended to assist the general reader in locating vehicles in this book where the popular name is known rather than the official designation.

2. Chronological Vehicle Index

The following index takes the form of a chronological country-by-country list of the tanks as they appear in this volume, keyed to the pages on which they appear. This is intended to permit the reader to examine the chronological development of tanks in each country at a glance, besides providing an easy to use index to the contents of this book.

GERMANY

GREAT BRITAIN

HUNGARY

ITALY

JAPAN

NEW ZEALAND

POLAND

SWEDEN

U.S.S.R.